D1076383

The Nation Holds Its Breath

The Nation Holds Its Breath

GEORGE HAMILTON

MERRION
PRESS

First published in 2021 by
Merrion Press
10 George's Street
Newbridge
Co. Kildare
Ireland
www.merrionpress.ie

9781785373732 (Cloth)
9781785373756 (Epub)

A CIP catalogue record for this book is
available from the British Library.

Typeset in Sabon LT Std 12/17.5 pt

Cover design by Fiachra McCarthy
Front cover photograph by Stills Photographic
© Marie Therese Hurson, 2021
Back cover photograph by Ray McManus
© Ray McManus/Sportsfile

Merrion Press is a member of Publishing Ireland

Contents

To Brenda and Eddie,
there every step of the way

1

Paradise in Solitude

What county man are you? That's a question I would be asked frequently when on parade for RTÉ. It's an Irish way of enquiring exactly where you're from, framed in the context of the country's most popular sport, Gaelic football, which is organised on county lines, itself hugely ironic when you consider who drew up the boundaries in the first place. Not being from that tradition, I was baffled to begin with, for county allegiance meant nothing to me.

Where am I from? I'm from Belfast. From the top of the Cregagh Road. Belfast doesn't easily subdivide into districts like Dublin or London would. The nearest arterial route tends to be the identifier, so your schoolmates might come from the Malone Road, while the boys on the opposing rugby team could be from the Antrim Road.

The Cregagh Road is in east Belfast, just over a mile of suburban highway, beginning for no apparent reason where the Woodstock Road ends. There's no major intersection, no perceptible change in the geography. If it wasn't for the street signs, you'd never know.

And it doesn't actually go anywhere. Now, it meets the dual carriageway that's part of the city's Outer Ring. In my childhood, the T-junction where it ended gave onto a simple country thoroughfare, known as the Hillfoot Road, an acknowledgement that, from that point on, the ground rose sharply to become part of the Castlereagh Hills.

The steepest ascent is the Rocky Road, a 20 per cent gradient round a left-hand bend that, in no time, delivers the most commanding view over the city below, stretching from the Lagan Valley, across to Divis Mountain, and on to the blue expanse of Belfast Lough, a place to stop and draw breath after the taxing ascent.

As you take it all in, you'll notice some streets in the foreground, rows of three-up two-down semi-detacheds leading in the general direction of those bright yellow hulks, Samson and Goliath, the two huge Krupp cranes at the Harland and Wolff shipyard that dominate the city skyline. One of those streets is Rochester Avenue, which is where I grew up.

Those cranes weren't there when my parents bought their new home in 1948. These houses were part of the post-Second World War building effort. There were almost a hundred of the semis on our little road alone.

The names of the streets – Rochester, Stirling, Sunderland – all had connections with another big Belfast employer, Short Brothers and Harland. Shorts was the first aircraft manufacturing company in the world and had its principal base at Rochester in Kent. In the 1930s, it developed the Sunderland flying boat and Stirling bombers, both of which played prominent roles in the British war effort.

Around this time, they expanded into Belfast, opening a manufacturing facility at the harbour in partnership with their neighbours, the shipyard owners Harland and Wolff, and building an airstrip for the factory that is now the runway at Belfast City Airport.

After the war ended, Shorts moved their entire operation to Belfast, and by the time I came along, they had a sports ground down the back of where we lived. This was where I had my first taste of real live football, my father's Saturday afternoon stroll with his little boy inevitably ending up on the touchline.

* * *

I was Jim and Gretta Hamilton's only child. In those post-war years, it wasn't uncommon for families to have only one offspring. My best pal was another – Peter Blaikie – one of at least half a dozen I can think of in the vicinity.

My parents had met at the tennis club on the Ormeau Road, where my mother lived at the time. My extended family owed a great deal to that sports facility in Ballynafeigh. It was where a lot of love stories began.

Going back a bit further, the history, on my mother's side at least, becomes a little more complex. My father was from Fermanagh, born in Irvinestown, one of the six children of Annie Moore, from Tempo, and Stewart Hamilton, who was a land steward.

I never knew my grandfather. It seems ill health led to a move to the city and he died when my own father was not long into his teens, which propelled my dad into the workforce as a breadwinner.

My mother, though, was Belfast through and through, originally from the Shankill Road, with a father who was the son of a cooper in a workshop in the centre of the city. But her mother, by dint of the abnormalities of nineteenth-century northern Ireland, was Scottish.

The love story that began in the hills above Larne in east Antrim seemed like a recipe for disaster. Annie McClelland, the girl from the big house, was a Protestant. John O'Neill, a local cattle drover, was a Roman Catholic. They did what they had to do and eloped.

They settled in Clydebank, just outside Glasgow, and had six children, three boys and three girls. And, in the way that they did at that time, the boys took their father's religion and the girls were brought up Protestant.

With the children grown, Annie and John decided to return to Ireland, and Maggie, my maternal grandmother, came too. They settled in Gransha, in the Castlereagh Hills, and soon after, Maggie met William Leathem. In 1907, they were married at McQuiston Memorial Presbyterian Church on the Castlereagh Road in east Belfast. My mother, Gretta, was the middle daughter of three in a family of five.

William Leathem was a champion baker – I have his Hovis medal from 1937 – but his success counted for nothing when a wartime indiscretion caught up with him. At the height of the rationing that was a feature of life in Belfast during those years, my grandfather took the fateful decision to augment his family's meagre allowance with some butter and sugar from the bakery. That was the end of that.

Out on the street, there was nothing else for it but to set up on his own. That he managed to do so and build a successful home bakery business is a tribute to what I can confirm was a grim determination.

He secured premises on the lower Woodstock Road – a converted terraced house with a glass counter mounted on a terrazzo floor, the stairs and rooms above used as stores, the backyard remodelled into an extensive bakehouse.

He rose at five to catch the first trolleybus into town and begin his day's baking – white pan, Toasties (batch loaves he'd source from a commercial bakery and brown to heighten the flavour in his own ovens, which became a local favourite), wheaten bread and those staples of the Ulster Fry, soda and potato farls. His offering was augmented with an extensive range of pastries, which quickly built up a sizable following from the small homes in the side streets around.

Those parlour houses as they were known – front doors, opening straight on to the footpath, giving instant access to the one downstairs room, leading to a kitchen, known as a scullery, out the back – were short on facilities, and Christmas would present a particular challenge. How could you cook the turkey?

Nanda, as we called our granddad, solved the problem, putting his ample ovens at the disposal of his customers. He'd spend Christmas morning behind the counter, roasted turkeys occupying every available space, ready to present the steady stream of locals with the centrepiece of their particular festive feast.

If Christmas involved a day's business at 'The Woodie', as it was known to us all, New Year was strictly a family affair. Hogmanay at my grandparents' home followed the traditional Scottish template, right down to the First Footing, where it was deemed good fortune if a dark-haired male bearing a symbolic gift of a lump of coal – to signify that the household would lack for nothing in the coming twelvemonth – was the first foot across the threshold after midnight.

My father, with a full head of hair that was yet to go grey, would make a discreet exit just before the witching hour, heading for the backyard and the coalhouse. As midnight chimed, the doorbell would ring. The dark-haired 'stranger' would be standing there with his lump of black gold. My Scottish granny's New Year was off to the perfect start.

It became my father's duty to perform this ritual, as the other visiting adult male, my uncle Fred, failed to qualify in the full-head-of-dark-hair department. A joiner in the Belfast Gasworks, Fred McMurray was an outstanding cricketer, a batsman and wicket-keeper for North Down and an Ireland international, making a single appearance, against Scotland in College Green in Dublin in 1939.

In this extended family of sportsmen, Fred's diminutive brother Tom, all five feet and two inches of him, was the star. He played professionally in England – football with Tranmere Rovers, Rochdale and Millwall, and cricket with Surrey.

Tom was involved in thirty-three first-class matches over six years and became the first Ulsterman to play in a Test, appearing as a substitute at The Oval when England faced Australia, Don Bradman and all, in 1934. He was a demon fielder, by all accounts.

My dad was a football player of some distinction, a free-scoring centre forward as he'd have been described in the jargon of the time. He played for Cliftonville in the Irish League and scored a hat-trick on his debut, a feat that put him on the front page of the sports paper that Saturday night.

Cliftonville, the oldest football club on the island of Ireland, founded in 1879, was amateur when my father played for them – just like Bohemians in Dublin. The pair faced off once a year, playing alternately in Belfast and Dublin, for a trophy called the Pioneer Cup. Years later, my dad drove me half demented trying, in those pre-internet days, to pinpoint the location of the original Jury's Hotel where Cliftonville would have stayed when they played in Dublin. We found it on Dame Street, just in front of Trinity College.

When I first joined RTÉ, I had an early marking at a Bohemians game in Dalymount Park. Job done, I was invited for a drink in the bar below the stand. The late RTÉ broadcaster Frank Hall, a fellow northerner – those of a certain age will recall his satirical revue, *Hall's Pictorial Weekly* – had spotted me in the press box and, knowing I was new in town, thought I could probably do with a few introductions.

It was like a grown-up version of my dad taking me into the Whitehouse – Cliftonville's version of Fulham Football Club's Craven Cottage, an incongruous addition to the stadium's architecture – to meet everybody who was anybody in the club and be made instantly welcome because of who had brought me in.

I still have a vivid image of that winter Sunday evening, the cosiness of the surroundings, a proper Dublin pub, and the unforgettable discovery that a key component in Bohemians' success that day – they'd just beaten Cork Celtic 6–0 – their right half Tom Kelly, was toasting their success in vodka and bitter lemon. I'd never realised that sportsmen drank spirits!

My dad loved telling me of Cliftonville's training sessions back in his day, which consisted mostly, it seemed, of endless laps around the cinder track that enclosed the pitch, followed by sprints up and down the terracing. That told you that though they may not have been big-time Charlies in the League, they did have a decent ground.

A trip to Solitude, Cliftonville's grounds – so called after a grand house that had once stood on its site near the Belfast Waterworks – was a small boy's heaven. It was a world away from the open spaces of the Shorts playing field behind our house, where my dad used to take me when I was a nipper.

That bit bigger now, I could be taken on the bus (we didn't have a car in the 1950s) to see the team universally known as The Reds. The other thing that made a trip to Solitude a no-brainer for a dad with a small child in tow was the fact that, as an amateur side in a league of semi-professionals, they hardly ever won a match and so had next-to-no support. In an era when association football in Ireland drew sizable crowds, there was never a danger of Cliftonville breaking any attendance records.

In a serendipitous twist, the number 33 trolleybus that plied the Cregagh route transformed itself at the terminus into a number 35, so becoming one of the few that actually crossed the city to a destination on the other side.

The 35 to Carr's Glen brought you into town, then departed in the direction of the Ballysillan Road, a journey that took you out to Carlisle Circus, then past No. 84 Antrim Road, where my father's elderly Aunt Emmy lived with her cats, before turning left onto the Cliftonville Road. My dad's old school was on the left; there were some fine houses on the right. Up the hill, Cliftonville

Cricket Ground sat behind high hoardings and just opposite, like something from an English mill town, was Cliftonville Street, a sweet shop on the corner and straight ahead, down at the end, the big red gates behind which was paradise – Solitude. No football ground was better named.

My father would take me into the Whitehouse and chat to anybody and everybody; those who knew him from years gone by, those who wondered who on earth he was. He'd take me into the dressing room, where I'd shyly proffer an autograph book and those guys about to go out to play would happily sign: Kevin McGarry, a medical doctor who'd have become a top international if he hadn't been devoted to his profession; Ernie McCleary, a towering centre half who taught French and still managed to win a cap for Northern Ireland; Ossie Bailie, the goalkeeper – in GAA parlance, he'd be a dual star, for he was a stalwart cricketer too, with Ballymena, the place where a tousle-haired young lad who did ball boy at Cliftonville in those years would also come to prominence: Jim Boyce, who not only became captain of Ballymena Cricket Club but also went on to become Vice-President of FIFA, world football's governing body.

With the scent of the embrocation still fresh in my nostrils, I'd be taken onto the terrace, my preferred position behind the Cliftonville goal, so that not only could I observe my team's custodian up close, I'd also have the best chance of seeing goals going in!

My father, ever the realist, was never too bothered when our afternoon out ended in another defeat. It was the way of our world. But we loved it.

* * *

Looking back, I can see how the commentary gene got a chance to develop itself. My mother would do a Saturday shift in my grandfather's bakery, so it was my dad and me putting in Saturday together. If we weren't going to Cliftonville (and that would be every other week – we didn't bother with away games), we'd be at home listening to the BBC *Light Programme* which provided second-half commentary on a top English League fixture, followed by *Sports Report*, presented by an Irishman who became one of the biggest stars of British broadcasting, Eamonn Andrews.

I was hooked. I got a present of a football game. Newfooty it was called. It was played on a table. You'd flick little celluloid players on self-righting bases at a rather oversized football. There were proper goals with nets (I was fascinated with the nets). The goalkeepers were attached to skinny wire handles you could use to make them dive. Perfect for two kids to while away an afternoon. Except there weren't two kids – there was just me.

In our little living room, we had what was known as a drop-leaf table. There wasn't enough space for a regular one, so our table spent most of its life folded away, opposite the fireplace. Underneath the window, there was a settee. The other wall accommodated a sideboard.

When it was time to eat, one leaf of the table would be raised so that our small family – mother, father and son – could dine.

The table was my mother's pride and joy, though goodness knows why. It was neither antique nor heirloom – just something halfway decent that they'd bought and it was as good as what they could have got, as much as they could have afforded. No rich, deep mahogany top. No fancy legs at each corner. No Chippendale.

My mother polished and shined it.

When the food was about to be served, up would go the extension, the supporting leg would be pulled from underneath and it would be covered by a big brown heat-resistant mat. A pristine white tablecloth would be laid out on top, to complete the look of respectability.

But, on a Saturday afternoon, or whenever the mood would take me and the folks were otherwise engaged, I would extend not just the section we lifted out to have our tea. I'd drag the contraption away from the wall and out into the middle of the room. I'd open up the leg that spent most of its time up against the wall so that the table was as extended as it could be.

There wasn't much space in the room, with the sideboard at one end, the settee under the window at the other and the hearth getting in the way.

I'd roll out the big brown heat-resistant mat. I'd long before taken a crayon to it, to mark it out like a football pitch. And, of course, I had my box of tricks, my Newfooty. My twenty-two plastic players wore striped shirts. Red-and-white against blue-and-white. Sheffield United against Sheffield Wednesday – it had to be.

I'd flick the little men at the football and play against myself, chirping a commentary as the game went on its merry way. Great practice.

It's surprising how many only children have ended up in broadcasting – not just in the commentary box but also as DJs, in solitary confinement in studios they operate themselves, all alone, playing the music and prattling on in between.

In Ireland, they are legion. My good buddy Jim Neilly of the

BBC is one. RTÉ, the state broadcaster in Ireland, boasts Ger Canning and Marty Morrissey, not to mention Jim Sherwin and Fred Cogley who went before.

A late, great BBC Radio 2 jock from Liverpool, who shared a birthday with me – Ray Moore (who was probably Irish as well) – was one of the prominent only children who charmed audiences in the UK.

Apart from Newfooty, I played football on the street with the other kids, jumpers for goalposts and all of that. There was a slight incline, so it always helped if you were playing down the hill. Few of the households had cars, so there was precious little traffic to interrupt our high-octane contests. What was of more concern were the kerbstones and lamp posts that could play havoc with the perfect pass you'd picked. So there wasn't that much passing to speak of, more football of the kick and rush variety.

We were way ahead of the times in that we allowed girls to play. The best of them was from No. 61. Marion Freud was her name. Her dad, Karl, was a Viennese jeweller who had somehow ended up in Belfast, married a local woman and settled in our avenue (we weren't allowed to refer to it as our 'street' – too common – though there wasn't a tree to be seen).

Karl Freud was one of the few with a car, and its appearance meant a short pause in our late afternoon combat while he drove past. I can still see the Vauxhall swing right into the driveway a short way down the hill, and the Viennese jeweller emerge and make his way in through his front door. In time-honoured fashion, his evening meal would be waiting for him.

Marion would be fully engaged in pursuit of the decisive goal

– the dinner gong would soon be sounding for us all – when her mother would appear at the top of her front step.

'Marion,' she'd call, though the use of the word 'gulder' from the local vernacular might be more appropriate given the tone and the accent. 'Marion, come in fer yer tea.'

Mrs Freud would turn on her heel and be gone. Marion, a feisty character like her mother, still had a score to settle. She'd remain on the tarmac pitch.

Some minutes later, the front door of No. 61 would open again and the same message would be delivered, with a somewhat higher decibel count, and an additional adverb at the end of the sentence – 'nahr!'

Dinner was clearly being served. But the winning goal was proving elusive. It soon became clear that it wouldn't be Marion who would score it.

The door opened for a third time and the ultimate arbiter emerged with a demand that could not be ignored. 'Marion. Come in for yer tea. Nahr! Or I'll knock yer pan in!'

Mrs Freud wasn't the only character on the street. There was the fearsome Mr Abbott in No. 41. We made sure that the goal at the top end was well down from his front gate, for if the ball were to end up in his garden, it would be the last you would see of it.

Another from the German-speaking world was Anna Redlich, who lived alone in No. 24. I say alone; a pack of dogs occupied the premises too. She drove a little van and wore wellington boots at all times.

Then there was Bob Warwick at No. 52. Open-air Bob, we called him. At the first sign of fine weather, he'd be out at his front gate, checking up and down the road to see what was going on, his attire a pair of trousers topped by a singlet.

Harold Mitchell, a Yorkshireman who lived in No. 51, was cricket mad. He'd put his son Ian in to bat at the back of their driveway and come roaring in across the road to bowl at him at top speed.

We would have done something similar up the side of our house, though fast bowling was off-limits for safety's sake. But spinners can invite a mighty whack. And when our next-door neighbour, Peter Long, tossed one up to me abreast of their kitchen, I couldn't resist the temptation to send it on its way to an imaginary boundary.

Unfortunately, my aim of scoring four runs by sweeping it low away to leg, which would have resulted in a resounding thud off the gable wall, somehow transformed itself into the kind of shot that, on a real-life pitch, would have cleared the ropes and earned me a six. Its trajectory took it straight through the Longs' kitchen window!

Opposite us were the Smiths, an English family with two boys and two girls. The craziest thing happened when both our households acquired new cars. Our smoke-grey Ford Popular was the first motor we ever had. It bore the registration number 1910AZ. Gazing absent-mindedly out the front window, I noticed a gleaming white Ford Anglia on the Smiths' pathway, with the plate number 1909AZ. I couldn't quite get my ten-year-old head around how two families who lived directly opposite each other could end up with cars that had consecutive registrations.

The dad, Bryce Smith, had a men's outfitters in Howard Street in town and would often appear on the new ITV channel as a spokesman for the business community. From my pal Paul, his second son, I would hear the inside story of how you couldn't wear a white shirt on television; it had to be cream or a pastel shade, so it wouldn't create glare.

Paul and I were both into media when media was principally print. He created a little local newspaper, the *Glenburn Gazette*, and I was effectively its head of production, for I was the proud possessor of a typewriter.

Fascinated by newspapers from a very early age, I pestered my parents, and lo and behold, one Christmas, a second-hand Remington appeared at the end of my bed. Determined that I make the best use of it, my mother brought her secretarial skills to bear – she was employed as a bookkeeper for a timber merchant near my grandfather's bakery – and taught me to touch type. She attempted to add shorthand to my skill set, but I didn't have the patience for that.

By way of my typewriter, Paul's prose made it into print. But our foray into newspaper publishing didn't last long. Just like in the real world, television was taking over. Not that we actually made any programmes, but we did have some fun pretending to.

Our garage became the set for a TV quiz show. Paul created the hardware and operated the 'cameras', which were beer crates, with the insides of toilet rolls attached to one end, making them look like the lenses on the real thing. Close pals became the contestants, those who drew the short straw made up the audience and I was the quizmaster.

It's terrible I didn't persevere with the partnership. I went on to front *Know Your Sport* for RTÉ; Paul Smith created *Who Wants To Be A Millionaire* and turned himself into one in the process. He wasn't the only Smith to make it big in the media. His sister Susy was the editor-in-chief of *Country Living* magazine for almost twenty-five years. I actually ended up working on occasion with his other sister, Claire, who directs sport on TV.

While the *Glenburn Gazette* was in its pomp and the TV quiz was finding its imaginary audience, I was going through school, Downey House, the prep department of the Methodist College, and then Methody itself – the biggest school in the United Kingdom at the time, it was said. It was certainly huge, in every way, occupying a magnificent elevated site across the road from Queen's University in south Belfast.

I thoroughly enjoyed the academic side of things, the arts more than the sciences. When I was there, there were three state examinations to be taken. First, there was the Junior Certificate, which you sat at age fourteen. It was immediately scrapped after I had completed it. The other two exams lasted longer in the form in which I took them – GCEs or the General Certificate of Education at Ordinary Level, aged sixteen, and the Advanced GCE when you were about to leave school at eighteen.

On the basis of your results in the 'Junior', you were graded for the eight subjects you would take to O-Level. One of these had to be science and, after sitting the Junior paper, I fully expected to earn myself a place among the dunces. It was a series of questions with multiple-choice answers and I hadn't a clue what the half of it meant. So, like some once-a-year punter trying to predict which horse will win the Grand National, I resorted to the tried and trusted method of closing my eyes to make my selection.

I was rewarded with a distinction and a place in the top set for Chemistry. Looking back, I reckon I was lucky to get out unscathed. There was one memorable incident, a minor explosion involving sulphuric acid – I even remember the formula, H_2SO_4 – which left me with several little holes in my school blazer and in the handkerchief I had used to try to remove the offending liquid. Not to be recommended. I got out with an O-Level pass and left it at that. German, French, English and Economics would receive all my attention for the next two years.

I particularly enjoyed A-level English. Our teacher was Walter Grey, whose bald head and horn-rimmed glasses made him a dead ringer for an American entertainer with a big following at the time. *The Phil Silvers Show*, shot in black and white giving it an added edge, was the vehicle for this bespectacled, bald-headed comedian to play the role of an American soldier for laughs. His name? Sergeant Ernie Bilko.

Bilko Grey's ready acceptance of his moniker – though he would never acknowledge it, we just knew – made for a great relationship with his students. With great good humour, he'd take us through the syllabus, and it was a favourite part of my day, since it featured Irish writers. We'd James Joyce's *Dubliners*; we'd Frank O'Connor's *First Confession*; and we'd Pegeen Mike and Christy Mahon. Synge's *Playboy of the Western World* came alive in Bilko's classroom.

* * *

I've never quite been able to understand why but, as a northerner born and bred – and christened in the same east Belfast Presbyterian church as the great footballer George Best – I've always been fascinated by life in the south.

'*Genau Genommen Ein Anderes Land*' read a headline in the West German political weekly *Die Zeit*, referring to the eastern part of the country controlled by the Soviet Union and known as the German Democratic Republic. Strictly speaking, it's another country.

That, I think, was the nub of it.

The south of Ireland was an attractive holiday destination, because things were different there, from the green postboxes to the street signs in Irish and the fact that a packet of Rolo contained much smaller caramel chocolates than the ones we were used to up north.

Our neighbours, the Longs, went off on a southern safari one summer and came home with two cats they called Dingle and Kerry. When my parents bought me a transistor radio as a prize for passing the eleven-plus, I was fascinated by the names on the dial. I couldn't pick up Hilversum or Lyon, but if I went to the opposite end, to the BBC, there would be a strong signal from Athlone.

So, I took to listening to Radio Éireann, as my connection with this exotic other. I'd been brought up with *Listen With Mother* and *Children's Hour* on the BBC Home Service. Here was something completely different. Fifteen-minute segments promoting confectionery (over nine million eggs are used every year in the baking of cakes by Gateaux), the Irish Hospitals Sweepstakes (which also bought time on Radio Luxembourg) and music ('If you feel like singing, do sing an Irish song'). And then they'd go off the air for the afternoon, playing 'O'Donnell Abú' on a loop as the station identifier until the schedule restarted at teatime.

Those shows opened up the Irish entertainment scene to me. Showbands seemed so much more a part of a world you could belong to than the stars who emerged after the Beatles burst onto the UK scene.

Not that I ignored them; 208 on the medium wave – Radio Luxembourg – was my bedtime listening, and when the British pirate ships came along – Radio Caroline, Radio Scotland, which at one point was anchored off the County Down coast – they became favourites too.

I'd buy the pop paper *Disc and Music Echo* every Thursday to see who was going to be on *Top of the Pops* that evening, but I read *Spotlight* magazine as well to keep track of the Irish dance hall kings – Joe Dolan, The Swarbriggs, Dickie Rock and the Miami.

My formal music education had begun much earlier. My father had a fine voice and sang regularly with local musical societies. I still have the programme from an appearance in the Grand Opera House in Belfast. My mother too could hold a note, so there was always plenty of singing in the house. They were keen that I should make the most of whatever musical talent I had, so they enrolled me for piano lessons.

When the time came for the nine- and ten-year-olds in the music class at school to be pressed into service as a rudimentary orchestra for the annual concert, a show of hands was requested from those who were learning the piano. The rest would be taught the fundamentals on the violin, which uses the treble clef, the stave you start with when you're being taught to read music. The pianists could read the bass clef, the lower notes, so they could get going on the cello because they'd be able to read the score.

So began my association with music which has been the source of enormous pleasure ever since.

I will confess a degree of reluctance to devote myself to the considerable practice required, but it paid off as I went through the grades on the piano. With the cello, it was different. I learned on the job, playing in a proper student orchestra.

I took Music as a subject in my O-Levels and owe a considerable debt of gratitude to our teacher, Henry Willis. He only had a handful in his class, but those of us who were left with a deep appreciation of precisely what was going on. I think of him often when I'm playing the tunes on Lyric FM.

* * *

Sport was a major part of life at Methody. The prep school at Downey House is set in over forty acres of playing fields, Pirrie Park, named after the chairman of the original owners, the shipbuilders Harland and Wolff. There aren't too many degrees of separation in Belfast.

What is now the 1st XV rugby pitch was once home to Queen's Island, an Irish League football team that took its name from an earlier club formed by workers in the shipyard. When I was at Downey House, Pirrie Park's boundary wall at the top of Ardenlee Street, behind one of the goals, still bore evidence that once there had been turnstiles there.

Queen's Island, now the Titanic Quarter and home to the shipyard, was formed from deposits dredged from Belfast Lough as the port was being developed. The engineer in charge of that project was William Dargan from Carlow, the man who designed and built Ireland's first railway between Dublin and Dún Laoghaire. They named the reclaimed land Dargan's Island, but following the visit of Britain's Queen Victoria to Belfast in 1849, Dargan was relegated. Queen's Island it became.

Beside what's now the rugby pitch at Pirrie Park, the little grandstand survives, as does the banking that served as standing accommodation for supporters of the Queen's Island football team. During my time, they built new dressing rooms behind the other goal.

My father scored his hat-trick on that pitch and I played on it too, though it was rugby I was playing, at full back or scrum-half, and I never did make it, like he did, to the first team.

The 3rds was my XV, the middle one of the five teams Methody ran every Saturday morning. One of my rare promotions to the 2nds, due as I recall to an injury to the usual full back, led to a bit of an altercation later with the teacher in charge of my regular squad, a surly individual by the name of Cowan, who had earned himself the unpleasant nickname of 'Sleg', presumably because of how he was in the habit of putting down those in his charge.

I'd been pleased enough with my performance to believe I might have earned another go, but when I went to the noticeboard where they posted the following weekend's line-ups, the name in the full back position on the 2nds was the guy I'd replaced, recovered, presumably, from whatever was ailing him.

Fair enough. So, I looked at the 3rds and saw I wasn't there either. A decent enough showing in a winning team had earned me a demotion to the 4th XV.

I sought out Sleg. 'What's the story, sir. I'm not playing on Saturday?'

His answer: 'You didn't show up last week.' Thanks for your interest, Mr Cowan.

But I really wanted to be playing soccer. That, though, was an absolute no-no at schools considered elite like Methody. So, my only outlet, until I got to university, was local summer leagues. Along the way, though, there was an unusual event that somehow I'd got involved in.

An older gent by the name of Davy Bennett, a kind of a soccer missionary, had created a network among the grammar schools of Greater Belfast from which he could draw a team, made up of boys like me who were stuck in a system that wouldn't allow them the opportunity they really wanted. There were a couple of us from Methody and we found ourselves selected for a game that would take place at Solitude, against an XI of similarly deprived young men from the south – a Leinster Grammar Schools selection.

We met for a pre-match lunch at Isabeal's, an old-style Belfast restaurant and from there, we were taken to Solitude, where we donned the Cliftonville kit of red shirts with a white shamrock crest. I took the field proudly wearing the colours my father would have worn, with the number three on my back.

My dad and my cousin Stuart, Fred McMurray's son, six years older than me and the nearest thing I had to a brother, were in the fine grandstand. But there was nobody in the press box and, sadly, I've no recollection of how it ended. Still, I do have fond memories of my first official appearance as a left back.

Maybe it was in my genes, but cricket was the game that I enjoyed the most success at in school. I opened the batting for the 1st team. I did have my Sleg Cowan moment there too, though. The way it worked, the umpires would be the teachers in charge of the team, so at one end you'd be facing your own man, at the other, the opposition's.

On the beautiful square in Pirrie Park on a fine summer Saturday, it was me against the top bowler from Belfast Royal Academy. He wasn't in any way intimidating. I began well and was confident I could build up a score. Then nepotism stepped in.

I was wearing typical cricketing kit for the time: whites, with white boots complete with protective toecap. In came the bowler. I was ready for whatever he delivered. This one was pretty loose and I went for a cover drive. I missed. The red leather sphere clipped my foot on its way into the wicketkeeper's gloves. 'Howzat!' he howled, as you do.

'Howzat!' screamed the bowler, in the midst of a histrionic turn towards his mentor. Off my bat, I am gone. Off my boot, I am not out. To my absolute amazement, their schoolteacher standing as arbiter, their paragon of social rectitude, doubling on this Saturday morning as the court of last appeal, put all fairness aside and raised his finger. I'd been caught. I was out. My bat was clean. I pointed to my boot, with the bright red stain on the toecap where the ball had connected. I got a wry smile in return. All is fair in love and war. Or not, as the case may be. I walked.

2

Superfan

I suppose it was during my youth that what would become the central thread in my working life was seeding into the fertile earth of my imagination. During those days of Saturday-morning rugby matches, on Saturday afternoons I was also a regular among the crowds, and crowds they were then, watching Irish League football.

Cliftonville, the Reds, were my team, but their status as perennial also-rans brought no street cred at school, where they used to poke fun at my classmate Howard Ruderman for supporting Crusaders, a team from north Belfast with no tradition, having arrived in the elite league only to fill the void left after the controversial withdrawal of Belfast Celtic in 1949.

Celtic, formed in 1891 and modelled on the great Glasgow club that had been set up three years before, was the green half of Belfast's equivalent to Scotland's Old Firm. Their arch rivals were Linfield, the Blues, whose teams were made up exclusively of Protestant players.

Between them Linfield and Celtic had won thirty-one of the

forty-six Irish League titles contested before the Second World War intervened, with Celtic having completed five-in-a-row. They were crowned champions again at the conclusion of the first post-war season in the spring of 1948, so when they visited Linfield's home at Windsor Park for the traditional Christmas derby the following December, with the Blues three points clear of them at the top of the League, it was sure to be a tense affair.

And so it turned out. By half-time, Linfield were down to nine men, having lost two of their players to injury. I'll let Malcolm Brodie of the *Belfast Telegraph* take up the story … 'Linfield's Scottish-born centre-half Bob Bryson was carried off in the 35th minute with an ankle fracture after an accidental collision with [Jimmy] Jones,' he wrote:

> [T]hen Jackie Russell, the Linfield forward, collapsed after being hit point-blank on the chest by a ball and he too was stretchered to the dressing-room.
>
> The Windsor Park tinder box was ready to explode and an undiplomatic half-time announcement over the public address system that Bryson had broken his leg didn't help matters. Indeed it was like a red rag to a bull.

When two players, one from each side, were sent off in the second half, fighting broke out on the terraces. Celtic were awarded a penalty and took the lead. With four minutes to go, Linfield equalised. There was a pitch invasion, repelled by police with batons drawn.

When the final whistle sounded with the score at 1–1, the crowd again poured onto the pitch, this time jostling the Celtic players. Jimmy Jones was singled out and attacked. 'I think the crowd must have had it against me for the Bryson incident,' he would recall. He was thrown over the parapet that surrounded the pitch and onto the terracing below. When the kicking and beating stopped, the *Telegraph* reported the following day that he had 'received multiple injuries, including a broken leg which might incapacitate him from football'. He was only twenty at the time.

Jones recovered to continue a prolific scoring career, his total of 647 goals setting an Irish League record. But Belfast Celtic would never be the same again. In a statement, they expressed their outrage at the 'concerted attack' which 'in its gravity is without parallel in the annals of football'. They were further appalled that the sanction against Linfield amounted to the closure of Windsor Park for just two games. Celtic decided enough was enough and, at the end of the season, resigned from the League.

Their ground on the Donegall Road in Belfast lived on into the 1980s as a greyhound stadium, before being sold off for development into what is now a dreary retail park.

If Howard Ruderman was having a hard time as a Crues supporter, can you imagine how much more difficult it would have been for me to persist with my allegiance to the Reds? At least Crusaders had won a couple of minor trophies since their elevation to senior status. Cliftonville's most recent success had been winning the Gold Cup, now long forgotten, back in 1933, when my dad was one of their players.

I was a teenager, though, and didn't need to be associated with an outfit that lost every week. I had to be able to boast. My team had to be winning things. The obvious choice was right on my doorstep, the team of east Belfast – The Cock 'n' Hens, The Glens, Glentoran.

After Celtic's sad departure in 1949, Belfast's 'Big Two' rivalry became a location as opposed to a religion-based thing. Protestant Linfield from south Belfast weren't really so different from east Belfast-based Glentoran with its predominantly Protestant fan base. Indeed Bill Heaney, whom you will meet later as a broadcasting colleague, used to say a visit to Glentoran's home, The Oval, off Mersey Street, used to fill him, as a Roman Catholic, with a good deal more dread than any trip to report on Linfield at home. Both venues are in fervently loyalist areas, but around Windsor Park, perhaps out of deference to its status as the home of Northern Ireland, allegiance tended to be shown in the flying of flags. On the other side of the city, the graffiti would have suggested a smidgin less tolerance.

The irony is that Linfield, known as the Blues on account of the colour of their shirts, complemented by white shorts and red socks, still only engaged Protestant players, while Glentoran, based in what was perceived as a more intensely loyalist area, had a tradition of hiring the best from wherever they came.

John Colrain, a player-manager who features later in this tale, played for Glasgow Celtic. Just before he arrived, the Glens' star player was a Dubliner by the name of Terry Conroy. He went on to have an illustrious career with Stoke City and won twenty-seven caps for the Republic of Ireland. He had a crucial role to play in the Irish Cup Final of 1966.

When it came to prestige fixtures, The Oval, Glentoran's home ground, was the second choice, after Windsor Park. If Linfield reached the Cup Final, it would be switched to The Oval, so they wouldn't have home advantage. If it was Linfield against Glentoran, they tossed a coin to decide where it would be played, and that led to one of the greatest of Irish Cup Finals, that 1966 game, played at Glentoran's home ground.

The Linfield fans chanted 'Pope of The Oval' every time Terry Conroy touched the ball. Terry delivered the perfect riposte, scoring both goals as Glentoran won 2–0.

It was a no-brainer. The Glens had to be my team.

The Oval became a favourite place for me. There was a park nearby. We went there during one school holiday to play football and it made me feel like I was playing for the Glens.

Glentoran, in an ambitious move aping the big boys across the water, had bought a sports facility on Donovan Parade from a local engineering company, Sirocco Works, to be their training headquarters. This acreage was in a housing estate in the east Belfast suburb of Castlereagh. The developer had obviously been a horse racing fan, for the streets of semi-detached houses that he built there were named to immortalise winners of the Epsom Derby. Donovan himself was first past the post in 1889. Donovan Parade is just off Ladas Drive, which leads to the main intersection on the Castlereagh Road. Grand Parade is on the opposite side. Ladas won the big race in 1894, Grand Parade did so in 1919. My father Jim's mother lived in Manna Grove. Manna's winning year in the Derby was 1925.

You'll also find Parades, Drives, Gardens and Groves commemorating Cicero (winner in 1905), Orby (1907), Pommern (1915), Trigo (1929), Blenheim (1930) and also Ard Patrick from 1902 (though the builder must have been Protestant, for he rejected the Irish presentation when he named Ardpatrick [sic] Gardens!).

I was becoming a Glentoran superfan and I would even go along to watch Glentoran's reserve team. On a particular Saturday afternoon, they were playing Dundela, a side from the second tier, whose base at Wilgar Park – affectionately known as the 'Hen Run' – was but a five-minute stroll from The Oval, so they would count as local rivals.

Normally, at that time in the Irish League, the reserves would play in the main ground every other week, when the first team was playing away. But now the Glens – like Liverpool at Melwood or Manchester United, then at The Cliff, had this other facility and that's where the second string would be at home. Like Shorts' ground at the back of our house, this was just playing fields with a clubhouse. No terracing, no grandstand.

And in this, the Irish League 'B' Division, where I would soon experience the realities of junior soccer as secretary of the Queen's University Association Football Club, there were no linesmen either, just a referee. The two teams would each provide a referee's assistant. A member of the Glentoran II's backroom staff was on one touchline. Dundela's twelfth man – there was only one substitute back then – ran the other.

I took my place on the grass beside the pitch, where I was passed at frequent intervals by Dundela's sub, a gent in his thirties who, I learned quickly, was called Herbie. Ready for action in case he might be called upon, he was wearing Dundela's colours, green shirt, white shorts, green stockings with white tops and, of course, football boots. He topped off this ensemble with a Crombie overcoat and bore in his hand a white handkerchief. No official linesman, so no official flag.

The necessity to patrol the touchline with a degree of vigour was leaving him somewhat short of breath and I was becoming increasingly distracted by the Herbie sideshow. Then, in an instant, disaster struck. Herbie's officiating, which was proving to be about as much exercise as he could cope with, was about to come to an abrupt end.

One of the Dundela players competed courageously for a 50–50 ball. The young Glentoran reserve emerged unscathed; the somewhat older gnarled 'B' division veteran remained on the ground. The trainer, as the team attendant was known in those days, trundled to his aid, rudimentary first aid kit – that is water and sponge – in hand. He assessed the damage, then turned to the touchline and, with a rueful shake of the head, made eye contact with Herbie.

'Holy fuck!'

It was the first time I had ever heard that particular expletive. Herbie reluctantly shed the Crombie and joined the fray, to complete what was probably the worst afternoon of his life. I was laughing too much to pay any further attention to the warp and weft of the footballing drama. My only focus was my erstwhile touchline companion, now pressed into service at the end of a career that had clearly gone one match too far.

***

Added to the hours spent following the Irish League, another colourful sporting thread ran through my childhood which piqued my lifelong love of football. In 1955, the European Cup was established, the brainchild of one Gabriel Hanot, a former French international who went on to become the editor of the

Paris sports newspaper *L'Équipe*. Take all the champions of the continent. Throw them into the mix and see what comes out.

Distillery against Benfica. The Irish League title-winners against the storied stars from Lisbon, among them a twenty-one-year-old who'd go on to become one of the game's greatest – Eusébio. Benfica had followed Real Madrid's five-in-a-row with a two-in-a-row of their own. And a thirteen-year-old kid from the Cregagh Road in Belfast went with his dad to see them play.

Distillery, back in the day the recreation club of lads who made whiskey for Dunville's off the Falls Road in West Belfast, had been the first club in Ireland to have floodlights. But their ground at Grosvenor Park, just below the Royal Victoria Hospital, couldn't have staged an event like this. So we Hamiltons found ourselves on the Railway End terrace at the international stadium, Windsor Park, right next to my Latin teacher at school, Joe Harris. Schoolmasters are human too!

The Whites – as Distillery were known – made the most of this opportunity by hiring Tom Finney, a headline name at the time, one of English football's greatest wingers with seventy-six caps to his name but by now forty-one and coming out of retirement for this one last hurrah.

It was obvious he was inspiring the part-time professionals by his very presence in their colours. Distillery led twice, Eusébio scoring the second equaliser, and though they went behind on the hour, it finished all square, 3–3. That was a one-off, of course. Benfica won the Lisbon leg 5–0.

Then there was Linfield. In 1967, the year that Celtic were plotting their path to the first British triumph in the competition in another of the Portuguese capital's sporting venues, the blue half of Belfast was celebrating reaching the last eight. Yes, Linfield of the Irish League made it to the quarter-finals of the European Cup.

The Bulgarian champions, CSKA, ended their journey, though it was close. The first leg in Belfast ended 2–2. Linfield lost in Sofia by a single goal.

My adopted Belfast team – Glentoran – would also reach a European quarter-final, in their case in the Cup Winners' Cup in 1974. But in September 1967, they entertained the Portuguese champions at The Oval on Mersey Street. John Colrain put them ahead from the penalty spot in the tenth minute, and for much of the rest of that Wednesday evening, east Belfast dared to dream.

But in the 86th minute, Eusébio put his name on the night. Eusébio, winner of the Golden Boot at the World Cup in England the year before, when Portugal finished third. He conjured an equaliser, which will forever more have an asterisk beside it. Two weeks later, Glentoran produced an heroic performance in the away leg and held these European giants scoreless, the first time that had ever happened to Benfica at home in Europe.

So, 1–1 on aggregate. Eusébio's late intervention in Belfast proved decisive. Benfica progressed on the away goals rule. This was the first time an away goal had decided a tie in Europe's premier competition.

Who knows what might have followed had the Glens managed to score in the Estádio da Luz. Life is full of forks in the road. Glentoran resumed the defence of their Irish League title which ultimately proved successful. And Benfica journeyed through Saint-Étienne, Budapest and Turin, where they overcame Juventus to arrive at Wembley on the last Wednesday evening in May 1968, where they would bow before the majestic magnificence of

Manchester United. Blue shirts, no crest on the chest, never mind a sponsor's logo. Bobby Charlton, Brian Kidd and, of course, George Best, wheeling away arm aloft, having scored the third in a 4–1 after-extra-time victory over Eusébio and the rest. Of course, Celtic had won it the year before, but England had to claim this as a first.

To Distillery, Linfield and Glentoran, add Waterford. When the draw for the first round of the following season's competition was made, it was the top team in the League of Ireland that came out as Manchester United's initial opposition in defence of their title as champions of Europe. The first leg would be played in Ireland.

There was no way this game was going to happen at Waterford's home place, the infield of the greyhound track at Kilcohan Park. Dalymount Park, Bohemians' ground, where the Republic of Ireland played, would hardly do either, for its capacity was limited. Waterford approached the rugby authorities. Any chance we might host the tie at Lansdowne Road?

Association Football had only ever been played there twice before. First, pre-partition, when an Ireland team under the auspices of the Irish Football Association in Belfast played England in a friendly on St Patrick's Day in 1900, the first soccer international to be played in Dublin. Then, in 1927, when the Irish Free State team faced Italy in its first home international. What a moment this would be. Waterford against the champions of Europe at the country's principal international venue.

We were there, my dad and me. The circumstances were utterly preposterous.

It had begun with an attempt to buy two tickets. Northern folk were unaccustomed to how things worked in the other part of the island. The pair of us figured if we posted an application with an Irish stamp, it might be more favourably considered.

My father – a civil servant whose duties took him out to livestock marts – had an assignment in the city of Armagh, just a hop and a step from the border. So we put our request on paper and I travelled with him, and then, as he assessed whatever livestock came his way, I drove across the border into Monaghan and posted our application for tickets. Are you having a laugh? We heard nothing.

Undeterred, we set sail for Dublin on the day, thinking there would surely be a way we'd get tickets from a tout.

Having stopped off in Ashbourne for one of those awful pub lunches they offered back then – oxtail soup in a stainless-steel bowl, with two slices of white bread on the side – we were in the environs of the rugby stadium in good time for the late afternoon kick-off. Lansdowne Road had no floodlights.

There was plenty of black-market business going on and, in due course, we managed to equip ourselves with the means of entry – one four-shilling ticket, purchased for two pounds, the best we could do in the circumstances.

How was this going to work, I wondered. But my dad had the whole situation sussed.

We joined the queue on Lansdowne Road, shuffling forward towards the turnstile that would give us access to the promenade, as it was called, the space in front of the old west stand. Eventually, we came to the little tunnel, home to the gate man standing in his cage, his foot poised over the pedal that controlled the stile that gave spectators access.

Clunk. One went through. We shuffled further forward. Clunk. Another squirmed his way towards the terraces. Now it was our turn. Hemmed in by the queue, a line of faces anxious in case they missed the start, there was only one way out: through the turnstile in front of us. The two of us. With just the one ticket.

My dad pushed the precious ticket through the little gap in the grille and did what many a father would do for his son back then. He declared, 'I'm lifting him over!'

Now, I'm no giant, but at eighteen years of age I was way beyond the category of small boys to whom this magnanimity applied. As it turned out, though, the gateman in his cage wasn't about to invite the wrath of the queue behind us by debating the point. Our single tout's ticket sufficed. I clambered over the stile. And we were in.

We watched on as the game unfolded, these images off the black and white television brought to life in vivid red shirts. As half-time approached, we made our way down towards the Lansdowne pavilion, which was where the dressing rooms were located.

Up close and personal with Nobby Stiles, he's the one I best remember as they came off at the interval.

It was no mean performance by Waterford, to hold them to 3–1. Denis Law scored a hat-trick. George Best had a goal ruled out for offside. Law got four more in the second leg, which ended 7–1 in United's favour.

3

The Making of the Man

If I learned anything from all those years as a young football fan, one basic lesson stands out. Nothing is going to happen unless you put yourself in a position to make it happen. If I wanted to become a football player, it was entirely up to me.

I'd no chance of course. I can see that now, from the far end of a career in the game where I've had the improbable privilege of spending a working lifetime seeing it up close at the top. But, at the age of eighteen, I still believed I might make it as some kind of player at some kind of level. So, on the first day of Freshers' Week at Queen's University in Belfast, in September 1968, the stall I sought out was that of the Football Club.

I just wanted to play soccer on a regular basis. The way the world worked, schoolboys like me played rugby and, if we were good enough, we progressed to representative teams. Many of my schoolmates did just that.

But as a player, rugby didn't do it for me. I wanted to play football. And now that I was at Queen's, I could do so. I went to the desk in the Whitla Hall, Queen's University Belfast's Aula

Maxima. I signed up. And then I went to the noticeboard in the Students' Union, looking for clues. I hounded any names I got via the noticeboard. There was no internet. No mobile phones.

There was to be a training session. I turned up. There was no coach. No manager. This was all being run by the captain, voted into position by the club members at the AGM. He was the 1st team right back, a guy called Colm Quinn, known to all and sundry as Ginto.

This Methody boy, from Protestant east Belfast, had landed in the middle of an Andersonstown mafia. Not that these young men were in any sense of the word nefarious. Absolutely not. They certainly weren't excluding outsiders. On the contrary. Mickey McCamley from Tennent Street on the Shankill Road (clearly Protestant) was there. So was Andy McMorran, who became a major player in education in the state sector in Northern Ireland, another from a unionist background. Quite simply, it had never struck me that I'd be diving into a very different kind of pool to what I was used to.

But then, it was the same in the lecture theatre. In French, one morning, I got talking to the student beside me and we hit it off. Tom Egan was the very first Catholic friend I ever had. And very soon I realised that that particular badge had absolutely no relevance when it came to character judgement. I was the product of a segregated education system, one that's taking a very long time to sort itself out. How could it have been otherwise?

I was very well received in the soccer club and no one was more welcoming than the new chairman, Denis Clarke, a stalwart centre half on the 3rd XI, known as Queen's Colts. I was curious. He was obviously a bit older than me. 'What year are you in?' I asked.

'Academically third year,' he said. 'Chronologically, fifth!' A priceless answer. Fifty years on, when Queen's Football Club won the Irish Football Association's Intermediate Cup, its first major trophy after 108 years in existence, Denis was still the chairman.

He has overseen a lot of changes, not least in how professional the whole set-up has become. In my time, it was amateur in every sense and, with five teams competing in five different leagues, it needed an enormous amount of organisation.

Ginto and his mates ran the 1st team, which played in the same division as Herbie the linesman's Dundela. With no promotion or relegation then, this was where the elite intermediate clubs competed with the reserves of each of the twelve clubs in the Irish League proper. Quite how Queen's University found itself among them is anybody's guess.

Term time didn't match the football calendar, so fielding teams when the new season began in August was a proper headache. Students aren't the kind of people to forego a summer earning money abroad or simply living the beach life to come back early for the football. We could get away with it with the club's junior teams, by simply postponing their resumption in their respective competitions, but it was less straightforward for the 1st XI, who had a place on a calendar of fixtures that took the complete season to fulfil.

Now, there would be a computer to take care of all the various exigencies, but then it was all sorted out in a series of regular meetings in smoke-filled rooms where the representatives of the various clubs would come together to haggle over who played whom and when.

I know all of this because at the first soccer club AGM I

attended, at the end of my fresher year, I discovered my enthusiasm had attracted a proposer and a seconder to put me forward for the position of honorary secretary. So, it fell to me to present myself each Friday evening at the offices of the Irish League behind Belfast City Hall and find out the hard way how to navigate a path through the diary of a season. It was a pretty steep learning curve, but Denis was always available to ensure that I kept pointing in the right direction.

At the start of that following season, I found myself at left back on the 1st team by default. We just about managed to put out a full side for the opening game, away to Portadown Reserves. Each year, the club would equip the 1st team with new kit. What had been worn the previous season would be handed down to the team below.

It fell to me to organise the acquisition of a brand-new set of green shirts, white shorts and green socks from the leading sports outfitter in Belfast at the time, a gregarious former water polo international who ran his business under the title S.S. Moore, on Arthur Street, in the centre of town.

Nothing was too much trouble for Sammy Moore. When this cocky young student presented himself with the order, Sammy assured me there would be no problem supplying the merchandise in plenty of time for the trip to Portadown. Except that wasn't how it turned out.

It was to Sammy Moore's that my parents had gone one Christmas to source the red shirt that their little fellow was mad keen to have so that it would look like he was turning out for Manchester United. I was about to encounter an issue similar to the one they faced when they discovered that all the pristine red shirts, as worn by the team followed by all my little friends, were gone and all that remained were red shirts with white sleeves. And so I convinced myself that Christmas morning that Manchester United was no longer my team. It would be the one that wore the shirts with the contrasting sleeves. I duly became an Arsenal fan.

In fairness, it wasn't the absence of a shirt but rather the absence of a number that created the problem for the new Hon. Sec. of QUBAFC. It being a busy time of year in the sports shop, there was a delay in having the numbers attached, 1 to 11 as it was then, squad numbers not having been thought of. It was touch and go if we'd get the new kit in time.

On the morning of the game, I was down in Arthur Street, waiting to collect our order. Sammy emerged from the back of the shop, full of apologies. All the gear was there but they hadn't managed to complete the order. They were short of a number 9.

It would be the best part of an hour to Portadown. I needed the kit. 'It'll do,' I said. I'd packed the previous season's shirts just in case, so I headed out of Belfast in our family Renault, my own kit bag in the boot accompanied by two strips, the brand new one and last year's, looking a bit the worse for wear.

We all travelled separately for games. I arrived at Shamrock Park, Portadown's home ground just off the Armagh Road, about an hour before kick-off, with the goods in the boot. I took the kit bag full of the new gear into the dressing room. The shirts were enthusiastically ripped from their wrapping and handed out by the captain. When it was all done, Mickey Farnon had no shirt. He was the centre forward. He should have been wearing number 9.

'Mickey,' I explained, 'we'd a bit of a problem at Sammy

Moore's. They weren't able to give us a numbered shirt for you. We've a blank one here … or, I can go back out to the car and get you last year's shirt. It's a bit faded after thirty washes or so but it does have a number on the back.' It says something about male vanity, I suppose, but Mickey went with the one with the number and Queen's played in ten smart new shirts alongside a fellow in a faded green top that had seen better days.

Club politics decreed I wasn't a 1st team regular. I would say that, though, wouldn't I! Though I reckon I did play at some stage for each of the five teams that Queen's put out, I had enough of a run to have seeded the memory bank. One particular reminiscence stands out, if only because of the other party involved. He was Jackie Fullerton, a pacy winger who had a great career in the Irish League and went on to become a popular broadcaster, first with UTV and then with the BBC.

Jackie is the loveliest guy, a renowned crooner and a merciless mimic of the whole cast of the Northern Irish press corps. I remember walking into my local bookshop in Greystones some years back and being confronted by his smiling face on the shelf. I didn't know he'd written a memoir. I picked it up and took it to the till. Bernie, a friend from the local tennis club, expressed her surprise when she saw me proffering it as a purchase. 'Sure, you know him. Would he not have given you a copy?'

'Bernie,' I said, 'if I ever go to the trouble of writing a book, the last thing I'm going to do is give it away.' It turned out to be a terrific read.

That, though, is not the point of the story. The point is that Jackie, outside left extraordinaire, was coming back from injury and playing for Glenavon Reserves, Glenavon being the team from Lurgan in the Irish League who were regular contenders for honours.

On the Saturday in question, I found myself at right back. Whatever had been going on, we were clearly out of term time and a gap needed to be filled. I found myself marking Jackie and I don't mind admitting, I was perplexed at the prospect. We had a few old jousts out on the touchline, he trying to outfox his younger (oh, how he'll hate that) opponent, me trying to show him the line, the classic full back ploy, to make the winger go the long way round in the hope that he'd be cut off at the pass.

I was happy enough with the way things were going, when the ball was swept out Jackie's way and he went for it, backing his pace to take me on the outside and get in a cross.

The one thing I had back than was that I was quick off the mark, like a Porsche going from zero to sixty in no time. When Jackie played the ball past me and went to go round on the outside, I went with him. It was my wrong side, being left-footed, but never mind, the principle is the same. He got close to the goal line and went to cross. I arrived exactly as I'd hoped I would. He swung his left leg, I extended my right and there was the most almighty thud as I blocked his attempt and the ball spun harmlessly away. Jackie, the most charming of men, has a minor black spot in his memory. He says he cannot remember the day I got the better of him. In fairness, had he got his cross in and Glenavon scored, I wouldn't have remembered it either!

Finding myself in my mind's eye back on those playing fields at The Dub at Upper Malone, the memories come flooding back. There was the day we were out on a pitch up at the rear of the playing fields, which had once been home to Malone Golf

Club. You can just imagine an elevated green with bunkers all round. Off in the distance, down the hillside, two figures were approaching. As the ball went out for a throw-in and one of our players went to retrieve it, he recognised them. Returning to the touchline, he let us know who these potential spectators were. 'See them there,' he called, 'that's Father Farquhar and Father Farquhar's father.' His Belfast accent overlaid a generous slice of humour to the statement. The players convulsed as the words came out as 'Fahrr Farker and Fahrr Farker's fahrr'!

Tony Farquhar was one of the university chaplains and regularly brought his elderly dad along for the walk and an hour or so in the fresh air. He would eventually become Auxiliary Bishop of the Diocese of Down and Connor while serving as President of Queen's Association Football Club. On his retirement, on age grounds, in 2015, he was the longest serving bishop in Ireland.

His ministry had young people firmly in its focus and he'd often talk to them about his episcopal motto, *Sapientia Proficere*, which translates as Increase in Wisdom, or as he'd put it to the kids in the vernacular of his native Belfast, 'Grow up and wise up.'

Tony Farquhar isn't the only bishop I can call a friend. One of my classmates in German at Queen's was Donal McKeown, whose long sacerdotal career brought him to the Bishop's House in Derry.

The Football Club itself wasn't short on characters either, among them guys who weren't what you'd call the most diligent as far as training was concerned but were nevertheless most welcome because their readiness to run out on a Saturday meant we were always able to field five full teams.

Turlo Burch was one such. Tall and tousle-haired, he'd rock up just when you thought you were going to have to start with ten men and would then proceed to run riot up the right wing, terrorising the opposition defence. The pity was he was regularly too fast for the rest of us and his best efforts often came to nothing.

There was Herbie Artt, whose family name was a byword for honey in Northern Ireland. We'd have had the impression that Herbie would have been loaded, wanting for nothing with a big local business behind him. Not a bit of it. Herbie's kit was deficient in almost every department. In place of shin guards, he used to stuff copies of the *Reader's Digest* down his socks.

Patsy Hennessy was a jovial little inside forward, Neville Todd a striker. Neville's dad, Jimmy Todd, was a former amateur international, a devout teetotaller whose time as a player at Glentoran had ended in bizarre circumstances when he was accused of being seen the night before a game 'blind drunk on the Newtownards Road'. Jimmy walked out in disgust. When I got to know Neville, his dad was the manager of Crusaders and, unlike most in his position, he would conclude his weekend at the sparsely attended Sunday evening service in his local Presbyterian church.

At my first training session, Stephen Kingon leant me his suave Adidas football boots to replace the rugby footwear I had brought with me. Stephen went on to become one of Northern Ireland's leading accountants, the chair of Northern Ireland Electricity and the Northern Ireland Chamber of Commerce. Davy Hamilton – no relation – finished with football and became an international in lawn bowling, a particularly popular summer sport where I come from.

We'd a number of players from England. I remember signing Paul Noall during Freshers' Week. He was from Lancashire and had his dad with him. He'd come from a proper footballing background and was soon a fixture in goal, tall, slim, elegant, commanding and a fine shot stopper. Stevie Pearce didn't cut quite the same dash but was pretty effective as a bustling winger.

Jim McCrae, another Englishman, was what they called a mature student, somebody not straight out of school. As a prototype wing back, I supplied the cross from the left for Jim to head the winning goal at Holywood Rangers. It's the best part of fifty years ago now, but I still get a thrill from the recall.

Frank McGettigan came from north London and was an angular right back who reminded me of Harry Creighton, a stalwart in that position for Glentoran in the Irish League. Harry didn't really look the part, but he was effective, as was Frank. Years later – we'd lost touch in the way peripheral uni pals do – we bumped into each other at some bunfight or other and it was as if all the intervening years just melted away. He was now in a senior position at Channel 4 and I was with RTÉ. It's a funny old world. It was the late 1980s and I was over and back to England to cover football more or less every weekend. 'Next time you're in London …' said Frank.

When next I was, I gave him a call and was invited round to the office for a drink. It was Friday teatime – time to kick back. 'Come up and meet the boss,' he said. In no time, he was knocking on the door and ushering me in to be introduced to Michael Grade, Channel 4's Chief Executive, all red braces and bonhomie – one of the main players in showbiz in the UK, putting down the welcome mat for the guy from RTÉ because he happens to be Frank's mate. It was exactly like it's played in the movies: the huge office, the equally huge desk … and the bottle of whiskey.

Along with the good days, there were some bad days on the pitch too. Rod McDonald, a creative inside forward, broke his leg. Kevin Finnegan, a centre half who went on to become a County Court judge, emerged from an aerial contest with a deep gouge on this forehead that necessitated an ambulance trip to hospital. And not long after, he suffered serious injury in a gun attack at his father's off-licence.

Then there was the afternoon we were approaching full-time in our match when the unmistakable sound of an explosion rumbled our way from the centre of Belfast. It was only when we repaired to the clubhouse to refresh ourselves with the regulation shandies as we watched the football results come up on television, that we learned of the horror that had unfolded in town.

The news bulletin that followed the sports programme led with it. Two people had been killed and over 130 wounded in a terrorist attack at the Abercorn Bar and Restaurant in Arthur Square in the centre of town. On a busy Saturday afternoon, the place was packed with shoppers, most of them women, when a five-pound bomb exploded under a table in the ground-floor restaurant. We watched aghast as the BBC reporter, Andrew Colman, delivered the details before breaking down, apparently in shock, saying, 'I'm sorry, I can't continue.' It turned out that Andrew, a brilliant journalist who went on to head the BBC News operation in Belfast, in doing his best to get back to report on the horror barely half an hour after the attack, had sprinted the mile back from Arthur Square to the studio and was still breathless when the cue light went on.

The early years of the violence in Northern Ireland were the backdrop to my time at Queen's. The Abercorn atrocity was perpetrated on Saturday, 4 March 1972. The victims – Ann Owens and Janet Bereen, in for a coffee after a day's retail therapy – are recorded as victims 293 and 294 in the encyclopedia of the horror that is entitled *Lost Lives: The Stories of the Men, Women and Children Who Died as a Result of the Northern Ireland Troubles.* It is seared into my memory because of its awfulness and the circumstances in which I learned it had happened.

How on earth could life go on? But somehow, it just did. On my first Wednesday at Queen's, there had been a civil rights march in the centre of Belfast, which went off with the good humour you'd expect of a Rag Week parade. But, of course, things could be a lot more serious, and mid-week evenings in the McMordie Hall, as the space in the basement of the Students' Union was then known, would regularly host protest meetings. At these, those who would become prominent in wider politics, such as Bernadette Devlin as she then was, would regularly harangue the audience.

With all the wider issues unfolding around me, football was my recreation and I was learning how to act in the best interests of the club I was serving as secretary, posting team selections on the ground-floor noticeboard and regularly checking to see who had ticked to show their availability and who had not, sourcing replacements where necessary, the only way to ensure that those five Queen's teams would take to the pitch with a full complement on the following Saturday afternoon.

I was really enjoying my time as a regular football player. Where I'd played rugby because that was what you did, I was now involved in something I really wanted to do and do well. We trained twice a week. Denis Clarke would organise Mondays.

We'd meet at the gym in Sans Souci Park just off the Malone Road, then jog the two miles to the playing fields, where he'd oversee the exercises in the dark – there were no floodlights – and after our conditioning session, we'd jog back down the Malone Road to the gym. Then, Wednesday afternoons, we'd be up at The Dub, less of the training and more of the practice matches. That was most enjoyable.

The first manager would come later, a tall, rotund, red-headed individual our third team – the Colts – would have come up against when he played centre forward for Laurel Lodge in the Amateur League. His rubicund features were a tribute to his refreshment of choice and quite something in the bright tangerine sported by his team; it leant him an unusual look for a striker, but he was effective and, best of all, he knew his football. His name was Brian Halliday. He went on to manage Cliftonville and Larne, then emigrated to California, where he continued his involvement with the sport while establishing a successful insurance business and ended up with a radio show enthusing over soccer for an American audience. He passed away in 2019.

Without a manager, though, and with a committee that had little interest in involving itself in the nitty gritty of running the club as long as it gave them their game at the weekend, as secretary I was left pretty much to my own devices. And as long as I kept the fixture calendar ticking over by attending the various League meetings and developing relationships with the other clubs involved, it was very much plain sailing.

It was over a beer with guys from one of the other sporting associations that I learned that the university had what was called a Games Fund. If you could come up with a project that looked like it would work to the benefit of the club, the Games Fund would back you with hard cash.

Remember, I was studying German, as well as French. I'd gone on a student exchange to the Black Forest while still at school. I'd been on a student trip to Paris. I liked travelling. What if I could convince the Games Fund that the Queen's University Football Club should go on tour?

I put my plan to the committee, who shrugged in that non-committal undergraduate way. Sure, we'd be for it, if it ever happens. I was by no means discouraged by this underwhelming indifference. On the contrary, it was par for the course. I knew if I could make it happen, there'd be no shortage of volunteers.

My proposal was for a week-long trip during the Christmas holidays, taking in New Year's Eve. It was all remarkably straightforward for this rookie nineteen-year-old tour operator. The people at the Games Fund were enthusiastic. Nobody had ever tried anything like this before. My enquiries led me to a travel company based near Ostend in Belgium, which was able to translate my request for three fixtures into a week-long itinerary. If we booked our flights, they'd have a coach at the airport to meet us and transport us to the hotel they'd arrange in the Belgian coastal city. There would be a game in Ostend itself and another not too far up the motorway, with the third across the border in the Netherlands.

On the morning we were due to leave Belfast, the phone rang at home in Rochester Avenue. I was flabbergasted to be getting a call from Belgium. It was just the final confirmation of the arrangements, together with the assurance that I'd be getting a commission from them for putting the business their way. The thought of being paid for this was the last thing on my mind. I expressed my doubts about whether this was appropriate. The voice on the other end of the phone assured me that that was how it was done. Their contribution was a most welcome addition to the beer kitty when we got to Belgium.

The three games were unremarkable. My clearest memory is of being pressed into service as an outside left under floodlights at the Dutch venue, then finding when we were received in the clubhouse after the game that we were expected to pay for the food that was laid on. In Belgium, we had been welcome guests. There had been no question of money changing hands.

The other distinct recollection is of our sortie, amply fortified, into the centre of Ostend to celebrate New Year in the deserted streets. Our revelry alerted the local constabulary, who arrived keen to transport us to one of their establishments where we would likely have been charged with disturbing the peace. It was the ensuing dialogue in French that ensured we actually spent the night in our own lodgings. I had clearly found an appropriate expression for contrition in my second language.

We had a lot of fun on that trip. I fondly recalled it on many an occasion subsequently as the time I took Queen's Football Club into Europe. The fun continued on the journey home. With no direct flights, the routing with British European Airways (BEA) as it then was, took us from Brussels via Heathrow. In those early days of 1970, the Belfast route from London was served by a Vickers Vanguard turbo-prop aircraft, with a single flight a day operated by the new Hawker Siddeley Trident jet.

It just so happened that the most favourable connection for the second leg was on board the Trident. For a group with precious few flying hours between them, travelling on a three-engined jet was an adventure in itself. We were all excited when we boarded our late afternoon flight. Now this was January, of course, and it was pretty chilly. The journey across the Irish Sea was uneventful and the announcement duly came that we'd be landing at Belfast's Aldergrove airport in ten minutes or so. We descended in the darkness. We awaited the thump as the tyres made contact with the tarmac. But there was no thump, just an almighty roar from those three jet engines at the rear as the aircraft clambered skywards again.

Another announcement duly followed – there was frost on the runway. We'd go round again and make another attempt to land. Ten or fifteen minutes later, the same scenario played out and we were roaring away from the ground again. This time, the captain assured us, he'd been able to have a really good look and he'd decided that he would be able to land if he came in for a third time.

At this point, the colour had drained from the cheeks of several of our party. There were others wondering if we mightn't have been better off on the old reliable turbo-prop Vanguard that would have been more forgiving in the conditions.

We prepared for our third approach and descended towards the south-west, lining up on Runway 25. The landing lights picked out the hoar frost on the fields adjoining the airport. Down, down, down, until … that roar again. They weren't going to risk it.

'Ladies and gentlemen, came the announcement, the captain has decided it is potentially unsafe to attempt a landing given the frost on the runway, so we are diverting to Dublin.'

The groans were audible. It was now well after six o'clock.

It would be another thirty minutes or so before we would land. And Belfast would be the best part of three hours away, up the road or however they chose to get us there.

Touchdown at Dublin was straightforward and within minutes we were disembarking. We collected our baggage and awaited further information. It was decided that we'd be put on the train to Belfast, so transport was being arranged for the transfer to Connolly Station on Amiens Street.

I found a public telephone and with a degree of difficulty – it was 1970 and dialling Belfast wasn't a function that was available – I placed a call to my dad. He'd have learned when he went to collect me at Aldergrove that we'd been diverted and they'd have told him we'd be coming by train. So he'd be at Great Victoria Street station for our late-night arrival.

Our historic trip was ending dramatically. The nascent newsman in me smelt a story. I asked my dad to call the newsroom at the *Belfast Telegraph* and see if they'd send a reporter round to meet us off the train. They did better than that. Our bedraggled and weary squad emerged from the platform to be met by a photographer. Queen's FC had never had such coverage. The story, and the picture of the returning tourists, featured prominently in the sports pages the following evening.

We'd good players at Queen's who went on to make a name for themselves in the semi-professional game. Jackie McManus was one – our number 10, our inside left as they were then known. He became a central defender at Dundalk and, in 1976, won the League of Ireland championship with them, the first major trophy under their legendary manager Jim McLaughlin.

Davy McMillan and Davy Malcolmson were two who went

on to have solid careers at the top local level. I like to think I might have followed them.

In the summer that followed my first season as secretary, my second year at Queen's, I signed up for a coaching course, intent on earning my badges. It was being held at our own playing fields at the Dub, so I felt very much at home.

Most of those taking part were Irish League players, hoping to cement a long-term future in the game. The one I remember best was Billy Sinclair, a Scot who played for Glentoran, the team I followed. In a practice match, I was playing on the same side, in my regular position of left back. He was in his regular midfield slot, in possession, looking in my direction and barking instructions. 'Go away, go away,' he called and I did so, stepping back to give him more room to approach the touchline. 'No, no,' he shouted as the ball went out of play. 'I didn't want you there.' It was only then that I realised I'd misheard the call. His rich Scottish brogue wasn't intoning 'Go away.' He had wanted me to go wide, the better to receive his pass!

One of the coaches in charge was another Scot, Gibby McKenzie, who was a bit of a legend in Irish League circles having managed Portadown for twelve years already, taking them to within a missed penalty of the League title in 1962. I had obviously made some kind of impression on the pitch alongside regular players from the top level, for at the end of the week, Gibby took me to one side.

'Who do you play for?' he asked.

'Queen's,' I told him.

'Would you fancy coming to Portadown?' I couldn't believe it. Here I was, only two years into regular football and here was this seasoned old pro inviting me to join one of the twelve teams in the top League. I really want to say I jumped at the chance. But I couldn't. Year three at Queen's was actually a year out for language students, spending the time abroad, becoming fluent. I was due to go to Germany that September.

Embarrassed, I told Gibby I couldn't take up his offer. 'Never worry,' he said. 'Come back to me when you're home.'

* * *

I had first visited Germany on a school exchange in the summer of 1967. I travelled to London with my friends, the Leckey boys, to meet up with a group from all over the United Kingdom who would be heading to Freiburg im Breisgau, a beautiful old city on the edge of the Black Forest, tucked into a little triangle where Switzerland and France meet the south-western corner of Germany.

Bertram Burgert was my host, so to speak, the seventeen-year-old who'd put his name forward to take part at the German end. He was the youngest of three brothers. His dad was a guard on the railway, a duty that would often take him away overnight. His mum, a lovely jolly lady, ran the household on the first floor of what is known in Germany as a *Mehrfamilienhaus*, an apartment building for several families that typically takes in two or three storeys. Not your typical high-rise at all. It's interesting to note that, even in 1967, the three families in the household shared a bathroom. That is to say, there was a toilet and basic washing facilities in the flat, but if you wanted a bath or shower, off you went with your towel to the bathhouse outside.

They were three idyllic weeks, when I found myself somewhere completely beyond my sphere of experience.

I'd been paired with the family because I'd put football as a major interest of mine. They were huge into one of the local teams, lesser lights these days, Freiburger FC. The first Saturday I was there, I was taken along to a match, introduced to all and sundry, then given a little tin can to rattle in front of spectators as I implored, '*Spendieren Sie ein bißchen für die FC Jugend?*' (Would you care to spare a few pfennigs for the FC Youth Team?)

The next weekend, the 1st XI had a game in Mannheim, two hours away up the autobahn past Stuttgart. That was a thrill, as I piled into the family's Volkswagen Beetle with the three Burgert boys for the trip to the game. We hardly had an M1 in Northern Ireland and the south of Ireland barely had a flyover. Now, here I was hurtling up one of Europe's state-of-the-art motorways. Talk about an education!

This, by the way, was a regional league game, which we'll say no more about because Freiburg lost 4–0. The interesting thing here is that the Bundesliga, Germany's top tier, only came into existence in 1963, so the kind of history that I heard talked about in terms of English, or even our own local, football didn't exist. Professionalism was anathema on the continent. Getting paid would have tainted the purity of sporting endeavour.

Prior to 1963, there was a collection of regional amateur leagues. The fact was that when I was watching Mannheim and Freiburg in what was one of the five geographically organised sections of the West German second tier, Eintracht Braunschweig were setting out to defend their Bundesliga title, only the fourth team (after FC Köln, Werder Bremen and 1860 Munich) to have won it.

Our visiting group went to language classes each morning, in the Berlitzschule in the centre of Freiburg, close by the Münsterplatz, a cobbled square dominated by the beautiful Gothic cathedral, which boasts the only church tower in Germany to have survived intact since the Middle Ages. One random memory is of the young teacher's car, a French Simca. Whatever happened to that marque?

At weekends, the family would take me on trips into the Black Forest, up to the local vantage point, the Schauinsland (which literally means 'look into the countryside'), to swim in Lake Titisee and have lunch in one of the many local taverns. This was where the inadequacy of my schoolboy German would emerge. The only word I recognised on the menu was *Forelle*, German for trout, and that only because of Schubert's famous quintet that bears the fish's name.

I had similar issues when I went to buy a bar of chocolate and a drink one afternoon. I had my script word perfect for the shopkeeper. It was only when he replied, offering a choice, that I was stumped. I hadn't a clue what he was saying. That's the thing about learning languages from books. It doesn't prepare you for using the words in the real world.

Of course, this was all just a foretaste of what would lie ahead of me when I signed up for my degree at Queen's. If I'm honest, I only ended up on a language course because of the absolute inadequacy of the career guidance at school.

Scott McAlpine, a bit of a bluffer who taught geography, doubled as the careers master. The standard advice he dispensed was to follow your grades into third level. I was good at languages, so the suggestion was to go and do a languages degree. And where would that lead me? Well, I was assured, there would be many opportunities.

Indeed. Neither of my parents had been to university. The only third-level graduate in our family was my cousin Stuart, who had taken a Bachelor of Arts in Spanish and French and had gone into schoolteaching. There were no dissenting voices at home when I said I was going to go for German and French.

It was only on one of my first days at Queen's, meeting a young man called Des Perry, that I realised I had the qualifications to go down the path he was following if only I had known. Des was doing a law degree. In 2010, by then a District Justice, obliged to impose a fine on a speeding motorist, he famously set the tariff at one penny, on the basis that, in his opinion, the case should never have been brought. I don't know that I'd have fancied a term on the bench, but I might well have enjoyed the cut and thrust of the courtroom from a position by the counsel table. It wasn't too late for me to change tack, but I suppose I didn't want to challenge the family decision that I was on the right track and, in any case, I quite fancied the idea of the anticipated year away.

That year turned out to be seminal, formative for me. I learned to speak German and I learned a lot about life – you might say it was the making of the man. I would spend three school terms there as an English language assistant, the native speaker who helps students hone their language skills. On the forms I filled in, I'd again mentioned football as my main recreational interest, so I was assigned to a school in a town called Mülheim, on the River Ruhr, right at the centre of the beating heart of the Bundesliga. In the end, I didn't play much football. I joined SV Heißen, who had a cinder pitch near where I had lodgings, but it was difficult for me, as a temporary resident, to get past the regulars and into a place on the team. I did go training twice a week, though, and I learned the on-pitch vernacular of a German footballer.

While there wouldn't be too much going on for me in terms of on-pitch action that year, Dortmund, Duisburg, Essen, Köln (Cologne), Mönchengladbach, Oberhausen and Schalke – seven of the eighteen teams in the top division – were less than an hour away from where I was based.

The year began with a week's acclimatisation for the squadron of twenty-year-old students who would be spending the next nine months at locations all over West Germany, offering examples of English as it is spoken in a variety of regional accents. We were briefed at a cultural centre in the small town of Altenberg, not far from Cologne, and on the Friday morning, we were let loose.

I boarded a train for the fifty-minute ride north to my new stomping ground. Through to Düsseldorf. Past the airport and on towards Duisburg. As we slowed on approach to the station that serves the world's largest inland port, situated where the Ruhr flows into the Rhine, the floodlights of the Wedau Stadium stood tall beside the tracks. MSV Duisburg, one of my new local teams, played there.

It's only five minutes from Duisburg to Mülheim and in no time I was ringing the doorbell at the bungalow on Fichtestraße, in the suburb of Heißen, right next to the boundary with the city of Essen, that would be my home till the following summer. I was taking over the lodgings that the previous year's assistant at my school had used and they'd come highly recommended.

Maria Lehnhoff was a sixty-something widow whose husband

had designed and built this fine residence, a touch on the dark side inside because of the preponderance of heavy wood, but a welcoming home nonetheless. I wasn't the only lodger. There was a married couple at the end of the hall who were saving to buy their own property and a gentleman from Augsburg in Bavaria whose duties as a salesman brought him into the area several days a week.

Frau Lehnhoff had lunch prepared and we hit it off straight away. She suggested I take myself back into town and familiarise myself with my new surroundings. I took her advice and boarded the tram for the ten-minute ride down the hill towards the river. I began what the Germans would call a *Stadtbummel*, a stroll through the streets, and in due course found myself outside the offices of one of the local newspapers on Schloßstraße. As was the fashion then, the *Neue Ruhr Zeitung* pinned that day's edition in the front window for passers-by to read, so I stopped to see what was happening in my new neighbourhood. It turned out that MSV Duisburg had a game that evening, at home to Eintracht Braunschweig. I hurried back up to Fichtestraße to say I'd be skipping the evening meal and went straight back out to find my way to the stadium in Duisburg, which turned out to be nowhere as near to the station as it seemed when I'd seen it from the train earlier on. It wasn't exactly the most glittering introduction to the Bundesliga. The match ended 0–0.

The following day, I'd arranged to meet one of the English students who'd been at the induction in Altenberg. Denis, from Sheffield if I'm not mistaken, would spend his year in Essen, and on that Saturday, the local team – Rot-Weiß – had a derby against rivals from just the other side of my town, Rot-Weiß

Oberhausen. Great names. Red-and-White Essen against Red-and-White Oberhausen.

Essen normally played in a small stadium on the north side of the city, but for this season they were based in the rather grand setting of the Grugapark. The pair of us met up early to make sure we got in and secured ourselves standing positions on the vast bank of terracing behind one of the goals. The Gruga Stadium, like most in Germany then, included an athletics track. It was probably on that day that I came to realise what, apart from the track, made the venues there so different to those I was used to.

Back home, and in England, football grounds tended to be in the midst of built-up areas, down the end of streets of terraced houses. Here in Germany, they were mostly on the edge of town, often surrounded by parkland. It wasn't bedroom windows you saw between the stands. It was trees.

Over fifty years on, a local derby between two teams nobody outside Germany knows much about any more might not be worth recalling. But this was drama of the highest order. We were two lads, at the start of an adventure, with a foreign football game for the ages. Essen was one of six teams sharing top spot in the table at this early stage of the season, Oberhausen one of three of the eighteen in the top division with just a single point to show for their efforts across four weekends before that Saturday in September 1970.

Neither of us had a clue about any of the players we were watching. I was just high at the thought of a year in this place, a whole calendar of first-class football on my doorstep. It soon became clear that the home favourite was a Dutch winger by the name of Willi Lippens, known on the terraces as 'Ente', the

German for duck, because he had a peculiar waddling style when he ran.

Ente Lippens was no slouch, though, and came to Essen's rescue after they went 1–0 down early on. He rose to head the equaliser and give us our first taste of a proper German fan roar. Things went downhill for his team from there on and Oberhausen cruised into a 3–1 lead.

I looked at my watch. It was twenty to five. 'Can't be long left,' I said to my new pal and Denis nodded, the pair of us schooled on the old First Division in England where a 3 p.m. kick-off and a ten-minute half-time meant that twenty to five was when the referee started playing injury time.

But this game went on. Ente Lippens put Günter Fürhoff in for a second for Essen and suddenly, at 3–2 to Oberhausen, it was now all about how long the ref would play. We looked at each other. There was no injury time to speak of. Why were they playing on so long? And then it dawned. Traditional kick-off time in Germany is 3.30 p.m. not 3 p.m. on a Saturday afternoon. We were now in the final fifteen minutes and Essen still had a chance. They kept knocking on the door and then it happened. Another cross and there was Ente Lippens once more, rising to head the goal that saved the day for Essen. Denis and I had plenty to discuss when we made it back into town for what was quite possibly the first Stauder Pils – the Essen brew – of our year by the Ruhr.

I don't remember the Monday morning headline after that particular derby, though I would certainly have been aware of it. Frau Lehnhoff, who took the *Westdeutsche Allgemeine* newspaper, always made sure that the sports section was on the breakfast table for whenever I appeared. But I do remember a later headline from the round-up of the final matches of that Bundesliga season. '*Böses Foul von Beckenbauer*', it read ('Bad Foul by Beckenbauer'), introducing the report on a game I'd attended on the final weekend of that season – MSV Duisburg against Bayern Munich. I was on my own in the Wedau that day. By now, I was well into the Bundesliga and knew all about the various characters, so I was no longer starstruck by Bayern, who boasted so many top international players – Sepp Maier in goal, Beckenbauer himself, Franz Roth, Paul Breitner, Uli Hoeneß. Gerd Müller was suspended for this final game.

I refound my inner underdog. Bayern were top of the table on goal difference, ahead of Borussia Mönchengladbach (which has to be my favourite team title of them all). Gladbach were away to Frankfurt and were expected to win but if Bayern could see off Duisburg, who were mid-table, with nothing to play for, they would clinch the title. So far, so straightforward.

It was all arranged. Blue light escort to Düsseldorf airport after the game and a flight back to Munich where the fans would be waiting to acclaim the champions. Except that Duisburg had other ideas. And the bad foul by Franz Beckenbauer emerged as a kind of symbol for how Bayern had lost the sympathy vote.

They're known now as FC Hollywood for the glitz, the glamour and the money. I still have a soft spot for them because they are a Munich team. But I'll let Ulrich Hesse-Lichtenberger take up the story, as he related it in his English-language history of German football, which he called *Tor!* – the German for goal: 'It's hard to pinpoint when people began viewing Bayern as evil incarnate but what's certain is that it happened a lot earlier than is generally believed today. Take the last day of that memorable

1970–71 season. Bayern travelled to Duisburg, level on points with Gladbach.'

I can't believe it, I was there. 'The Bavarians were not yet a superpower, having won just two titles … When the players ran out, Franz Beckenbauer was "shocked at the hate" confronting his team.'

Beckenbauer's bad foul – I remember it well, the cynical challenge that it was. Bayern lost 2–0. Gladbach won at Frankfurt. It was their title. There would be no blue lights down the autobahn to the airport.

I read the headline over my Westphalian ham and cheese at Frau Lehnhoff's breakfast table the following Monday morning. It was a seminal moment, reading that in the *Westdeutsche Allgemeine* about a German World Cup hero. And I've loved recalling it since, a reminder of how, to an outsider, all is not necessarily as it seems.

The year in Mülheim was memorable for many reasons. I enjoyed introducing a little novelty to the classroom. I'd bring my guitar along, play the kids Simon and Garfunkel, and James Taylor, and then we'd discuss the lyrics. That went down very well, even if my attempts at imparting my mother tongue left something to be desired. One of the boys, Franck Förster, wanted to express his appreciation and reached for an English equivalent of the German *'Sie sind schwer auf Draht!'* What he came out with was a literal translation – 'You are heavy on the wire, Mr Hemmilton' – when what he really wanted to say was, 'You're really switched on.' I left them speaking English of a sort, with a distinctly Belfast accent!

The year was hugely educational for me. It was noticeable on public transport that the reserved seats were for pregnant women, the elderly and war wounded, a reminder that this was only twenty-five years after the cessation of hostilities in the Second World War. The number of men you'd see on the street missing a limb was quite astonishing. And then you wondered about the tram driver that you kind of got to know because you were always travelling the same route in a small town; was he once maybe a member of the Hitler Youth?

The regional education ministry laid on a week's visit to West Berlin, really a propaganda exercise to emphasise that the Soviet Union had only a small portion of what had once been Germany's capital. It was quite an experience. The Kurfürstendamm, developed by Bismarck from the old route out of town to the hunting lodges of the aristocracy, had been turned into a kind of Fifth Avenue, a German Champs-Elysées, with all the leading department stores and an abundance of restaurants, bars and retail. Berlin's old main street – the broad avenue of lime trees named Unter den Linden – was beyond the Brandenburg Gate, behind the Wall, a dull shadow of what had once been one of Europe's most fashionable boulevards. Rising high above it was what remains Germany's tallest structure, the television tower built by the government of the German Democratic Republic – the Deutsche Demokratische Republik (DDR), familiarly known as East Germany – as a symbol of communist power.

Three hundred and sixty-five metres tall, with broadcast antenna on top, the slim column features a spherical structure, 200 metres up, designed as a reminder of the Soviet Sputnik satellites, housing a viewing platform and a revolving restaurant. In bright sunlight, the stainless-steel tiles of this dome reflect an image in the shape of a cross, an irony prompting Berliners to remark that this was the Pope's revenge for the secular socialist government's removal of crucifixes from the churches of East Germany.

It was to be a do-as-you-please week. We travelled by train from the West, armed with all manner of promotional material from the tourist office at our destination. We checked out the sights and came to the conclusion that there might well be more worth seeing in the East than what was on offer amid the bright lights of the Kurfürstendamm.

The Berlin U-Bahn – the underground – was managed out of West Berlin. The network featured a number of so-called ghost stations, stops that were now in East Berlin and had been closed by the authorities there. The lights were on but there was nobody home. East Berliners were not allowed passage into the West. By contrast, the overground system, the S-Bahn, run by the DDR state railway, operated throughout the city. We ended up spending most of our days on the other side of the Wall.

There was no issue about us, as foreigners, entering East Berlin. We could have walked through history at Checkpoint Charlie, but that would have been a roundabout way of doing it. Instead, we took the train to Friedrichstraße, alighted there, presented our papers, completed the obligatory exchange of a minimum of twenty western Deutschmarks into Ostmarks at parity, the cash useless if we didn't spend it in the East, then descended the staircase from the platform to the street.

The first morning, we turned right for Unter den Linden and in no time at all, were accosted by a young man keen to buy whatever item of clothing we might be prepared to sell – jeans, a pair of shoes I'd bought on a Queen's French Society trip to Paris, anything. Western gear was obviously a status symbol.

Apart from the fact that we'd have looked pretty silly wandering around half clad, it didn't seem like a good idea to be engaging in any kind of trade that might bring us to the attention of the authorities.

It was a strange kind of freedom, wandering streets bereft of traffic, looking in shop windows that offered little.

On Alexanderplatz, the central square that was used as the title of Alfred Döblin's great novel on the decline and fall of the Weimar Republic, the vast pedestrian concourse offered an eloquent summary of the state of the nation. Having walked for half an hour beneath the lime trees that gave the avenue its name, past the historic Humboldt University, on across the island in the River Spree, home to the cathedral, just as the Île de la Cité in Paris has at its heart Notre Dame, pausing to take it in before gazing up at the TV tower that was the next landmark, Alexanderplatz was stark, brutal in appearance.

A communist-state department store called Centrum dominated, the grey of its exterior matching the depressing dullness of what was on offer inside. A well-stocked bookshop a little further along was little more than a literary *trompe-l'œil*, offering a vast selection of tedious state-censored fiction and a huge array of political propaganda. Mind you, it did my student street cred no harm when I returned to Queen's with a copy of Karl Marx's *Das Kapital* that I'd actually bought in East Berlin.

The vista beyond Alexanderplatz told another story. As far as the eye could see were Soviet-style high rises, apartment blocks for the proletariat. Twenty-five years behind the Iron Curtain and East Berlin had diverged down an entirely different architectural track to its other half back beyond the Wall.

Returning for the World Cup in 2006, I arrived at the magnificent central station that had been developed after reunification. On the taxi ride to our hotel, in the old Soviet sector, I got talking to the driver about how things had changed. He was an East Berliner, a graduate engineer, who had enjoyed a comfortable lifestyle under the communist regime. The apartment that came with his status was spacious, his children's education was free, as was the family's health care. He'd had a car and really wanted for nothing.

But with the fall of the Wall, everything changed. He told me of the manufacturing plant that had produced the vast majority of brassieres for the Soviet bloc. When western management marched in to run the place, they concluded it wasn't fit for purpose and closed it down. With it went the livelihoods of many families. My taxi driver's employer was taken over by a big West German engineering conglomerate (Siemens) and things changed dramatically. He now had to pay for services the state had provided before. And as the parent company rationalised, so his part of the business was closed down and he was now driving a taxi.

His story reminded me of a conversation I had with a German friend, a man you'll meet later, for he was alongside me in Stuttgart at the famous Euro 88 match when Ray Houghton put the ball in the English net and everything changed, changed utterly. Walter Johanssen would go on to lead German Television's Olympic coverage in London in 2012. When the Wall came down, I asked him how he viewed the prospects. He was not alone as a West German, a resident of Hamburg is his case, in questioning what it might mean for people like him and his family who would be hit severely by what reunification would cost. He wasn't suggesting it wasn't for the best for Germany, merely that it was going to have to be paid for somehow and it was his generation who would have to stump up.

My year in Germany came to an end and I headed back to Belfast ready to join Portadown for pre-season. It was then that my dad broke the news. Gibby McKenzie had been sacked and no longer had a club. My career at the top level had ended before it began.

4

Does a Duck Swim?

The news of Gibby McKenzie's sacking was disappointing. I wouldn't be signing for Portadown, so my mates at Queen's pressed me into another year as secretary of the club and I carried on playing, happily enough. I didn't know it at the time but it would be my final season as a soccer player.

My mother's sister Isobel worked in the BBC. She was important enough to sign the cheques when her boss was on leave. I can't be sure when my fascination with broadcasting started, but I put it down to those Saturday afternoons with my dad, waiting, waiting, listening to the light music they played – 'Arrivederci Roma' is lodged in my mind – tunes they played on the *Light Programme* while they waited for the teams to emerge at the start of the second half, the only part of a game they were allowed to broadcast. Right up until my time working in London and beyond, it wasn't permitted to say which match was being covered until kick-off time. It's hard to believe now, with wall-to-wall football on TV, that the football authorities' fear of affecting attendances prevented the BBC from announcing which match would be featured until the crowds were actually in, and even then would only allow commentary on the second half.

Those were the days when the complete football programme kicked off at 3 p.m. on a Saturday afternoon. At five minutes to four, the commentary would start and I would be spellbound for the forty-five minutes, kicking a little ball up and down the hall, living the ebb and flow of the match. Just as well it was only my dad and me. I think my mother would have feared for the safety of her ornaments.

Subliminally planted, the flair for broadcasting would flourish further when we got our first television. I reckon this would have been around 1957, for we had had the black and white set for a while, with just the BBC to watch, before Ulster Television came on air at Halloween in 1959.

The *Belfast Telegraph* was delivered every evening and my father would always read the editorial, which was presented in the left-hand column on the front page under the title 'Viewpoint'. The media held me spellbound. Already addicted to the '*Tele*' – always starting at the back with the sports reports – I took the notion that I might have some fun if I pretended to be a television presenter and read the Viewpoint column aloud. I'd do this like the men (and they were all men at the time) who did it for real on TV in those pre-autocue days, attempting to avoid glancing down at the script as far as possible, so they could look straight down the lens of the camera.

There I was, with all these hours as a sitting-room broadcaster racked up, about to begin my final year at Queen's, facing the prospect of entering the world of employment, uncertain what I could do with my modern languages degree.

Despite the fact that my year in West Germany had made it clear to me that I did not feel at home in the classroom, I applied for a place on the HDip at Trinity in Dublin. I thought teaching might be my only option. I was accepted.

I also took the Northern Ireland Civil Service entrance exam – with an Arts degree, that was a possibility. Parental encouragement was a factor. My dad would have been more of a free spirit. My mother's ambition for me was a 'staff job', with a pension at the end. When you're twenty-two, imagining yourself as a sixty-something cashing in your chips is not at all appealing. I was offered a place in the Civil Service.

'Procrastination is the thief of time' was one of my father's favourite aphorisms. I can't imagine he knew he was quoting an eighteenth-century English man of letters. Edward Young's long blank verse poem 'Night-Thoughts' includes this passage:

Be wise to-day; 'tis madness to defer;
Next day the fatal precedent will plead;
Thus on, till wisdom is push'd out of life.
Procrastination is the thief of time;
Year after year it steals, till all are fled,
And to the mercies of a moment leaves
The vast concerns of an eternal scene.

So true. Sadly, I was proving to be a master of procrastination. With an offer of a place on the Master of Business Administration programme at Queen's, I was able to put off joining the Civil Service for a year. I kicked for touch. And I went to see my Aunt Isobel.

Her cheque-signing shifts were proof she was well enough up the food chain in Ormeau Avenue to know what was what and who was who. I was well aware that the contributors to the Saturday evening sports round-up were not professional broadcasters. They were schoolteachers, mostly, and solicitors, civil servants too, people with day jobs who made a few bob at the weekend going to matches and talking about them. Was there any way I could become one of them?

It was a question that had to be asked. I had to confront reality. This itch had to be scratched. I could not enter the world of work without at least giving the broadcasting game a shot.

'Well,' said Isobel, 'there are auditions periodically and I can certainly put your name down for one. But after that, it's up to you.' If she'd been a footballer, my aunt would have been what they called a no-nonsense centre half.

She was as good as her word, though, and in due course, I got the call. Yes, they were holding auditions – that would involve going to a game, compiling a report, coming in to present it and then conducting an interview with a 'personality' to see how that would go. Great, I thought. And then my heart sank. They were oversubscribed with football reporters. Could I do something else?

Well, I'd played rugby at school. I followed Ireland. Sure, I'll give that a go. Malone Rugby Club wasn't far from our house. Ironically, it was about a hundred yards from Aunt Isobel's front door. In the days when club rugby was where it happened, Malone were decent, regularly represented on the international scene.

The following Saturday, they were hosting Academy, a club originally established by former pupils of the North Belfast grammar school that had given me such grief years before when their less than impartial umpire had brought my knock as Methody's opening bat to a premature end. Belfast Royal Academy, or BRA as it is known in the city, is some way down the Ulster Schools' Cup roll of honour, but one of its old boys is, according to the assessment of the Irish Rugby Football Union, the greatest ever Irish rugby player. The gentlemen of the Fourth Estate held a similar view. This is Paul McWeeney in *The Irish Times*, evaluating his contribution to Ireland's victory over France at Ravenhill in 1953:

> They seek him here, they seek him there,
> Those Frenchies seek him everywhere.
> The paragon of craft and guile,
> That damned elusive Jackie Kyle.

Kyle had been part of Ireland's first Grand Slam-winning team in 1948. Not that Academy were boasting.

There wasn't anything particularly special about the meeting of these two that Saturday afternoon in 1972. For goodness sake, those were the days when, in Irish inter-provincial matches, players wore the shirts and shorts of their province but were expected to play in their club socks! They weren't exactly sprinkling stardust when I rocked up at Gibson Park, Malone's well-appointed base on an east Belfast side road that's known to all and sundry from the vicinity as Daddy Winker's Lane.

Malone Rugby Club was like any other on the island of Ireland. Spectator facilities were concentrated in the clubhouse. There was a panoramic view from the bar or, if you were prepared to brave the elements, you could stand on the touchline.

That's what I did, as I compiled my very first match report. I took home my notebook, wrote up what I had seen – re-worked and polished it. Finally, and this was ten days later, I had the ninety seconds they had requested, ready to deliver.

I presented myself at reception in Broadcasting House. And at some point, on my way from the front desk to Studio 3 where my audition would take place, I was introduced to the most wonderful, exuberant, over-the-top absolute character – her catchphrase, 'Christ, dahling' – the lady who gave me wings, Joy Williams.

Auntie Joy, to all who knew her, was a woman in a man's world, the number two to the head of sport who was, in BBC parlance, designated by a set of initials. Malcolm Kellard was SPO – Sports Programmes Organiser. That put him below a Head of Department. Looking back, that told you how much sport mattered then.

Malcolm was a thorough gentleman, a gregarious individual who had progressed from fronting the television news to leading the group who put sport on the air, a position that fitted his personality perfectly, given the conviviality that came with a welcome from those who were only too happy to have their sporting organisations reach a wider public.

When I was poking and prodding, trying to find a way through the front door, the BBC Northern Ireland Sports Department didn't even live in the building. It had rooms down the street, in an office block called Bedford House. When its programmes, such as they were, would go on the air, they were given the space usually occupied by Radio Current Affairs, which only operated on weekdays.

So, on a Friday afternoon, on Bedford Street, which leads from the back of Belfast City Hall up to Shaftesbury Square and the university beyond, you would see a short procession of what appeared to be business people bearing files. This was the Sports Department of BBC Northern Ireland decamping for the weekend to the place where they belonged.

The venue for my audition was at the end of a corridor on the third floor, just beyond the office Sport took over at the weekend, one of two fully equipped radio studios that I was to learn handled the bulk of the local input to BBC Radio 4. I was shown through the control room and a very heavy door into a larger space with a round green-baize-covered table and chairs in the middle, and a microphone suspended in mid-air. On the table were several pairs of headphones, a little coloured light bulb on its stand in the centre (the cue light that would flash when it was time to speak) and – ever-present in every BBC radio studio I ever worked in before I returned to Dublin in 1984 – a small, Bakelite ashtray.

Joy sat beside the sound engineer on the other side of the soundproofed glass. The cue light flashed. I delivered my script. Then, through the headphones, I was invited out to listen back.

Two adjacent sentences in the report noted pressure from Malone and the surprising counter-attack that followed. My adverb of choice to conjoin these two statements was 'however'. Joy drew my attention to this, then asked me to tell her as I would over a cup of coffee just what had taken place.

So, I began. Malone were getting on top and looked like they might score, but then Academy broke away. She stopped me right there. You didn't use however, did you? She had cut to the quick in an instant, identifying the requirements of a narrated report as opposed to what might appear in print. You'd never use the word 'however', she said, if you were simply telling me the story. So it doesn't belong in a voice piece.

Reliving the moment reminds of what my good friend Jim Neilly is fond of remarking when he hears someone on the air who is less than adequate. Remind me again, he'll say, of what the middle B in BBC stands for.

I'd another example of the care and attention the British Broadcasting Corporation paid to these matters some years later, when, as an established contributor, I was invited to a session with Roy Williamson, who had moved on from a lengthy career as a newsreader on Radio 4 to become, effectively, the head of standards.

He had me read aloud a recent report I had done. I chose what I thought was a good one, about a recent unsolved killing. Somewhere along the way, I had noted that the police had no leads, introducing this information with the phrase 'One of the most baffling aspects of the case', which I delivered stressing the second 'of' as I had heard many a time on the air.

Roy smiled when I got to the end and said, 'Very good. I'd just like to pull you up on one thing. You spoke of the case being baffling. Would you read that sentence again, please?'

I did so and he asked me, 'What's the key word in there?'

I thought for a moment and replied, 'Baffling.'

'Indeed,' he replied. 'So why did you stress the word "of"?' I had no answer. It had been done for effect, aping others I'd heard who'd put pretentious delivery ahead of proper speech. It's easy. You just need to pay attention.

Back at my audition, I excised 'however' and returned to the studio for Take Two. It was warmly received. I was then introduced to a man whose face was familiar from local television screens. John Bennett was a teacher at Strandtown Primary School in east Belfast and, like a number in his profession, had found another outlet for his talents as a communicator. John presented the weekend sports preview on the teatime television news each Friday and doubled up as a football commentator.

He was so highly regarded in this capacity that they laid on a private plane to get him back from Wembley after a mid-week international between England and Northern Ireland, so that he wouldn't miss school the following morning.

John had been pressed into service as a stooge for the audition. He was to be the subject of my interview. Except that I wasn't interviewing John Bennett. This was role play. I was interviewing the manager of the Northern Ireland judo team!

Now, all that I knew, and indeed know, about judo could be written on the back of a postage stamp. And John Bennett wouldn't have known too much either, given the quality of his answers. But then, I suppose, that was the point. A difficult interviewee would give those judging my performance as an interviewer a better indication of how I might handle a real live situation.

To use a word from the lexicon of Ulster-Scots, I sprachled through somehow. They thanked me for my interest and I left with a valediction I wasn't sure I wanted to hear: 'Don't ring us, we'll ring you.'

They did, the following Thursday. I answered a page at Queen's and took the call in a phone booth by the Great Hall, looking out across the immaculately manicured lawn of the quadrangle.

It was Rosemary Clarke from the Sports office. 'Can you do a game for us on Saturday?' she asked.

'Does a duck swim?' I was tempted to reply. I couldn't believe it.

That, I suppose, was the moment my career as a player came to an end. If this was to develop into anything, my Saturdays would be spoken for. And back then, they didn't play soccer on a Sunday in Northern Ireland.

So instead of donning my kit and running out at the Dub playing fields, I'd be taking my place on the touchline of their principal rugby pitch, notebook and pen in hand, to watch the students take on one of Ulster's top teams, Ballymena RFC. They were led by the redoubtable Willie John McBride, with four Lion's tours under his belt already and soon to be captain of the invincible tourists in South Africa in 1974.

I must have stood out like a sore thumb among the sparse attendance because, in no time at all, I'd been joined by a man who introduced himself as Ed Curran. I knew the name, for sure, and I recognised him from his photograph in the paper. He worked for the *Belfast Telegraph* and would eventually become its editor.

He was at the Dub on assignment for the *Ireland's Saturday Night*, commonly known as *The Ulster*, or even *The Pink*, as it had begun life as the *Ulster Saturday Night* and, as was the practice with sports papers, was published on coloured newsprint. Like the *Tele*, it too came through our front door, and its arrival, around eight o'clock each Saturday evening, was one of the most anticipated events in my adolescence.

Ed Curran was like so many of those I would meet on early markings: engaging, interested in what I was up to and, above all, helpful. We watched the game together on that touchline, engaging in the 'who-done-whats' that I was to discover were a vital aspect of life in a press box, despite the absence of one at our venue – confirming identities at key moments, checking the time of the incident, all the little details that would show up for sure if you were to get it wrong. The sporting press is the most wonderful confraternity.

Game over, I took myself off down the Malone Road, which had been part of our regular evening training routine as soccer players. Part of my past now.

The office by the studio was a hive of activity as the squad of part-time reporters compiled their contributions, and those who'd been entrusted with a tape recorder listened back to their booty before taking it off to be edited. Every seat at the big table in the centre was taken, the sound of the clattering typewriters filling the room.

Standing at one end was Larry McCoubrey, the front man of the television news on weeknights, who was also BBC Northern Ireland television's football commentator. He was one of the principal personalities in local broadcasting, bags of charisma complementing a smiling face and a sharp brain. Larry was engaged on Saturdays to provide a review of the sporting press, which he did with characteristic humour. He didn't type, so a secretary was engaged to create his script as he dictated at her shoulder.

The clock ticked on remorselessly. Before you knew it, it was showtime. We filed into the studio, the one beside where I'd done my audition only ten days before. Similar set up, only the other way round. You turned left instead of right to reach the round table at the centre. The presenter, Ira Milligan, a man who seemed a lot less at ease in person than he did when I'd listened to him over the years, was already in position, and opposite him was an empty chair.

Those of us who would tell our tales of sporting endeavour that afternoon took our places on the seats around the perimeter of the studio, lined up according to where we figured in the running order. If I thought Ira Milligan was a little on the nervous side, it was nothing to how I was feeling.

I looked on agog. I was listening to voices that were so familiar, but now I was sitting only a matter of feet away, observing their mannerisms, noting the military-grade shine on primary teacher Harry Thompson's brown shoes and the suave urbanity of Bill Heaney (a man from the catering college) as they delivered their verdicts on the top Irish League football games. I tensed up as solicitor Brian Parker moved centre stage to add his observations, for he covered rugby and that meant I was next.

Deep breath. Move in. And wait for the cue. Ira wasn't nervous at all. It was just that his script trembled a little in his hands as he spoke. He was generous in his introduction, welcoming the new cub and, handing over, he fixed me with a smile. I could not have asked for more.

I can't tell you, though, how nerve-wracking the next minute actually was. Yes, I had a perfectly typed script in front of me and yes, I'd read it aloud time and again walking up and down the corridor outside the office. But here, with a microphone in front of me and all eyes in the studio and on the other side of the glass upon me, all I wanted was to get to the final full stop.

Thankfully, I made it, without pressing the accelerator too

hard. At around ten to seven on a Saturday evening in September 1972, my initiation was complete. I had become a part-time radio broadcaster.

At the end of the show, we all made our way to the BBC social club. It was like heading for the bar after a round of golf. Except in 1972, you wouldn't have been going to a bar in downtown Belfast. The *Sportsound* crew had, I learned, been habitués of the Elbow Room across the way on the corner of Bruce Street at the bottom of the Dublin Road. But public houses were no longer safe havens, with licensed premises deemed legitimate targets by paramilitaries on both sides.

We headed to what was known as simply 'The Club', round the back of the BBC site, on Linenhall Street. In the upstairs lounge, it was just like a regular rendezvous for old friends. Joy Williams was master of ceremonies, a big character who really loved her tribe. She would have had overall charge of the programme. Malcolm Kellard, though not directly involved in the Saturday show, would come for the crack (I can't be having 'craic' – it's a made-up word).

Every Saturday evening, we'd all be there, mulling over the events of the past week. Joy would have her scotch; it would be gin and tonic for Malcolm. I was developing a taste for G&T myself. Harry Thompson would have his whiskey and ginger, John Bennett his pint of Harp. For Bill Heaney, it would be two bottles of stout before heading home for a fry, the perfect end to his Saturday.

Inevitably, we'd be joined by the doyen of the Belfast sporting press, the *Telegraph*'s sports editor, Malcolm Brodie. A sociable Scot whose family had been evacuated to the city during the

Second World War, he had stayed and found his way into journalism. As a child, I'd followed his dispatches from the World Cup in Sweden in 1958, Northern Ireland's first involvement in the game's biggest tournament.

Now, here I was, rubbing shoulders with the great man, who'd come hotfoot from the newspaper's offices, where he'd overseen production of *The Ulster* after filing his own match report. He brought with him a copy for everybody in the bar.

Those *Sportsound* Saturdays became a regular part of my week. I kept up my football, playing five-a-side at the gym, and rationalised the extra-curricular activities by reckoning it was good to have a couple of outside interests as distractions from the heavy workload of preparing for my finals at Queen's.

What I had not been aware of, when I'd been forced to opt for something other than soccer as the key that might unlock the door to an involvement in sports broadcasting, was that I was actually pushing an open door.

Rugby on BBC Northern Ireland had been the province of one of the game's Ulster greats. Sammy Walker propped for Instonians in Belfast, played fifteen times for Ireland and captained the British and Irish Lions on their tour to South Africa in 1938. In my teenage years, he was the commentator on the radio when Ulster and Ireland played. When Sammy had died in January 1972, his place had been taken by Tom Cromey, a senior civil servant in the Northern Ireland Office in Belfast. But with the deteriorating political situation, Tom's day job was becoming ever more demanding, and a sideline that required occasional weekend overnights away for interprovincials and internationals was no longer an ideal fit.

When I came along looking for a start the following September and began a satisfactory run in the team, the pieces of the jigsaw could be put into place. Without having to push too hard, I was going to get my chance as a commentator.

Harry Thompson and Bill Heaney would take a tape recorder with them to their football assignments and do what's known in the trade as lift-and-lay – record snatches of commentary if it looked like something might be about to happen.

I remember wondering, as a listener, where these bits of coverage came from. Were the games being broadcast somewhere that I didn't know about? Now I understood the magic. Not so much a trick of the light as a trick of the sound. I too would get my chance.

I was overjoyed when I first saw my name on the commitments sheet with 'plus Uher' beside it. Uher was the German manufacturer of the broadcast quality reel-to-reel devices used right across the industry. That 'plus Uher' was not only my opportunity, it also meant an extra £1.50 on the £5 fee!

5

Let the Pictures Tell the Story

They used to say that getting dropped from the Irish rugby team was more difficult than being selected in the first place. Well, as a variation on this theme, I've always maintained that the hardest thing about getting any kind of a career is getting in the door in the first place. So I was delighted with myself when I discovered that, inside the BBC tent, there was a host of opportunities to be exploited.

I was introduced to H.N. Gilbert, the Head of Radio Current Affairs (the N. stood for Niall but he was 'Dan' to all and sundry). He was responsible for *Round-Up Reports*, the precursor of the breakfast marathon *Good Morning Ulster* that I would have the privilege of launching on New Year's Day 1975.

Dan was a nautical man whose greeting of choice was, 'What ho, dear boy!' He was a distinctive character in so many ways, favouring open-necked shirts and knotted kerchiefs instead of ties, striding forth from his office on the corner of the corridor on the third floor of Broadcasting House on his latest mission. He was something of a hero too, as evidenced by the story of

Florence Chadwick, a long-distance swimmer of whom I became aware as a kid on holiday in Donaghadee, on the coast of the Ards Peninsula in County Down.

From Donaghadee to Portpatrick in Galloway is roughly twenty-one miles, the same distance as Dover to Calais. It's not the shortest route across the North Channel to Scotland, the passage from Ballycastle to the Mull of Kintyre being only half as long, but the currents there are stronger, the water is much colder and it's plagued by jellyfish.

Donaghadee to Portpatrick is still a difficult stretch for a marathon swimmer, so a perfect challenge for an extreme sportswoman like Florence Chadwick. She was a celebrity at the time, with reports of her attempt front-page news in Fleet Street, as well as in Belfast and Glasgow.

Florence was the daughter of a San Diego cop, who'd made her mark in long-distance open-water swimming off the California coast before turning her attention to Europe. She had already swum the English Channel in both directions – the first woman to do so – and the Strait of Gibraltar, breaking records as she went, before she turned her attention to the stretch from County Down to the Scottish shore. The combination of tides and the cold had beaten every previous attempt to swim it bar one. Tom Blower from Nottingham had made it across in 1947. It took him fifteen hours and twenty-six minutes. In Donaghadee, everybody knew that name. Tom Blower was spoken of with awe.

Florence had been in the little coastal town preparing while we'd been there on holiday. Crowds would flock to the harbour to watch her set out on her training routine. There wasn't that much to see. This greased figure would enter the water and glide off, like a seal, in the direction of the nearby Copeland Islands.

At 5.20 on the morning of Tuesday, 3 September 1957, Florence Chadwick slipped into the water at Donaghadee pier to begin her front crawl towards Portpatrick, the bright cap on her head fading into insignificance with each stroke, the presence of a few small boats the only indication that she was in there swimming at all.

Among those aboard the little flotilla that accompanied her was Dan Gilbert, described in *The Glasgow Herald* as a young Belfast journalist (which he was), though, according to *The Northern Whig* in its lead story the following morning, he was there as a lifeguard.

After almost twelve hours in the water, Florence Chadwick's adventure came to a dramatic end. Blue with cold and unable to do much more than tread water, the swimmer was in danger of expiring. Dan took the initiative, stripped off his tracksuit and dived in. He probably saved her life. This was the man who gave me my start in radio current affairs.

This was just as well, for it wouldn't have been possible to sustain a career on what sport could offer at the time. There was no regular sports news as such. It was all pretty basic and restricted, by and large, to Saturdays. On radio, there was a five-minute preview programme at lunchtime and the teatime round-up *Sportsound*. On television, a short local results sequence, tagged onto the end of *Grandstand*, followed a preview on the Friday teatime news.

There were occasional outside broadcasts too, but nothing like on the scale of coverage that has developed over the years. Gaelic games scarcely got a look-in. It was association football, rugby, hockey, rowing, athletics and, in the summer, cricket and bowls. Shortly after I became involved, a Sunday edition of *Sportsound* was launched specifically to cover GAA.

So, current affairs it was. In the newsroom there were staffers, correspondents and reporters. In Dan Gilbert's little empire, the foot soldiers were paid per engagement.

That summer of 1973, another former Methody boy got in through the door of Broadcasting House. Mike McKimm and I joined others like Wilson Harte, Clive Ferguson, Alasdair Jackson – young men of our own vintage – and more seasoned reporters – Malcolm McCalister and Alan Giff – contributing to a programme whose main presenter was Barry Cowan, a soundman who had moved to the other side of the glass and become a formidable broadcaster. He had a brief spell with RTÉ, but his forensically incisive interrogations proved too much for the sensibilities of the southern audience at the time.

Barry alternated with a part-time broadcaster called Frank Hanna whose day job was in his father's solicitor's office. Frank too was a powerful presence in the studio, who also liked to party, making conspicuous contributions on the piano, his brow glistening with sweat as he hammered out the singalong songs.

The craziness of this was that we were living in a kind of parallel universe, for the heavy-duty field reporting was being done by the newsroom. Our assignments were in areas that were not necessarily directly related to the violence that was such a part of daily life at the time.

I found myself heading for the seaside town of Bangor one afternoon, to interview the new head of the RUC Drugs Squad. This was a sensitive enough mission, as somebody in his position was clearly going to have been careful about his own security, so arrangements had to be watertight before I arrived at his suburban bungalow just after lunchtime.

I was welcomed into the front room and sat down with my tape recorder. My host was clearly somewhat unnerved by the prospect of what we were about to embark upon, for it seemed that I was the first to hold a microphone in front of him since his elevation to his new post. His training would not necessarily have equipped him for the PR side of the job and he was going to have to learn on the hoof. Very much what I was doing myself, though in fairness, I had been advised about the basics, like, ask the question and then encourage the answer by nodding appropriately. And don't put your hand in your pocket and jangle your coins as you're conducting the interview. It won't sound very good.

The policeman had a tough act to follow. His predecessor was a sergeant by the name of David Dunseith, who had emerged as a television personality on the back of regular appearances warning about the dangers of drug-taking. The fact that he was articulate, fashionably dressed and wore his hair long in the style of the time, only added to his aura. Ulster Television was so impressed by the debonair detective, they offered him a presenting job and he went on to become one of the most respected political broadcasters in the region.

His successor was understandably concerned about how he was going to come across and asked if we might rehearse the interview. Now, with a nervous or uncertain subject, this is never a good plan. It only increases the pressure.

'Sure, I'll talk through what I'm going to ask you,' I told him, 'and I won't start recording until you're comfortable.' He had an idea. Will we have a drink?

A bottle of Bushmills whiskey was produced and we partook as I proposed where our conversation might go. The afternoon proceeded and the anxiety evaporated. He had reached a point of fluency and the interview went well. He thanked me for my patience and I thanked him for his hospitality. It was a learning curve for both of us and I like to think that neither of us looked back.

Not all of my encounters with the local constabulary were quite so convivial. On a Monday evening in October 1973, a bomb exploded in a pub in Ballyhackamore in east Belfast. There had been a fatality. I was dispatched to the scene. There was a crowd milling around, and in my naïve attempt to get a steer, I found myself eavesdropping on a conversation between two gents who turned out to be plain-clothes policemen. They were in no mood to help me with my enquiries. I was told, none too politely, to make myself scarce.

I'd no more joy engaging with any of those around. Nobody wanted to commit their voice to tape. I went back to base empty-handed, made my apologies and asked if there was anything else they might need of me. 'No,' came the reply, 'we have enough for the morning.'

Tuning in at 8.25 a.m. next day, I had my abject failure con-firmed. The vastly experienced newsroom reporter David Capper, whom I hadn't even noticed at the scene, had gathered enough for his news piece to be able to offer some eyewitness accounts to *Round-Up*. I was still very wet behind the ears.

It wasn't all hard graft and grief. Another producer keen to employ me was a lady by the name of Pat Lindsay, who was in charge of a weekly half-hour called *Countrywide*, which ran in the slot just before the lunchtime news. It was a human-interest magazine that steered well away from the contentious.

My fondest memory of working with Pat was of the day she sent me off to mid-Ulster to a big house near the village of Moneymore. I've long since forgotten why we were featuring Mrs Lily Letitia Thompson, but I've never forgotten the name. She was a member for a time of the Northern Ireland Hospitals Authority, that much I do know.

My appointment was for mid-morning and I was most graciously received. There was none of the Drugs Squad detective's diffidence. Quite the contrary, in fact. I do recall she gave me so much material that when we were done, it was close to one o'clock.

'You'll stay to lunch, won't you?' It would have been rude not to. We were served in the grand style, starched linen in the dining room, her staff presenting our food on the finest china. It was a long way from what I'd have been going back to in the BBC canteen.

In fairness to it, though, the canteen wasn't the worst. A welcoming space at the top of the old five-storey building, it played host to early shift breakfasts, roast lamb lunches, dinner if you were working late, and everything else in between. Coffee time always brought much mirth.

Broadcasting House in Belfast opened in 1941 and by the time I had become a regular contributor it was fair to say it was showing its age, clearly the creation of a different era, with its thick walls separating the offices spaced along its lengthy corridors.

The small lobby housed the reception desk, a waiting area, the entrance to what would have been its concert hall, and the lift which plied its course to the fifth floor in the space in the centre of the stairwell.

The original concert hall was now home to the BBC Northern Ireland Orchestra, a thirty-strong house band which would break from rehearsals mid-morning. This would obviously lead to problems upstairs, if they arrived en masse in search of elevenses. The orchestra's diminutive bespectacled harpist was one of Ireland's most distinguished musicians. Derek Bell was a multi-instrumentalist who was part of The Chieftains. He was also very good at strategic planning.

When the orchestra's conductor would call for a coffee break, Derek, a small figure in sports jacket, collar and tie, would break from the studio, emerging into the lobby at pace, pressing the lift button as he progressed to the stairs, up which he ascended at a gallop, floor by floor, calling the lift at each landing, ensuring his place at the top of the canteen queue. Derek's daily dash became part of the lore of the building.

* * *

My freelancing was coming along nicely. Opportunities were presenting themselves. Joy Williams, who would soon become the first female head of sport in all of the BBC when Malcolm Kellard moved to a similar position in Scotland, had taken on the role of mentoring me. And I wasn't the only one. She was always on the look-out for new talent. Mike Nesbitt was another she started. Mark Robson too.

Joy introduced me to Virginia Hardy as a potential contributor. Gin Hardy was the BBC World Service's representative in Belfast and produced a weekly magazine covering Northern Ireland from a Portacabin in the yard out the back of Broadcasting House. I was welcomed with open arms. When she learned that I'd arrived at the BBC with a degree in German and French, Gin immediately suggested I make use of my languages. The BBC German Service, in particular, would welcome stories from Northern Ireland, given the turmoil the place was going through.

I was put in touch with a producer, Donald Armour, and a very fruitful relationship was born. Not only did I get to broadcast in German for the BBC, my pieces were picked up abroad, and in no time I was acting as a stringer for several stations – WDR in Cologne, Süddeutscher Rundfunk in Stuttgart and Radio Studio Zürich in Switzerland.

And I got to do some commentating. Tom Cromey was in the process of giving up broadcasting due to the demands of his job in the Northern Ireland Office and I was being eased into his seat. The Uher tape recorder had been put to good use. The snatches of 'lift-and-lay', the actuality of a try being scored, they were enough to encourage Joy Williams to let me loose on a live broadcast. I would be heading for Lansdowne Road for my debut in the commentary box: Leinster against Ulster, Saturday, 15 December 1973.

Only fifteen months after getting my first commission, it was going to be my voice describing the action, and at Lansdowne Road too, a venue I'd only ever been to twice before: once, on a rugby weekend with Methody, when we'd played against the Masonic School in the morning and gone to watch Ireland play

Scotland in the afternoon from behind the goal on the packed south terrace; then, for Waterford's European Cup tie against Manchester United, when my dad and I had blagued our way in on a single black market ticket and taken our places on the promenade in front of the West Stand.

Now, I was going to have a seat in that grandstand and the chance to do what I now realised I had always wanted to do. Soccer or rugby – that was neither here nor there. To say I was overjoyed at the prospect would be a mad understatement.

The fun started on the Friday. We were to travel the day before the game on the team coach. My father, by now retired from the Civil Service and filling his days doing deliveries for Zerny & Carson, a wallpaper and paint merchant in the centre of town, drove me to Ravenhill in his little green van.

I boarded the bus and took my seat alongside Joy, among the committee men and their wives at the back. I would get to know them over the next few years – men like Ewart Bell, Dudley Higgins, Jimmy Nelson and Paddy Patterson, all key figures in the Irish Rugby Football Union. Joy made the introductions.

I was obviously more familiar with the players. I'd been at school with Annesley Harrison, the regular out-half who'd lost his place and was among the substitutes on this trip. Graham Crothers, the full back, never tired of telling the story of how I once did him a huge favour when he trying to get back on the 1st XV at Queen's following an injury. As secretary of the soccer club, I'd arranged a run out for him with one of the junior teams to build up his fitness.

Belfast to Dublin in those days was a good two-and-a-half to three hours and the only town on the route that had a by-pass was Dromore in County Down, not far into the journey. We trundled through Banbridge, Newry, crossed the border, still with its checkpoints, carried on through Dundalk, Castlebellingham and Dunleer, before reaching Monasterboice to start our descent down that long stretch into Drogheda.

The slow crawl through the town, ten days before Christmas, the festive illuminations twinkling in the dusk of a December Friday afternoon, light cascading from the open doors of the three churches, the pavements thronged, the excitement palpable, it was very much a highlight of the trip.

On through Julianstown and Balbriggan, Swords, then the red bulk of Holy Child, Whitehall and down through Drumcondra to the railway bridge that announces to every northerner that you've finally arrived in Dublin.

We pulled up outside the Shelbourne Hotel. In those days, you didn't do things by halves. I'd never stayed anywhere as grand as this. Checking in, Joy was hailed by a gentleman descending the stairs by the lift (geographically, an arrangement similar to that in the BBC back home but aesthetically a thousand miles removed). Casually attired in cardigan and carpet slippers and looking very much at home, this was the sports editor of the *Belfast News Letter*, whose travel budget extended beyond that of the entire BBC, never mind the Ulster branch. He'd been in residence at the Shelbourne since earlier in the week.

This trip would classify as an initiation for me. Friday evening it was drinks in the Horseshoe Bar before dinner in the Saddle Room – smoked salmon followed by rare roast beef; the house speciality I was told. I was taking my lead from Joy.

The following morning, we had a leisurely breakfast. I had

plenty of time to go through my notes before we made our way down Baggot Street to the ground, where I would deliver a preview for the ten-to-one slot on the radio.

The thrill of it all. Going in through the official entrance, up to the press box. In those days it was still pretty rudimentary, tucked underneath the upper tier of the West Stand. The commentary boxes were on the forward lip of that upper deck, approached along a gangway above the heads of those seated in the West Lower, then through a door into a space where there was scarcely room to stand. In a compartment to the left sat the sound engineer. The commentary seats were to the right.

The slanted, sliding windows could be removed, the better to let the crowd noise pervade, though on a wet day they were a very necessary inconvenience. I'd learned that the ideal spot for a television camera to cover a football pitch was thirty feet back and thirty feet up. That's exactly where we were in our BBC commentary box. It provided the perfect view.

All of that I remember well from repeated visits to the venue. As for the match, not a single snapshot remains in the mind's eye.

I have Paul McWeeney's match report in the following Monday's *Irish Times* to thank for filling in the blanks. It was, he noted, 'a bitterly cold afternoon with an icy breeze blowing across the pitch'. Ulster dominated from the start and took the lead in the fifth minute. Wallace McMaster – known to his teammates as 'Squeak' – was put clear by Graham Crothers and touched down. 'Squeak' subsequently pulled a hamstring, which brought my old school chum Annesley Harrison back into the team, and he it was who stretched the lead, converting two penalties. With a try then worth four points, that put Ulster 13–0 up with a little under half an hour gone.

However – this is the written word, not the audition – Leinster finally came to life and conjured a try of their own, scored by Vinny Becker. 'The wing,' said *The Irish Times*, 'stretched out to leave the pursuit trailing over fully 85 yards and his team were back in business.' They most certainly were. Three unanswered tries – from Johnny Moloney, Becker again and Jim Flynn, the last of them converted by Tony Ensor – secured victory for Leinster – 18–13 – and crowned Munster, 'who may not have been specially attractive to watch' in McWeeney's view, interprovincial champions for the first time in five years.

Back in the Shelbourne, it was very much a case of Take Two, with the Horseshoe Bar and the Saddle Room hosting animated discussions on the course the afternoon had taken, while the two teams and officials attended their own dinner.

And that was the start of it. A gentle enough introduction to a world in which, I would soon discover, not every destination offered the kind of basic creature comforts available at Lansdowne Road that December afternoon. Why, there were even hot water pipes at floor level to keep the chilblains at bay. I might have been making progress from windswept touchlines, but grandstands can be every bit as draughty.

I reckon I could use just about every Christmas cliché to de-scribe that period in my life. Christmas had come early for me in 1973 and what followed certainly made it seem that all my Christmases had come at once, for, nine weeks later, I was making the step up to what was then still the Five Nations Championship. Apart from my schoolboy visit to Ireland against Scotland,

I'd only ever been to one rugby international. That was in 1969, when I'd gone with a party from Queen's on a week-long field trip to France. We were staying in student accommodation in the 5th arrondissement, the Latin quarter, not far from the Panthéon and the Sorbonne. My roommate was Vincent Trainor, a young man from Mourne country in south Down, as inexperienced as I was in the matter of Parisian bathroom accoutrements. Ours featured, aside from the usual bath, shower, sink and toilet, a low porcelain basin with taps and a stopper, which caused much head-scratching. We reckoned it must be for some fancy continental way of washing your socks. We'd been baffled by a bidet!

Vincent was as keen as I was to sample some local sport. On the Friday night, we found a Ligue 1 football match in the northern suburb of Saint-Ouen. Seeking the match report in the sports paper *L'Equipe* over breakfast the following morning, we realised we'd lucked out in terms of somewhere to go that Saturday afternoon. France were hosting their final match of that season's Five Nations at Stade Colombes, against Wales, who, two weeks before, in Cardiff, had denied Ireland what would have been only a second Grand Slam.

It was once an impressive venue, the main stadium for the Summer Olympics of 1924, where the races that would inspire the film *Chariots of Fire* were run. It also hosted the 1938 World Cup Final, when Italy successfully defended their title, winning the third edition of the event by defeating Hungary 4–2. Now, though, it seemed no more special than any other suburban football ground, which is what it was soon to become, replaced by the revamped Parc des Princes much closer to the heart of the city.

The Métro didn't go to Colombes, so we took the train and rocked up in good time for the game. We'd no tickets. Sure, we could pay at the gate. Oh, the sweet innocence of it all. Well, we did get in, part of an attendance of almost 35,000 who saw France, themselves defending Grand Slam champions, follow three straight defeats by scratching out a draw – 8–8 – against Wales.

Three weeks later – in those Five Nations days, matches were spaced out – Wales hammered England by 30 points to 9. Only that draw, that Vincent and I had happened upon, denied them a Grand Slam of their own.

Five years on, I'd a ticket for what would be only the third rugby international I'd ever attended – a ticket for a seat in the commentary box at Twickenham. England against Ireland. I wasn't actually on the air, though I was unaware of that at the time. I thought I was repeating my Lansdowne Road experience with Ulster. Nobody told me otherwise, but BBC Northern Ireland was taking the network commentary. I had an audience of one.

Joy Williams was determined that her protégé should have the best possible start. He'd come through his first audition. He'd satisfactorily negotiated his first season as a reporter and he'd moved onto the foothills of commentary. Leinster against Ulster at Lansdowne Road was the stuff of an inside page.

She had every faith and boy, was I grateful for that. And she wanted me to have the best possible backing. So, she arranged for my commentary at Twickenham to be relayed back to Broadcasting House in central London, where the Head of Radio Sport would be watching the match on TV with the sound turned down, listening to Joy's new find. Some compliment to Joy. Some compliment to me. Not that I knew it, but I'd have nowhere to hide.

That Head of Sport just happened to be Cliff Morgan, an iconic Welsh rugby out-half, familiar to anybody who's ever followed the game. (He played with Bective Rangers in Dublin for a time.) I commend him further for his involvement in what's been called the greatest rugby match ever played, the Barbarians meeting with the All Blacks in Cardiff in 1973.

Cliff wasn't playing. He was the commentator. And he was simply ... awesome. Rich Welsh cadences, complementing the action, interspersed with staccato interventions of a single word or maybe two or three.

'Brilliant! Oh, that's brilliant!' he called, as the BaBas turned early defence into attack. Then, 'Great dummy!'

'This is Gareth Edwards', no more, no less than we needed to know as the scrum half broke the cover. And the conclusion to the move that led to the dramatic opening try: 'What a score!'

Let the pictures tell the story. As the man himself said: 'Brilliant!'

Bread of heaven, they sing at matches in the great rugby cathedral in Cardiff. England against Ireland that February day in 1974 delivered sporting heaven for the rookie commentator. A 26–21 victory for Ireland, crowned by the most magnificent try, England bursting out of their 25 as it was still known, the kick ahead eluding Dick Milliken, the counter-attack still threatening until Tony Ensor bravely intervened, his pace as he picked up the loose ball carrying him clear of the initial cover. Drawing the final tackle, he released Cameron Michael Henderson Gibson (known simply as Mike), Belfast solicitor, North of Ireland FC and Ulster, and one of the finest players ever to wear the green, who was in for his second try of the afternoon. The commentator from the Cregagh Road could not have asked for more. In my elation at the finish, I hadn't time to be disappointed when I learned that I wasn't actually on the air.

6

Pearls of Wisdom

After the excitement of the afternoon at Twickenham, we were driven back to Broadcasting House to meet the man himself. When you've been following sport since you were a nipper, and names and personalities have implanted themselves in your mind, it's a surreal feeling to be told that one of those people has surrendered his Saturday afternoon to the equivalent of a schoolteacher's marking session and that he's now staying behind to await your arrival and make your acquaintance. 'Cliffie is expecting us,' said Joy.

This was my first time in Broadcasting House. If broadcasting was a religion, this would be the Vatican. Oh yes, Ormeau Avenue in Belfast was Broadcasting House too, just like the other regional bases of the British Broadcasting Corporation. The same, only different, and on a much smaller scale – different details: for Art Deco, read neo-Georgian; for Portland stone, read sand-faced bricks – though they all had the same multi-paned windows, the same thick walls lining lengthy corridors with offices off. You half expected somebody in flannels and a sports jacket, with a pencil moustache and Brylcreemed hair, to emerge from one, smoking a cigarette. It was the 1930s come to life.

Cliff Morgan rose from behind his desk. I was in the presence of one of rugby union's all-time greats. With the broadest of smiles, he offered the warmest of handshakes. If I was Joy's newest recruit, he was going to make me most welcome.

The office was spartan. The Head of Radio Sport lived in a small enough space, which gave onto a larger meeting room. There was the television he'd watched with the sound turned down, listening instead to me describing the action. And he was about to offer his verdict on what he'd heard.

'Well done,' he said. 'That was some game, wasn't it?' I was in total awe. This voice off the television, this face so familiar, those memories melding in a moment into all of the response I could muster.

'Thank you!'

'You know,' he said, 'radio commentary and television commentary are totally different things. You can worry about TV commentary if you ever get to do it.'

I thought back to how he called that Barbarians game. A veritable masterclass. I got it. On TV, everybody can see what's going on. You're there to complement it. All these years on, I can't but suggest that it's a crying shame that so many who are granted the privilege of commentating on a game on television do not realise that the last thing they should be doing is stating the bleedin' obvious.

Cliff handed me a sheet of paper. It was the BBC Radio commentator's bible on one A4 page. The bullet points summed it all up. Score. Time. Geography. Accuracy. Start from there and carry on.

You're on the radio; you're the one and only link between the listener and the action. So, they must know first and foremost what is the score. They need to know where we are in the game. They need to know who is where. And they need to know what is going on. Simple, really.

It's easy when a game kicks off. Arsenal, in their red shirts, white sleeves, white shorts and white socks, playing left to right, against Bayern Munich, in their away strip, all in silver grey. There you are. You have the picture.

But what if you're late tuning in? You need to know if it's all square, how far we are into the game. Five minutes is too long to be wondering. And twenty-first-century radio commentary forgets this all too often.

Four basic rules. Cliff didn't tell me what he thought of how well I'd kept the story on track that afternoon at Twickenham, but however happy he might have been with how I'd sounded, he made it clear that this was how radio commentary worked.

And then he expounded on the personal business of covering a game. Make sure you're wearing the right clothes for the weather. Make sure you're at ease, so you're not distracted. Stand if it feels better. (I do, a lot of the time.) If you're a smoker (remember, this was 1974, when every studio was furnished with an ashtray), light up a cigarette if it helps. The last thing you should be doing is distracting the listener by mentioning your circumstances.

Never let yourself get in the way, Cliff cautioned me, among many other pearls of wisdom he imparted. You're there to help, to bring the event to the audience. Your conditions mightn't be ideal – you might be out in a howling wind, you might be soaking wet. But forget about it. They don't want to know. They want to know the score and how it's going. Get on with the job.

Your job is to bring them the game, not your problems. They've tuned in to you to find out how their team is doing, to hear the match described, and what's happening on the pitch is all you should be talking about, unless what you're saying adds to that, like the floodlights are on because a winter's evening is drawing in.

Tutorial over, Cliff took us out the back door of Broadcasting House, down Hallam Street and into the basement lounge and restaurant that was The Rugby Club. Jeff Butterfield, a former England captain and a Lion, had left behind his teaching career to develop a venue that celebrated the game. As Cliff Morgan's guests, the new commentator and his mentor were treated like rugby royalty. And I had double cause for celebration. Ireland's campaign was concluding in a fortnight's time, when they were to host Scotland at Lansdowne Road. Radio 4 Northern Ireland would have dedicated coverage of its own and I'd just been told that I would be at the microphone.

The build-up to my Five Nations debut wasn't without drama. During the week before, I'd taken the family Renault into town for some reason or another, to a workshop on Corporation Street where the car was due for inspection. I remember this vividly, only because of what happened next.

When the business in the garage had been concluded, the car had to be driven onto a turntable, so that it could be lined up to leave the premises – unusual enough to leave an imprint on the mind. On my journey home, I had further business to attend to, so I was emerging from a junction that wouldn't normally be on my route when I missed the green light and found myself first in line to effect a right turn onto the main road when the lights changed.

Red. Red and amber. Green again. I moved forward and into a thundering impact from the right. With singular good fortune, I had been slow off the mark and the oncoming car had smashed into the side of the Renault's engine compartment. Had I been a split second earlier, I'd have taken the full impact through the driver's door. My car spun and, in the impact, my head smashed off the seatbelt mounting on the door pillar.

I emerged from the wrecked vehicle in a daze. The two cars were write-offs. Unbeknownst to me, in the car behind me and a witness to the whole thing was Fred Wylie, a colleague at the BBC. The driver who'd broken the light had attempted to flee the scene, for he'd had a drink or two. He'd no luck there. Fred was out of his car in a flash to apprehend the miscreant and was now sitting on him in the middle of the road.

And then another acquaintance appeared out of nowhere. Brian Dean was a year ahead of me at school and had gone on to become a hospital doctor. He took a look at my head and said, 'You need to go to the hospital, mate.' To cut a long story short, the headphones I'd be wearing on my international debut would be covering four stitches above my temple.

That, though, was the last thing on my mind when I set off with Joy for Dublin, on this occasion on the Thursday before the game. 'Lots to prepare on the Friday, darling. We need to be there in good time,' she told me. Not that I was complaining about an extra night in the Shelbourne.

We were up bright and early, and, fully breakfasted, headed down Kildare Street towards the playing fields of Trinity College, where the Scottish team would be having what would now be known as their Captain's Run, the final training session before the game.

The players were already on the pitch when Joy and I arrived. On the touchline, among a knot of individuals one stood out, tall and with a shock of dark hair, wearing a light-coloured trenchcoat. It was Bill McLaren, the top rugby commentator of the era, on duty for BBC Television.

'Christ dahling, there's Bill.' Joy's voice always led. 'Come on,' she said and marched me over to interrupt their conversation. Of course, Bill was pleased to see her. Everybody was. She had such a magnetic personality. Excusing herself to whoever had been enjoying the company of this most genial of people, she introduced me to the man himself. 'This is my new boy, George. Commentating for the first time tomorrow.'

I was standing there, completely gobsmacked. Hardly having had the chance to process the fact that I was seeing Bill McLaren in the flesh for the first time, here I was being introduced to him and here he was talking to me, excusing himself to the others and suggesting we take a walk up the touchline, just the two of us. Maybe it was the schoolteacher in him – his day job was as PE master in the Scottish Borders – or maybe it was just that he was the heart and soul of decency. He would always have a driver standing by to take him to the airport after a game, so that he could be back home in Hawick to enjoy what was left of Saturday night and the whole of Sunday with his nearest and dearest, his wife Bette.

I'd had the formal induction a fortnight before from Cliff Morgan. Here, now, in College Park in Dublin that Friday morning,

I was having a one-on-one with the leading exponent of the art.

As I blurted out my background, he surveyed the Scottish players going through their moves in a session of unopposed play. Those were the days before sponsored training gear and they looked a motley crew. 'If you can tell them apart dressed like that,' Bill said, 'you'll be halfway there when they trot out in their kit with numbers on their back. Though, mind you,' he went on, 'they won't always oblige you by showing their number when you might need it to identify them.'

'So,' he continued, 'there has to be something else. See the centres there. Renwick is the wee baldy one. McGeechan has the hair. And look at the forwards. Ian McLauchlan – the captain – he moves like he's a waddling barrel.'

It made absolute sense. Observe them so that you'll recognise them no matter what. Everybody has something distinctive about them – maybe the way they move. And it's the same with players.

Then Bill pulled something from an inside pocket. It looked like an envelope, but it unfolded into what it actually was – four sheets of A4 paper, carefully taped together, covered in intricate, colour-coded script.

'This is my dope sheet,' said Bill. 'I start when the teams are announced' – in those days, that would be well before the game, following a meeting of the selection committee – 'and I put the names on top, in the middle. I work on it through the week, adding information I think might be of use. By the time I'm heading off, it's more or less complete. I might add a few bits and pieces if anything develops while I'm here. And then, when I get to the commentary box, I open it up, spread it out before me and take it from there.'

There didn't appear to be room for much to be added. It was an absolute work of art.

'You've so much there,' I said to Bill and, in my total naïveté, added the question, 'How are you going to get it all in?'

'I'm not, son,' he replied. 'Ninety-five per cent of that is for the bin. I just won't know what to junk until the final whistle has gone. That, in a nutshell, is how you prepare for a commentary.'

The game the next day was soon forgotten – nothing like the excitement of Twickenham. Ireland took an early lead through a penalty converted by a wing forward of all people, Stewart McKinney. When the penalty was awarded, quite some distance out, McKinney informed the captain, Willie John McBride, that he felt confident he could put it over. He'd done something similar for his club Dungannon the previous week. Willie John, in the middle of a major international, was happy to let him have a shot and Stewart duly obliged. He had never kicked for Ireland before and I'm not sure he ever did again.

On the half hour, a try, scored by Dick Milliken, driven over the line by the pack following a line-out, was converted by the regular kicker, Mike Gibson, and Ireland led 9–0. Scotland could only muster two penalties in reply, both from Andy Irvine, who had also missed a sitter. Had he scored and the game ended 9–9, Scotland would have won the title, for, a fortnight later, in the final round of fixtures which was Ireland's fallow weekend, Scotland defeated France. But the point they missed out on in Dublin meant it was Ireland who won the Five Nations that year, thanks to the 9–6 win that had been a most significant milestone on my journey into a career at the microphone.

All rugby so far, but the following Tuesday, the stars aligned. As the only one working for the morning current affairs programme who had a sporting string to his bow, I was the obvious choice to be sent to cover a football match. *Round-Up Reports* wouldn't normally have been covering a football match – it only had twenty minutes to fill in the background to the news of the day and there was plenty of that given the turmoil the place was in at the time. But this was a significant occasion, above and beyond a run-of-the-mill midweek fixture.

Glentoran, the club to which I'd transferred my allegiance as a teenager when it was no longer cool to be seen to be supporting the perennially defeated Cliftonville, had reached the last eight of the European Cup Winners' Cup, and the first leg of the tie would be played at their home ground, The Oval, wedged between Mersey Street and the Sydenham Bypass in east Belfast.

In those days, when the European Cup and the Cup Winners' Cup were open only to a single team from each country, it was still possible, with the luck of the draw, for part-time players from a small league to make decent progress.

Linfield, Irish League champions in 1966, entered Europe's premier competition that autumn, confronting Aris Bonnevoie, a team from Luxembourg, whom they duly dispatched 9–4 on aggregate.

That earned them a tie against Norwegian opposition Vålerenga from Oslo. Playing away in the first leg, they achieved a magnificent result, a 4–1 win, with their final goal coming from a nineteen-year-old winger who'd make a big name for himself in the game. Bryan Hamilton, no relation, went on to play for Ipswich Town and Everton among others, winning fifty caps for Northern Ireland.

The 1–1 draw that followed at Windsor Park earned Linfield a place in the quarter-finals of the European Cup, the premier competition that morphed into the Champions League. They'd got past Christmas, further than the champions of England. Liverpool had gone out at this stage, eliminated by Ajax of Amsterdam.

At the draw for the last eight, Linfield were first out of the hat against the Bulgarian army team CSKA, so the first leg would be at Windsor Park in Belfast. Despite going behind in the second minute, they battled back into the game, and by half-time they were ahead. Two goals in three minutes just before the interval – Bryan Hamilton on the scoresheet again and then Tommy Shields. Though it finished 2–2, the Blues were still in the tie.

A single goal in the second leg a fortnight later would end their European journey, at the same point in the competition as no less a name than Real Madrid. They too made their exit, defeated by Inter Milan. The ten-time champions of Italy and winners of the European Cup in 1964 and 1965 went on to reach the final, where, on a Thursday afternoon in May, they met their match. That was the year Celtic became the first British and first non-Latin club to win Europe's most prestigious trophy.

Linfield hadn't exactly had the most glamorous opposition along the way to their quarter-final, and seven years later, Glentoran had been following a similar path with trips to Romania and Norway, until the quarter-final produced an ace from the hat.

They were drawn against Borussia Mönchengladbach, the West German Cup holders, a team in the midst of a golden age. National champions in 1970 and 1971, they would soon be adding three more Bundesliga titles in a row. This was a side that included five players who'd be part of West Germany's World Cup-winning squad less than four months later: Berti Vogts and Rainer Bonhof, who featured in the final, Gladbach's captain Herbert Wimmer, the goalkeeper Wolfgang Kleff and the striker Jupp Heynckes who went on to win the Champions League as a manager with Real Madrid and Bayern Munich. A quarter-final of the European Cup Winners' Cup, featuring one of the top teams on the continent, Germans to boot, and I was being sent to cover it.

A report enhanced by the inclusion of some comments from key participants was what was required. I recognised an opportunity. I thought of *Sportsound* and those crucial moments in the rugby contests I'd covered and caught for posterity on the reel-to-reel tape recorder. I had the same device over my shoulder as I headed to The Oval to record the post-match interviews. I'd earned my stripes. I'd done a live game. So why not do what I'd always really wanted to do and commentate on a football match?

There was just one aspect of all of this that would bring an added edge to the evening. Because I wasn't an accredited football hack – I was working for a current affairs programme – and because it was Mönchengladbach, the press box was full to overflowing, so I had been assigned a seat in the grandstand. If I was going to attempt this commentary caper, I'd have an audience, up close and personal.

Not that my neighbours minded in the slightest. Once they'd got over the novelty of finding themselves seated beside a young guy with a tape machine in his lap, they became far too engrossed in what was happening on the pitch to be bothered by my earnest efforts at describing the excitement as it unfolded.

The trick, of course, and not least to cover my self-consciousness, was only to press the record button when it looked like something significant might be about to happen and those around me were suitably distracted. I didn't have long to wait. Glentoran attacked from the off. The game was only in its eighth minute when what *The Irish Times* described as 'a blockbuster' from midfielder Roy Stewart was cleared upfield. The recorder was running. Two Glentoran defenders went for the ball, got in each other's way and in a flash, Jupp Heynckes was all alone on the edge of the area, able to drill a crisp right-footed shot past the advancing goalkeeper. The disappointment of the fan in me was washed away in the flood of euphoria that followed the realisation that I'd got the goal on tape.

Not every clip ended in excitement. There was plenty that would end up on the edit suite floor. But I had the Uher running again when Berti Vogts crossed from the right. Trevor McCullough, the keeper, could only palm it away and Horst Köppel finished. My commentary clips were in the bag.

I did my interviews, hotfooted it back to Broadcasting House in town and put together my two-and-a-half minute package for the morning – reportage, interviews and, the icing on the cake, the commentary on the goals.

Proud as Punch, I listened as it went to air. In the south Belfast suburb of Dunmurry, Malcolm Kellard was in his bathroom, shaving. He couldn't believe what he was hearing. The wee fella can do football too!

I was the talk of the place that Wednesday morning. Joy reported Malcolm's delight at developments. But the day ended with some dreadful news. While the *Belfast Telegraph* featured

Malcolm Brodie's match report in the sports pages at the back, the front was filled with an image of Roy Stewart and his wife, Pat, with some teammates. Pat and Roy had married the previous September and had tied in their honeymoon with Glentoran's trip to Romania in the opening round of the competition. Roy had skipped the post-match reception to head home to Bangor. In the early hours of the morning, he collapsed and died. He was only twenty-five.

7

The Point of No Return

If there is such a thing as a red-letter year, then 1974 was it for me. Not only had I made my debut as a commentator, I had also got myself a contract. The post of continuity announcer had been advertised shortly after I began freelancing for *Round-Up* and I had applied, but the job went to Edgar Martin, a well-known voice whose experience in the role at Ulster Television would have left the rookie reporter in the ha'penny place. I can't say I was that bothered. I was enjoying what I was doing, though it would have fulfilled another little ambition if I'd been able to go on the air and say, 'It's five to one, and this is the Northern Ireland News, read by George Hamilton.'

When I was growing up, it felt like something of a novelty to hear locally produced programmes. The BBC Home Service morphed into Radio 4 in 1967 and that was where the radio output of Ormeau Avenue was housed. Regional news bulletins and the sparse selection of indigenous programming – not just in Northern Ireland – were opt-outs of a nationwide service. The radio arm of RTÉ, with no mothership to tether itself to, simply shut down for several hours each day.

So, local newsreaders became household names. Maurice Shillington, Duncan Hearle, Walter Love, Michael Baguley. Michael, wonderfully televisual, immaculately groomed, sporting a huge moustache, the possessor of the most magnificent baritone broadcasting voice, had been elevated to Head of Presentation but was still making occasional appearances at the microphone when the position of announcer was readvertised, this time on the basis of a one-year contract.

Nothing ventured, nothing gained. I had another go and was summoned for interview. The Head of Programmes, a formidable man by the name of Ronnie Mason, whose first love was the theatre, was in the chair, alongside several colleagues who sat opposite me at the conference table. I had passed the audition, easing my tongue around potential pronunciation potholes like Magherafelt – don't drop the 'ghe' in the middle the way some would say it – and Cambrai Street, named after a First World War battle in northern France but never delivered as it would be there. There was, though, another word that had arrived in English by way of French and was of particular interest to the chairman of the board.

Ronnie pushed a piece of paper across the table towards me. 'How would you pronounce that?'

Had I opted for the regional vernacular and declared 'am-machure', I'd have been out the door. But with all those years of Modern Languages behind me, I wasn't going to fall into the trap. 'Amateur,' I replied, *à la française*, in my best broadcasting voice.

'Congratulations, Mr Hamilton.' And that was it. I was a BBC continuity announcer.

My first day was to be Thursday, 16 May 1974. I would shadow Michael Baguley on the evening shift. That involved reading the two scheduled news bulletins, ten minutes at 5.50 p.m. and then a shorter summary at close down at a quarter to midnight. That was the plan. But this was far from being a normal Thursday afternoon.

The unrest in Northern Ireland had led to the suspension of the Unionist-dominated Stormont parliament. Its replacement by a power-sharing executive, representing both traditions, in tandem with the Sunningdale Agreement, had been signed the previous December. It created a role for a Council of Ireland in which the Irish government would have equal representation to that of the Northern Ireland Executive. It was denounced as a sell-out by unionist hardliners.

The Executive, comprising six Ulster Unionists, four from the nationalist Social Democratic and Labour Party (SDLP) and one from the cross-community Alliance Party, met for the first time on New Year's Day 1974. Increasing loyalist resentment crystallised in the setting up of what became known as the Ulster Workers Council (UWC). When a motion before the Assembly that had replaced Stormont condemning power-sharing and the involvement of the Republic's government through the Council of Ireland was voted down, the UWC called a general strike. Thursday 16 May was Day 2.

On the newsstands as I made my way to the BBC, the evening paper, the *Belfast Telegraph*, had a banner headline in huge letters which read 'Shut-Down Almost Total'. It reported, 'The entire Citybus fleet in Belfast was withdrawn shortly after 8 a.m. today following the spate of hijackings throughout the city.' The front-page photograph showed hijacked lorries blocking the main route in from the east, the Newtownards Road.

The tension on the streets translated into an air of excitement in the building. It's the same with any major news story. Those covering it have something substantial to get their teeth into. Given all the circumstances, I made sure I arrived in plenty of time. Michael took me to his office and told me it had been decided to replace the hourly news bulletins from London with summaries from Belfast, and the first of these would be at four o'clock.

We headed for the newsroom on the first floor, where the scripts to be read were laid out as they were prepared, on a bench along the side. There would be an ad hoc rehearsal, as each one was timed. The editor would finalise the order, present the sheaf of paper and the announcer would depart for the radio continuity studio just off the Master Control Room upstairs. This was where announcements between programmes would be made, along with the shorter news broadcasts which involved only a reader.

It was a self-operated studio, meaning the announcer drove the desk without any technical assistance. A Northern Ireland opt-out meant taking Radio 4 off the air by flicking an insignificant-looking switch, which gave the desk in the continuity studio control of the output. The clue as to the importance of this little circuit breaker was its colour – red – and the fact that it was housed inside a shiny chrome switch guard. You wouldn't want to be closing down *The Archers* by accident.

Part of the process of shadowing Michael would be learning how to operate the studio. It had been explained to me that I'd simply sit and observe him in action over a few shifts, then it would be my turn to read the news and he – or whoever I would be shadowing on the day – would take a back seat and keep a close eye on me, to make sure everything was being done as it should be.

In through Master Control we went, the new boy briefly introduced to those on duty there, past the jack fields and the monitor screens and on to the little studio off to the side. Michael held open the heavy door and ushered me in.

I could just imagine myself playing the DJ in here: record decks to one side – vinyl discs were the music source in the 1970s – and a tape player, too, for recorded inserts. In the announcer's eyeline, the sound meters and, above the bank of faders, those sliding levers that adjust the levels, a single microphone suspended on its boom arm. Just about enough room for a script on the desk – a real one-person operation, all right.

Michael followed me in. I stood back to let him take the chair, but he remained standing and extended his arm. You sit down. You take it.

I hadn't time to be nervous. But I suppose almost two years of experiencing various aspects of the radio game, with a fair smattering of live broadcasting in there too, had prepared me for this moment. The smile on the face of the Head of Presentation – BBC Northern Ireland's most senior announcer – was reassurance too. Michael had no fear that I'd cock this up.

Radio 4 was on the speaker. The clock was ticking up to four. Michael talked me through what I needed to do and, of course, he was there to intervene should things go haywire.

Headphones on. Slide open the fader for the channel from London. Then flick that little red switch. Radio 4 still played, but now it was in my hands. The time signal would come through automatically. I could open my mic and wait for the two-second pause that would precede the pips.

Deep breath. Close the fader. And wait for those six familiar little beeps, the last one slightly longer than those that go before it. 'It's four o'clock and this is a special bulletin of the Northern Ireland News, read by George Hamilton.' And I was off, unscheduled but, in the circumstances, the biggest broadcast I'd ever been involved in.

The stories were of the developing crisis, power cuts, transport disruption, school examinations cancelled. This was the deep end without a doubt. Sink or swim.

During the two weeks of the UWC strike, the BBC was the primary source of information and my new position put me at the very heart of that. It was a time, you might have thought, when reassurance was what was required; familiar, trusted voices telling the story. Looking back, I'm astonished and flattered in equal measure that the BBC had such faith in me.

The Presentation Department covered television as well. Two announcers – David Gamble and Michael Nunan – did evening continuity, three nights on, three nights off, providing out-of-vision announcements between programmes and an in-vision read of the late news from a shoebox of an unmanned studio at the end of transmission. David, in particular, happily acknowledged that the working arrangements were great for the golf.

It wasn't exactly a hard station on radio either. The news bulletins were the primary focus and there were just five of those – ten-minuters at 6.50 and 7.50 in the morning, not counting a visit to *Round-Up Reports* around 8.30 a.m. to read a review of the local papers. Then the five-to-one and after that, there was just the 5.50 p.m. and the news at close down. The general shifts also covered the two daytime television commitments, a mid-afternoon summary and then the news-reading element of the teatime magazine *Scene Around Six*.

There was another aspect to the mornings, though, now that I think about it. You did have to ring the Met Office at the airport first thing to get the weather forecast. That was quite bizarre, sitting at a newsroom desk with the copy-taker's headset on, banging away on a typewriter as the meteorologist dictated the bad news about the kind of day we could expect, while the duty reporter who'd been up all night yawned at this noisy interference to the relaxed conclusion of his shift. There wasn't likely to be much new news at such an early hour.

I struggle to think now what I did all day when I was in from 10.00 a.m. until 6.30 p.m., but I do have vivid memories of the nights, particularly those two weeks of the UWC strike. The announcers' shift pattern in Belfast mirrored that at Broadcasting House in London, so when I came in that Thursday to start at four in the afternoon, I would have stayed on duty until nine the following morning. Colleagues across the water would simply have crossed the street after reading the midnight news, to rest in one of the rooms in The Langham, which had been a rather grand hotel – subsequently reinstated as such – but at the time housed office accommodation, a social club and dormitories for the BBC. A Belfast announcer, who tended to live not that far from base, would nip home for a few hours to the comfort of his own bed.

But this was a particularly dangerous period. The violence was at its height and now there was disruption piled on top. If you were to leave the building late at night, there was no guarantee you'd find free passage back.

There was no Langham across Ormeau Avenue from the BBC in Belfast, but what we did have was Walter. He came from somewhere in the north of England and I'm pretty sure he was an ex-army man. The Corps of Commissionaires, a British Commonwealth movement set up to secure worthwhile employment for armed forces veterans, would provide the smartly uniformed personnel who would staff the lobbies of BBC premises across the UK, checking credentials and offering appropriate guidance to visitors in the days before swipe cards and electronic keys.

Walter might well have been a commissionaire, but as he worked nights, he was never in uniform, though he did wear a permanent smile and, in the unpleasantness that was Belfast at the time, he was always positive, always ready with a solution no matter what problem might present itself, which, in my case on the overnight duty, was where to get a couple of hours' kip.

He had it sorted in no time at all. Off the reception, directly opposite the desk, was a little office with frosted glass windows onto the street, high up on the wall. I think it might have been the commissionaire's rest room during daylight hours. Anyway, Walter sourced a camp bed from somewhere and some pretty basic bedding, which included rough blankets I have not forgotten, but, given the times that were in it, his B&B was a godsend.

He topped it off with room service. At 5.30 a.m., to give me time for a quick wash and brush up, he'd appear at the door with a cup of tea and his big grin, before he told me what would be in the scripts awaiting my arrival in the newsroom to prepare for the ten to seven. At the height of the strike, when movement was proving particularly difficult, I was asked to stay on after one of my nights on Walter's guest list. I finished up by reading the news on *Scene Around Six* and then headed home. I had read every single bulletin over the preceding twenty-six hours.

In the *Round-Up* studio, I'd be meeting whoever came in for interview. As well as those with political points to make, there would be spokespeople for whatever services around the city were being affected, and one of those was a lovely gentleman called Hugo Patterson, the personification of everybody's favourite uncle, who could never have imagined he would find himself in this kind of situation. He was the spokesman for Northern Ireland electricity, not that that's what it was called at the time. The key to the UWC strike was the fact that the workers at the principal power station at Ballylumford on Islandmagee had joined the protest.

'Ulster is on the brink' became Hugo's catchphrase as he explained how electricity generation worked and what, if one part of the chain was no longer effective, the knock-on effect would be. Sadly, this became a refrain, Hugo doing his best to put a brave face on things but having to impart a pretty stark reality. There was the real possibility that Northern Ireland could actually be left without power.

Hugo became a household name then, a reluctant celebrity doing his level best to let us all down lightly when he knew that the whole thing could so easily end in tears for everybody. The journalist Robert Fisk summed it up in his book, *The Point of No Return*: 'A self-elected provisional government of Protestant power workers, well-armed private armies and extreme politicians organized a strike which almost broke up the fabric of civilized life in Ulster. They deprived most of the population for much of the time of food, water, electricity, gas, transport, money and any form of livelihood.'

The point of no return was a phrase also used by Hugo Patterson. Twenty-five years later, in *The Irish Times*, Mary Holland recalled it, explaining that Hugo was saying a complete shutdown of power in Northern Ireland had begun and could not be reversed. This, said Mary Holland, marked the climax of the UWC strike and led to the collapse of the power-sharing executive the same day, though the refusal of the then British Secretary of State for Northern Ireland, Merlyn Rees, to meet representatives of the UWC may very well have had something to do with it as well. In any event, power-sharing was over. The strike ended. And Northern Ireland, as it always does, picked itself up, dusted itself down and turned its attention to the next crisis, which was the continuing IRA campaign, the loyalist response to it, and the British government's attempts to sort it all out.

No longer in need of Walter's accommodation, I was able to do what every other overnight announcer had done before the crisis hit and break up my night shift by going home. There was one morning I was heading back in when, a couple of miles shy of the back gate to Broadcasting House that gave me the privileged access to the onsite parking spot that early morning radio heads were entitled to, my car began to behave badly, pulling strongly towards the kerb. I was on the Stranmillis Road, named after a sweet stream – the Sruthán Milis – that probably refers to the River Lagan which flows nearby on its way to Belfast Lough. A suburban street, some housing, some shopping, so not a lot of potential assistance in the event of a breakdown at six in the morning.

I stopped the car and got out to see what on earth could be the problem. A puncture, that's what it was. No chance of an immediate fix and, with a news bulletin to be read in a little under an hour, I had a decision to make. I could walk it but I might get there a little too close to transmission time.

I was thinking I'd set off anyway and take my chances with an early morning jog, when, like the deus ex machina, a plot device whereby a seemingly unsolvable problem is suddenly and abruptly resolved by an unexpected and unlikely occurrence, an armoured Royal Ulster Constabulary (RUC) Land Rover pulled up a hundred yards away.

Now, bear in mind, the Troubles are at their height – that's the reason the RUC Land Rover is armoured – and their early morning patrol is interrupted by a young lad rocking up at the driver's door. I'm surprised they didn't draw their weapons. Instead, the policeman looked at me quizzically. This clearly wasn't an attempted assault, more likely some fool who'd stayed out too late and was in need of the bus fare to get himself home.

I had been very circumspect in my approach, which was entirely appropriate. Once we'd got over the formalities – I have not come to mount a terrorist attack – he was willing to listen. As he did so, his colleague emerged from the shop outside which they were parked.

'Yer man is reading the news in an hour and he's got a flat tyre. Will we give him a lift?'

The constable colleague burst out laughing and said, 'Of course. Jump in.' Except, with only two seats in the front, I had to board through the rear doors. Climbing in, I found myself among bales of newspapers. 'We'll get you to the BBC, don't worry, we just have a few drops to do.' This RUC 'Meat Wagon' as they were known, was doubling as a newspaper delivery van.

I sat in the back of this vehicle, which was most certainly not designed to carry passengers in the rear, as it roared around the immediate vicinity, dropping parcel after parcel of precious cargo, before finally swinging into Ormeau Avenue and pulling up outside the BBC. It was half past six – a little later than I would have hoped to be there, but at least I was there. That was the important thing. Walter's shift wasn't quite finished. He followed me up to the newsroom with a cup of tea. And the ten to seven began calmly – on time.

Remarkably, in these appalling circumstances, it was still possible to get on with your life. Privations, there were many, without doubt. Sometimes, *Gott sei Dank* as the Germans would say, with humorous consequences. Shopping was an awful experience. Security gates at the entrance to Belfast city centre meant a search of whatever you were carrying and a patting down into the bargain. So, the Northern Irish consumer developed a reflex.

Shortly after moving south, my parents came to visit and my dad and I headed off to H. Williams, a 1970s discount store near to where I was living, to source some provisions. It was a vast barn of a place and, as we approached the entrance, I was aware my ageing father, whose arthritis meant he wasn't too steady on his feet, was shuffling rather more than usual. I turned to ask him if he was OK, only to realise that he was trying to prepare the shopping bag he was carrying for inspection by the security people at the door and it was refusing to co-operate. Of course, he'd no need to be concerned. What was de rigueur for Stewarts Supermarkets in Belfast didn't apply in Dublin 14. As an aside on social history, the ghosts of those long-forgotten brands, along with Quinnsworth, live on under the name of Tesco. And where once H. Williams piled 'em high, the southern tip of Dundrum town centre now stands.

While life in Belfast stuttered on, Ormeau Avenue was a happy place for me. I thoroughly enjoyed reading the news. I've fabulous memories of the camaraderie of delivering the stories compiled by great people like Norman Stockton and George McEvoy, Graham McKenzie and Diane Harron, and Denis McGrath.

The shorter summaries were read in the small continuity studio and the ten-minute versions, which would include recorded taped inserts, came from the larger managed studio where I'd done all of my earlier broadcasting, with a sound man on the other side of the glass and Denis, the calmest of men, sitting alongside as you read the longer bulletin, feeding you the content sheet by sheet, always with an eye on the clock to make sure you didn't crash the pips (run over time) – the broadcasting equivalent of a capital offence!

Occasionally, I'd be on TV. There was no autocue then and I worked hard at perfecting a reading style that would let me take in whole sentences, so I could deliver them straight down the lens without having to keep looking down at the script.

Twenty-first-century presenters have it easy, with technology delivering their words electronically onto a screen in front of the camera so they can appear to be speaking spontaneously while looking straight at you, when, in actual fact, they are just reading their lines.

Before that technology had been developed, there was the teleprompter, which involved a device being placed directly under the lens. The reporter would read from something resembling a toilet roll as it was spooled through a viewer. When I joined, the BBC in Belfast had a teleprompter and only one presenter used it. The political correspondent, W.D. Flackes, was accorded the privilege because of his status.

Billy, as he was known, had built his career at the *Belfast Telegraph* before moving to the BBC, a move that many top journalists in town would make, mostly for the money it's fair to say. He operated both at Stormont and at Westminster, and was equally well received in both parliaments. He's renowned for the scoop that announced the end of Stormont was nigh. Edward Heath, the British Prime Minister at the time, was so much at ease in his company that his guard dropped to the point that he let slip the fact that the Northern Ireland parliament was to be prorogued. Billy Flackes was an absolute ace at his job.

He wasn't that great with the teleprompter though. In his thick-walled office alongside the newsroom, he'd type up his script on the special machine that the roll of paper was fed through. In the studio, it would all be lined up. And then it would be showtime.

Now, an autocue is run by a computer operator who's rolling the script across the screen in time with the presenter's delivery. The teleprompter, however, was driven by a pedal that equated to the accelerator in a car. And who pressed the pedal? The presenter.

Billy was intense in his delivery. As he spoke, he would become more involved in what he was saying. This found physical expression in the pressure he exerted on the teleprompter pedal. Billy's pieces to camera had a unique style, beginning in relaxed mode and ending rather frantically as he read the words moving ever more rapidly through the viewfinder.

That summer, a young reporter called Jeremy Paxman came to the BBC in Belfast on a six-month attachment. The way the Corporation's graduate trainee scheme worked, successful applicants would be sent on placements to the various regions, building up experience on the way to being appointed to a permanent position. I'd met him a couple of years previously when I'd gone to visit my school pals, David and Geoffrey Leckey, in Cambridge, where they were at uni and Geoffrey was in the same college, St Catharine's.

Jeremy cut quite a dash then, very much the English charmer, a side he kept well hidden in his subsequent career as a tigerish interrogator. I was introduced to him at one of the many garden parties, a striking figure in a striped jacket and straw boater. One Sunday in Belfast, he was the reporter on duty while I was down to read the news. David and Geoffrey were home that weekend and I suggested the pair of them might like to come in to the BBC to see how it all worked, totally unaware that Jeremy was going to be there.

In 1974, it wasn't a problem bringing your mates in to show them around and Sunday was a good day to do it, for there was precious little going on and there were few people around in Belfast itself, never mind the BBC. On Sundays, after the early bulletin, I'd stroll down to the newsvendor at the City Hall – there were no shops open in town on a Sunday then – and come back with an armful of papers to pore over in the hours between commitments. So, I had ample opportunity to give the Leckey boys the guided tour. When we got to the newsroom, I don't know who was more surprised, my friends or the young reporter. Anyway, they had a good old catch-up and then we left him to it.

Half an hour before showtime, we were back. I had scripts to check.

I explained how it worked. There was the lead story and then several more that had to go in. Further down, there were what were rather disparagingly known as fillers, items that could be dropped to keep the bulletin to just five minutes. Those would be timed in advance and it was left to the reader's discretion whether or not they were used; so, depending on whether you needed twenty, thirty or forty seconds, you took your pick. And then there was the weather, which had to go in and it usually took about half a minute to read. All in all, there was a fair degree of mathematics and clock watching involved, as well as fulfilling the primary function.

I gathered up the pages, carefully crafted by Jeremy Paxman, and the three of us headed for the little continuity studio. I showed the boys the inner sanctum, let them sit in the chair and work the equipment, making sure they stayed well away from the little red switch. The staffer on duty in the Master Control Room was happy for them to watch the actual bulletin go out from his area on the other side of the glass.

I was well set up, ready to go, David and Geoffrey positioned outside about to watch the radio news go out live, and then Jeremy appeared. A major story had broken and it needed a voice piece to do it justice. It was too late to record one, so he was going to have to do it live. There was only one problem. The continuity studio was built for one, with no facility opposite the presenter for a guest. There was no room at the desk itself for a second chair and there was just a single microphone.

Needs must. I created as much space as possible to leave room for Jeremy to position himself alongside. He's a tall man. If he stood, he'd be towering over the microphone, which had to remain where it was because I had to be seated to remain in control of the desk. In any case, moving the mic while we were on the air would have created unacceptable noise. There was only one thing for it. Jeremy would have to kneel beside me.

Funnily enough, because he was so tall, when he knelt down, his head was almost level with mine, so he was perfectly positioned. We got going at five minutes to one and the two boys outside could scarcely believe what they were seeing, their schoolboy pal at the controls and their chum from Cambridge on his knees beside him presenting the Northern Ireland News. You could not have made it up.

But those were days when things still did get made up as they went along. I was warned of pranks that might be played. Walter Love had achieved legend status at Broadcasting House after the day one mischievous colleague had decided that the best way to test his mettle was to set fire to his script as he was live on air. I never did find out how he managed to get through that, but I was assured he did.

My initiation process was routine until I crossed paths with a studio manager called Alan Dickinson. Seated at the circular table in Studio 3, you would be aware of your technical colleague on the other side of the glass, but you wouldn't be engaging with him or her, unless there was occasion to use the talkback. You responded to the cue light, got on with your read and the studio manager took care of the rest. On this particular evening, Alan had something planned for the new guy.

I introduced a taped insert and by instinct, looked towards the cubicle where he'd have pressed play on the tape machine. Except that he was nowhere to be seen. Oh, the recording was going out all right but it seemed there was nobody manning the controls.

Before I had time to wonder if this could be a problem, an object rose slowly into the space where he should have been. It was a cardboard box with eyeholes cut in and flashing lights on top. He'd created this helmet of sorts to add a dash of slapstick to the scene. It was all I could do to get through the paragraphs that followed with a straight face and a steady voice. That's how it was back then.

* * *

I was settling into my new routine rather well. They were prepared to allow me to carry on commentating at events, so my rota included appropriate gaps. My first gig for television followed soon after, and with it came the realisation that if I was to make my way in this world, I was going to have to confront a particular phobia.

Having to make use of one specific type of 'commentary box' was almost inevitable as a sports commentator at the time – the tower of scaffolding with the most rudimentary flooring supporting a portable shed of sorts and all of it accessed by a series of ladders. I never was one for heights and vividly remember the build-up, or should I say climb-up, to my first TV commentary position. It was at Ravenhill, the home of Ulster rugby. The ground had one grandstand and facing it was an uncovered terrace. Quite apart from the fact the terrace was on the southern side of the pitch, which meant that should the sun deign to shine, it would not do so directly into the lenses of the cameras, shooting across towards the grandstand created a much better visual ambience for the game.

So far, so sensible. But then came the ladder and I recall standing at the foot of it thinking, what have I got myself into here? One deep breath later, having told myself that if this was what I wanted to do, I was just going to have to get over my angst, I climbed that ladder rung by single rung and on to the next level of my commentary career.

Something else happened in 1974 that had a profound effect on my career. Larry McCoubrey had become a bit of a role model, for not only was he the genial host of *Scene Around Six*, he was also the TV football commentator. I had actually met him years before, on the opening day of the 1966–7 season. In the midst of my teenage-era superfan status, I was at The Oval making use of my brand-new season ticket for the very first time. That summer, to much fanfare, Glentoran had appointed a new manager – not just a manager but a player-manager, a twenty-nine-year-old Scottish centre forward called John Colrain.

'Colrain to sign as full-timer!' trumpeted the *Belfast Telegraph*, the headline's exclamation mark indicating the excitement with which this development was met. Bill Ireland's piece began: 'What could be the first firm move towards full-time professionalism was taken in Belfast this afternoon when terms were agreed for the signing of John Colrain, the 27-year-old [*sic*] former Ipswich Town and Glasgow Celtic centre-forward.'

His first competitive action would be on the first Saturday of August, in a game against my pal Howard Ruderman's Crusaders.

They too had a new centre forward. Joe Meldrum was unusual for the times, a Roman Catholic RUC man. He was a weekday regular on point duty at the junction of Sunnyside Street and the Ormeau Road, just outside his station at Ballynafeigh in south Belfast; on Saturday afternoons, he would turn into a holy terror as he tore open opposing defences. He'd been part of the Distillery team that won the Irish League title in 1963, scoring forty-nine goals along the way, and went on to play in the famous European Cup tie at Windsor Park when they held the mighty Benfica of Lisbon, Eusébio and all – finalists in the three preceding editions and winners twice – to a 3–3 draw. Joe, an amateur international, left Distillery after six seasons, his 172 goals in 197 appearances a post-war record, and played junior football for a year with the police team.

His Crusaders debut marked his return to local football's top tier and would have been the headline of that afternoon had John Colrain not been centre stage. I was in position in the new lower deck of the grandstand. It had been a big deal when Glentoran had put on a roof and installed seating that summer on what had been the reserved terrace, where, for sixpence more at the gate, you could avoid the hoi-polloi! Now, it meant that Glentoran had the Irish League's only double-deck grandstand. To my right was what remained of the reserved terrace, out in the open, and it was from there, about twenty minutes into the game, that a figure emerged. He vaulted the dividing wall and chose a spot to sit, just a few empty spaces along from me.

I did a double take. This wasn't just another football fan. This was Larry McCoubrey off the television. This was who I wanted to be. He couldn't fail to notice the nosy teenager along the row who kept looking at him. So, up he got and, with a smile on his face, came and sat down beside me.

'What's the new fella like?' he asked me. And with that we were off, me and my new best friend. He could have left it at a wave, maybe signed an autograph if asked. Instead, he introduced himself to the curious and adopted him as his matchday companion. Little did I think that eight years on, I'd be sharing a broadcast studio with him, a colleague who was every bit as charming and accommodating as that football fan I'd met so many years before who had turned up late and wanted to know the score.

On Irish Cup Final day in 1974, I was in the BBC in Ormeau Avenue. Joy Williams was editing coverage of the game, which would be broadcast in the form of highlights that night. I watched Ards defeat Ballymena United 2–1 from VT, the area where the videotape recording took place. Larry was the commentator. Joy was pointing out how his role in recorded coverage differed from how it would be if the game were live. To accommodate contemporary technology, you had to be aware of potential edit points and restrict your commentary so you weren't talking when the shot changed. That way a clean cut could be made.

Crowd shots were used to cover the join, but you couldn't keep showing the crowd every time you needed to move from one point in the game to a later sequence. A player close-up followed by the dropping ball from a defensive clearance offered another option. And there were the action replays as they were known. Belfast's outside broadcast kit at the time didn't include the means to provide these on site. They would be added during the edit back at base. But the commentary had to be live, to maintain the integrity of the crowd noise. It would have sounded false if it too was stitched in afterwards in a silent studio.

I marvelled at how Larry was able to describe what had just happened in such a way that it would take account of a slow-motion replay he wasn't actually seeing, all the more so when I saw the finished product as the edit took shape. Minutes after the full-time whistle, the monitor filled with a shot of Larry standing on the TV gantry beside his commentary box, ready to provide a match report to be slotted into the results sequence fronted by Seamus McKee. With no autocue and precious little time to gather his thoughts, this would be a top-of-the-head piece to camera.

Flawlessly, word perfect, Larry delivered the requested sixty seconds on the button, consummate broadcasting from a professional at the top of his game. From Shorts aircraft factory at the harbour, through amateur dramatics and radio comedy shows, Larry had arrived at the pinnacle, with the perfect showcase for his talent; the warmth of his engaging personality would always be a bright spot in the continuing gloom of the political situation – prime-time television five nights a week and the joy and release of popular sports coverage.

On a Monday morning that June, just a matter of six weeks after he'd covered the Cup Final, Larry was driving his sports car, a Reliant Scimitar, from his home in Groomsport on the County Down coast to Ormeau Avenue to begin another week on *Scene Around Six*. He was at the wheel on the dual carriageway on the Belfast side of Bangor when he suffered a brain haemorrhage and died at the scene. He was just thirty-eight.

8

Good Morning Ulster

There wasn't much in the way of good news in 1974. The bulletins I was reading told of more grief and despair. One morning, in search of some light relief, alongside its current take on political developments, the *Belfast Newsletter* featured an offbeat editorial which made it into the review of the local press that it fell to me to read on *Round-Up Reports*. Another edition of the programme at 7.30 a.m. had been added to the local opt-outs, and plans were being hatched to develop a standalone station that could offer more extensive coverage of the continuing crisis and provide some home-grown entertainment as well.

I checked the script for the review of the papers and saw an opportunity to inject a little humour into the read. I gave it my best shot. Having breakfast at home, the Head of Programmes, Cecil Taylor, a gruff no-nonsense journalist, who'd been the first television reporter to be appointed in the region and had risen to No. 2 in the hierarchy, was impressed. 'Sounds like you have a bit of personality, young man,' he said when he summoned me to a meeting. 'We've big plans here and we want you to be a part of that.'

Good Morning Ulster, or *GMU* as it came to be known (a word, as opposed to a set of initials), which would run from 6.40 to 9 a.m., would be the new Radio Ulster's flagship programme, much more ambitious than anything that had been attempted before. I was their choice to front it.

They hedged their bets. I'd do it Monday to Thursday and on Fridays they'd bring in David Dunseith, the former Drugs Squad sergeant who was now king of the teatime news on the opposition television channel, UTV. It would be a six-month contract at reasonable but not significant money (though a hike on what I was getting as an announcer), with the promise that if I did OK, there'd be a generous increase in both duration and remuneration when I'd completed the period of probation.

Radio Ulster took over the local Radio 4 wavelength at 11 p.m. on New Year's Eve 1974 with an ecumenical service from Magee College in Derry followed by the chimes of Big Ben in London at midnight and what was billed as a New Year party. The following morning, bright and early, mine was the first voice to be heard at the start of regular programming.

There was a total of four hours of local output each day. The other daily flagship programme was *A Taste of Hunni*, presented by a top local personality, Gloria Hunniford, who went on to become a household name on British radio and television.

As the two main presenters on the new station, Gloria and I were pictured at its launch introducing the Radio Ulster logo, which would not have been the most inspired piece of graphic design, the R and the U combining in what for all the world looked like an illustration of the bathroom trap invented in 1880 by the English sanitary equipment specialist, Thomas Crapper.

I was using one of those automated hot-drink makers that were popular in the 1970s for my early alarm call. Somebody had given my mother a Christmas present of a Teasmade, but, diligent woman that she was, she'd never have countenanced staying on in bed to have her first morning cup. Coming from the waste-not-want-not school, though, she thought it would be perfect for my requirements, saving me precious minutes before my crack-of-dawn commute.

So, I'd set it for 4.30 a.m., but the problem was that it would start boiling the water to have it ready for the moment its buzzer would sound. So, from about 4.15 a.m. there would be a gentle gurgling sound, followed a little later by a hiss as the head of steam built up, then a rushing sound as the hot liquid poured into the pot. I was usually wide awake before the tea was actually made.

Despite the physical demands of the position – I wouldn't be what you would call a morning person – I was thoroughly enjoying the responsibility of it all. I was the sole presenter, so I got to interview all manner of people who'd come in for a live appearance. Politicians and churchmen, community leaders, leading lights from business and sport, all human life was there on *Good Morning Ulster*.

Following the UWC strike the previous year, Northern Ireland was now under direct rule from Westminster. Harold Wilson's Labour government legislated the setting up of a Constitutional Convention to try to work out a political settlement for what the BBC style book referred to as 'The Province'. Elections were announced for 1 May, almost a year after the two-week strike that had brought down Stormont.

As the principal, if still probationary, presenter of current affairs on the station, I was given the job of hosting Radio Ulster's coverage. This was a big step up for me and a huge vote of confidence from the management. They were putting me up to interrogate the heavyweights of the time – Harry West, Bill Craig and Ian Paisley on one side, Gerry Fitt and John Hume on the other, with Oliver Napier and Bob Cooper of the Alliance Party in the middle.

There would be analysts too, among them Conor O'Clery, then the Northern editor of *The Irish Times*. Conor and I shared a taste for a particular Swiss cigar, made by the Villiger company, which was square in shape. I had a stash at home, which I had bought duty free on my last trip abroad, and reckoned they'd be the perfect accompaniment to his ruminations. The presence of the Bakelite ashtray meant there was no issue with smoking in studio. Only on television, where everyone could see what you were up to, was it frowned upon. Gerry Fitt, I recall, would have taken most advantage of this absence of regulation.

On the morning of the first election special, I was packing up the paraphernalia that would see me through the marathon broadcasts – reference books, colour-coded constituency line-ups and press cuttings (no laptops then). There was only one item missing from my satchel. The box of Villiger cigars was nowhere to be found. I was damned if I was going to pay through the nose for full-price replacements from the local tobacconist, so I made a little pact with myself. If I could get through without them, I would stay tobacco-free till Christmas and resume my relationship with the weed only then. That's what happened. Poor Conor had to source his own.

On 1 July, my contract was renewed for two years and I got the pay rise I'd been promised – a whopping 25 per cent. But there was no change in the political situation. The Constitutional Convention never had a hope of leading anywhere, given that unionists, opposed to the very idea of power-sharing, had won a majority in it. And the Troubles continued.

On a sunny Tuesday afternoon in August 1976, Anne Maguire was wheeling her six-week-old son Andrew in his pram along Finaghy Road North in west Belfast. Alongside, on her bicycle, was Anne's daughter Joanne, aged eight and a half, and her toddler son John, aged two and a half. A few yards further along was another son, seven-year-old Mark. Just up the road, a car driven by an IRA man, Danny Lennon, was being chased by British troops in armoured Land Rovers. The soldiers opened fire on the car, shooting the driver dead. The speeding car mounted the pavement and crashed into the railings of a school, crushing three of the children in the process. Joanne and Andrew died at the scene. John was fatally injured.

The incident caused widespread revulsion. 'To blame either the republicans who initiated the chain of incidents resulting in the deaths, or the soldiers who had shot Danny Lennon as he drove through a heavily populated area in broad daylight, seemed almost profane: the core reaction of the community was one of pure anguish at the needless deaths.' Those comments and the description of the incident come from the website of the Peace People, a movement begun by the children's aunt, Mairead Corrigan, and a local woman, Betty Williams, soon to be joined by an *Irish Press* journalist, Ciaran McKeown.

Their demonstrations calling for an end to the violence attracted worldwide attention. Soon after, having breakfast with the *Good Morning Ulster* team in the fifth-floor canteen in Broadcasting House, I was paged. There was a telephone call for me from Germany. It was a radio journalist from the Süddeutscher Rundfunk in Stuttgart, who had been tasked with travelling to Northern Ireland to compile a feature on the Peace People. Within days, I was at Belfast airport, awaiting the arrival of Winfried Roesner, one of the most interesting individuals it has ever been my pleasure to meet. What began as a weekend of intense collaboration developed into a firm friendship with the very epitome of a Renaissance man.

Eventually Winfried escaped from current affairs and settled into an area much more in tune with his personality. He became a much-respected arts broadcaster. For many years he hosted a monthly miscellany called *Schatzsuche (Treasure Hunt)*, a potpourri of puzzles from the fields of music, literature and art.

Life had started out in a far more uncertain way for Winfried, though. He had been born in 1939 in what was then the German city of Breslau. Aficionados of classical music will be familiar with the place. In 1879, its university conferred an honorary doctorate in philosophy on the composer Johannes Brahms, and it was in recognition of this, and slightly mischievously, that Brahms composed his medley of student drinking songs, the Academic Festival Overture.

Breslau in the time of Brahms would have been quite the place to study, but when Winfried was born, the biggest German city east of Berlin was not such an inviting place to be with the Nazis in control. With a sizable Jewish population, the Gestapo had been in evidence there for several years already and with all that was going on around – it would be Hitler's invasion of Poland, less than 100 kilometres away, that would mark the start of the Second World War – Breslau no longer seemed safe. The Roesners moved west.

When post-war borders were redrawn under the terms of the Potsdam Agreement, Breslau found itself in Poland, to be known henceforth as Wrocław. As a West German now, Winfried wasn't able to go back to the city of his birth until the Iron Curtain collapsed and the Berlin Wall came down. By then he was fifty. Winfried Roesner's story intrigued me and I found it exciting that, alongside my growing experience as a radio presenter, I was getting some international exposure as well. That, after all, was what had led to his phone call that morning.

Many years later, I was in Wrocław myself, on the day my father would have been 104, 16 June 2012. It was my fifth game of Euro 2012 – the European Football Championship – that brought me there. The Czech Republic played the hosts, Poland, in the Miejski Stadium in the evening. By this time, though, I was also presenting for Lyric FM and the programme has followed me around whenever it can. Happenstance, one Saturday, I was in the city that took Brahms to its heart. So, an early Polish breakfast of fresh fruit and cold meats was followed by a 30-złoty (€5) taxi ride to Aleja Karkonaska 10, the home of Polskie Radio.

It was an imposing three-storey structure with a four-storey centrepiece built in the fascist style – well, it did begin life as a regional outpost of the Reichsradio. Now, having sprouted a modernist wing with a car park in front, it was right beside a suburban two-lane dual carriageway. I was met by Stan, my sound engineer for the morning, and a most genial host, who brought me to my studio and made sure I was plied with coffee for the three-hour show.

I wasn't expecting what followed. Stan was very proud of his workplace and wanted to show it off. He took me to the control room of a studio where a discussion programme involving mothers and children was in full flow. The production team was delighted to welcome an Irishman.

Then he set off to fetch some keys. Locked away was a little museum, a decommissioned studio that was full of all sorts of the paraphernalia that had made broadcasting possible from its beginnings in the first half of the twentieth century. There were old microphones and phonographs, and grainy black and white images of pioneers of the medium and of some prominent people from down the years, including the odd Nazi who'd come in to broadcast propaganda.

Just down the corridor, there was a concert hall. It had been built exactly seventy years before, while the Second World War was raging all around. While Hitler's army had been fighting on many fronts, back in Breslau (as it then was), they were creating a space for a symphony orchestra. Stan rattled off its vital statistics: perfect acoustics, room for the biggest of ensembles and 200 seats for an audience that couldn't get enough of the music. It's still there, pristine, a monument to the dedication and foresight of those determined that life would go on and the best of life would be celebrated.

* * *

Sport has taken me all over the world as the decades have rolled by, but in the 1970s it was a gateway to the world beyond Northern Ireland. Malcolm Kellard had moved from Belfast to become Head of Sport at BBC Scotland and Joy Williams had taken his place to become the first female Head of Sport in the history of the BBC. Her position had gone to Nevin McGhee, the former rugby correspondent for the *Belfast Telegraph*, who had made the leap into freelance broadcasting not long after I'd started freelancing myself.

My rugby commitments continued. I'd been promoted and was now part of the network team deployed on what was then the Five Nations Championship, though only for the Ireland games. The way BBC Radio arranged its rugby coverage mirrored how they brought soccer to listeners – two commentators who'd each broadcast a half of each half. In international rugby, the two competing nations would each be represented in the commentary box, so if it was Ireland against England, I'd share the duty with Peter West. For Scottish games, either of the two former internationals Ian Robertson or Chris Rea would be beside me. On Welsh games, it was the one of the Principality's best-loved broadcasters, Alun Williams. The order of appearance would be dictated by the venue. When Ireland were at home, I'd get to commentate on the conclusion of each half. When Ireland were away, I'd be on first.

The only games in which this arrangement didn't apply were those involving France. A second English-speaking voice would be required and that would generally be one of the team of journalists operating out of the Sports Room in London. Except that when Scotland played France, the new Head of Sport in Glasgow sent for the young lad he'd launched and I became the second voice on those matches, which meant extra trips in alternate years to Edinburgh and Paris. Rugby was being very good to me, giving me huge opportunities on radio now to add to the occasional TV commentary.

And there was football on the agenda too. Larry McCoubrey's sad passing meant there was no full-time sports commentator available in Belfast. Not that they needed a full-time commentator, for there wasn't enough sport being covered, but they did need a commentator who wasn't shackled by the demands of a job outside the BBC.

That applied equally to radio and television, which is how I found myself in Swansea one Friday evening in 1976.

It was the final weekend of the domestic football season. What was known as the British Home Championship used to deliver one of the great days out when it was spread right across the calendar. Alternately, England or Scotland would visit Windsor Park on an October Saturday afternoon and the Irish League would shut down for the day so that the spotlight could be trained on the big game. In the 1950s and 1960s, 60,000 would turn up to see the top stars in the flesh. England's World Cup winners were in town in 1966, just three months after winning the trophy at Wembley. The following year, a Scottish team featuring Denis Law and four of the Celtic side that had won the European Cup that spring were beaten 1–0. I was there on the Spion Kop for both, with the Scottish game an unforgettable experience thanks to the genius of one man – George Best.

By the mid-1970s, shorn of its previous prestige as something of an anachronism in the modern game, the tournament had been relegated to a round-robin series in May, when the serious business had been done. The fact that the unrest at home meant Northern Ireland played every game away for three-and-a-half years hadn't helped either. Football finally returned to Windsor Park with the visit of Yugoslavia for a European Championship qualifier in March 1975. There followed visits by England and Wales, then Sweden and Norway. Footballing normality had resumed. But still, the weekend before Swansea, Scotland had refused to travel to Belfast and Northern Ireland's opening game in the Home Championship was played at Hampden Park in Glasgow. They lost 3–0. A 4–0 defeat at Wembley on the Tuesday before meant Northern Ireland and Wales would be battling, if that's the right word, to avoid the wooden spoon, the Welsh having lost both their previous games as well. It's fair to say it was a pretty low-key occasion that Friday night at the Vetch Field.

The commentary set-up was the usual. I'd share duties with my new Welsh pal, Alun Williams, who'd been my partner at Lansdowne Road just a couple of months before when we'd covered the Five Nations game, a four-tries-to-nil 34–9 hammering of Ireland by Wales, the third leg of the journey towards a Grand Slam. Alongside us was Nevin McGhee, who'd travelled with me from Belfast as producer for the night. Reflecting the status of the event, there was no co-commentator or summariser as they were known in the BBC, and no studio panel. The whole broadcast was being handled from Swansea.

Alun was at the mic when the half-time whistle blew, with Wales 1–0 ahead thanks to a goal from Derby County's record signing, Leighton James. In those days, before wall-to-wall live television coverage on channels with ad breaks to squeeze in, the interval didn't extend to a quarter of an hour, but there would still be ten minutes to fill. Alun, one of the best-known broadcasters in Wales over a wide range of programming, was closely identified with the Principality's most popular sport. Had this been a rugby game, he'd have been in his element, but halfway through a run-of-the-mill soccer game that had thrown up few talking points beyond the single goal, he needed help. He called in Nevin.

There was no one more surprised than the former rugby correspondent of the *Belfast Telegraph*. A print journalist par excellence and a master at crafting a voice piece, Nevin would have been the last person to put himself forward as an off-the-cuff summariser and certainly not at a football match. The look on his face was priceless. With great good humour, he rose to the occasion and, between the three of us, we got through to the start of the second half.

Leighton James' goal decided the game and brought the curtain down on Dave Clements' eleven-game tenure as Northern Ireland player-manager. He had moved to the United States to join New York Cosmos and, with a World Cup qualifying campaign beginning in the autumn, the Irish Football Association (IFA) took the view that having the manager based 3,000 miles away wasn't going to work; they opted not to renew his contract.

They turned to the iconic figure of Danny Blanchflower, who had captained the Tottenham Hotspur team that in 1961 became the first in the twentieth century to complete the English League and Cup Double. It was Blanchflower who said, 'The great fallacy is that the game is first and last about winning. It is nothing of the kind. The game is about glory, it is about doing things in style and with a flourish, about going out and beating the lot, not waiting for them to die of boredom.'

He played on until he was nearly forty, then became a columnist with the *Sunday Express*, but he had never been a manager. Still, if the IFA was taking a punt, they were taking a punt with a popular figure who was very much the people's choice.

One of the first things he did on appointment was offer an invitation to George Best to resume an international career that had stalled at the age of twenty-seven, around the time his relationship with Manchester United was falling apart. He'd drifted, securing a shirt at a variety of destinations. He'd been in South Africa; he'd had several games with Stockport County. Cork Celtic thought they could cash in, but after three appearances, he was gone. The North American Soccer League offered possibilities. He spent the 1976 season with the Los Angeles Aztecs and his inclusion in the All-Star team alongside Pelé, Bobby Moore, Tommy Smith and Rodney Marsh suggested he could still play.

That brought him back to England. He teamed up with Moore and Marsh at Fulham, in the Second Division, and that's where he was, now thirty years of age, when he got Danny Blanchflower's call. Northern Ireland's World Cup qualifying group included Belgium, Iceland and the Netherlands, World Cup finalists in 1974 and third in the recent four-team European Championship. These were the Dutch of the Total Football era, the national side based on the Ajax team that won the European Cup three times in a row in the early seventies – Arie Haan, Ruud Krol, Johan Neeskens and, of course, Johan Cruyff. And as luck would have it, Danny Blanchflower's first match in charge would be against the group's top team, away, at the home of Feyenoord in Rotterdam. He would certainly need George Best.

Joy Williams was on leave from her post as SPO (remember that BBC fondness for reducing titles to initials) and it was the Assistant to the Sports Programming Organiser who was in charge when the offer of access to live coverage of the game came in. Nevin McGhee gave it more consideration than Joy would have done, for the hurdles to surmount were sizable. For one thing, BBC Northern Ireland could only opt out of the schedule on BBC1. And the kick-off time in Holland meant the match would run right across the *Nine O'Clock News* from London, which was sacrosanct. To use the word 'brilliant' to describe Joy is by no means over-egging the pudding, but she wasn't one to rock the boat. The newly installed No. 2 reckoned he had nothing to lose.

He took his time and composed a memo to the Head of Programmes in Belfast, Cecil Taylor. Ultimately, if this was to be a runner, Cecil would have to go in to bat for it at the very top in London. Nevin set out the case: the new manager, the people's favourite, the quality of the opposition, but above all else, the return of the prodigal, the one and only George Best. 'I would strongly urge and advise you,' wrote Nevin, 'to give live transmission your most serious consideration.' Cecil, no shrinking violet himself, I think, admired his balls.

He ran with the idea, taking it to London, where the significance of the request was immediately acknowledged. But there remained the problem of the *News*. You cannot simply record a news bulletin and put it out later – at that point it is no longer the news. It's the news from whenever it was broadcast. Not every broadcaster, in my experience, is quite so diligent as the BBC. Fair play to head office. 'Go for it,' they said, 'and we'll run the *Nine O'Clock News* again, just for Northern Ireland, once the match is over.'

Joy came back from her break horrified at what Nevin had done. But, inwardly, I'm sure the reflected glory made her proud as punch and, what's more, she hadn't had to agonise and, potentially, make the wrong call.

It was a coup for BBC Northern Ireland. Nevin and I flew to Rotterdam via Heathrow, finding ourselves seated beside a Dutch lady called Lennie on the second leg of the journey. She was intrigued to find herself beside two guys who watched sport for a living. And she knew enough about football to understand that this trip was a big deal for us. We shared our excitement and declared our absolute ignorance of the Dutch language, wondering, as we sipped gin and tonic, how best to go about ordering our refreshments in her country. 'Of course, everybody will understand English,' she said, 'but if you want to really do it like a Dutchman, go for a chaser. Order *twee bier, twee genever*.' That became the catchphrase of our trip.

We'd gone out on the Monday, so Tuesday was the day to do our homework on the opposition. We went to the national training centre at the central town of Zeist, described as the beating heart of Dutch football. We saw them up close and we began to get goosebumps at the prospect of seeing them in action, most likely mauling our gallant crew.

Matchday arrived. The Feyenoord stadium, because of its shape known as De Kuip (which is Dutch for bathtub), had 56,000 in that night, the vast majority sure the hosts' World Cup campaign would get off to the perfect start. Danny Blanchflower agreed. 'There is no way the Dutch cannot be made favourites. No way at all. If they don't beat us there is something wrong. That is not to say we won't be going out there to try.'

He invoked Martin Luther King. 'We in Irish football must be dreamers. Dreamers that we can beat all opposition. Sometimes dreams can come true.'

Danny had worked his magic in the dressing room. Within four minutes, Northern Ireland were ahead. Best fed McIlroy out on the left. He beat the defender and crossed. Chris McGrath, just signed from Tottenham by Manchester United – no transfer windows back then – was unmarked and able to pick his spot with a header. His feet never left the ground.

Then there was a moment of magic that those of us privileged to see it will never forget. Best had told a journalist, Bill Elliott, that he had something in mind to make his mark on the match. Elliott takes up the story:

> Best received the ball wide on the left. Instead of heading towards goal he turned directly infield, weaved his way past at least three Dutchmen and found his way to Cruyff who was wide right.
>
> He took the ball to his opponent, dipped a shoulder twice and slipped it between Cruyff's feet. As he ran round to collect it and run on he raised his right fist into the air.

The perfect nutmeg. He did it again, to Johan Neeskens. If Northern Ireland were to lose that night, they'd always have George Best's nutmegs.

It did indeed look like they might go down. Two goals in two second-half minutes – Krol hammered one in from distance, then Cruyff added a second from close range – threatened to throw a dampener on the night, but this wasn't the end of the tale.

Blanchflower sent on Derek Spence, who, the following day, would complete his transfer from Bury in the old Third Division to Blackpool in the Second, for the last quarter hour. Spence was a striker, but he'd never scored for Northern Ireland. Two minutes to go. A 2–1 defeat would have been an honourable result, but Blanchflower's boys were still dreaming. Sammy McIlroy took a throw, David McCreery sped on to it, past the defender and into the Dutch penalty area. His cross was spilled by the goalkeeper. 'Spence. A goal! It's there! Derek Spence has done it!'

Kees Jansma, the Dutch TV commentator next door to our booth, couldn't help but hear and he has never let me forget it. That goal shattered Dutch dreams – 2–2 and the match finished. One of Northern Ireland's greatest nights.

I did Kees a favour though. Down in the tunnel afterwards, George Best had been his usual accommodating self, happy to answer anything that was thrown his way. Alongside, the Dutch were waiting to interview their players. In the circumstances, they were taking a little longer to appear. We finished with George and Kees tapped me on the shoulder. 'Do you think he'd do one for me?'

'I'm sure he would,' I said and asked him. Kees got his interview and ever since, he's introduced me as the man who introduced him to George Best.

While all of that was going on, back in London, Kenneth Kendall was reading the *Nine O'Clock News* again, at half past the hour. It hadn't changed much from the original version. Just a new headline for the second edition: Northern Ireland have drawn 2–2 with the Netherlands in their World Cup match in Rotterdam.

9

It was all George Hamilton's Fault

'It was all George Hamilton's fault!' If you ever quote that to me as an opening line, I'll tell you who wrote the book. My very good friend Jim Neilly has been promising for years to commit his life story to print but, as far as I'm aware, he hasn't got beyond that first sentence. He has a tale to tell, for sure, after over forty years as one of the most recognisable voices in broadcasting.

After school at the Royal Belfast Academical Institution, known locally as Inst, Methody's great rivals on the rugby pitch, Jim had gone to Stranmillis College and by the time our paths crossed, most likely in the Eglantine Inn on the Malone Road in Belfast, he was teaching chemistry in the Boys' Model School in the north of the city.

The Egg, as the pub was known, was one of two directly opposite each other a quarter of a mile up the road from the university. In the 1970s, the Botanic Inn – The Bot – and The Egg attracted the recently graduated crowd. You were categorised by which one you favoured and Jim and I were Egg men, habitués of the upstairs lounge, where a lady by the name of Pauline ran the bar with fearsome efficiency.

We hit it off immediately, the fund of stories we swapped the basis of many an evening's high-octane entertainment. When I began on *Good Morning Ulster*, my early-to-bed regime meant my socialising was restricted to weekends, but that wasn't so bad, for the fact that David Dunseith had been hired to front the programme on Fridays meant I could start to let my hair down on a Thursday night.

It just so happened that that was when the Glenmachan Hotel in the Holywood Hills just outside Belfast hosted a weekly jazz session in its stables out the back. The fact that it had a late licence only added to its appeal. The Tuborg Gold and the smooth tunes flowed at a venue whose location helped keep its profile low enough to stay off the target list of those who were doing their best to destroy what little remained of the city's night life.

Jim's only issue was that he had to get up to go to school the following morning and there were only so many lab experiments he could safely assign to his class while he gathered himself in his office. Over time, the notion formed in his head that he too might like a crack at the lifestyle I was enjoying, where early morning starts were a matter of choice and not obligation. But that's all it was, an idea, for the teaching wasn't proving too taxing and he was still going strong on the rugby pitch, propping for Instonians – his Old Boys team – well enough to have earned a call-up from Ulster.

When we met for a beer one Saturday night, he told me he'd been listening to the report on his game and hadn't been too impressed by what he'd heard. Why don't you give it a try? I suggested.

Not long after, the stars aligned. Jim was on bouncer duty at the door of the Instonians clubhouse disco when an over-inebriated acquaintance attempted to gain entry. Whatever ensued left Jim with a broken hand. Playing rugby was off the menu for at least six weeks. And coming up was the very first Ireland 'B' international. They were to play Scotland at Ayr, on the coast south of Glasgow, not that far from the port of Stranraer. I was to cover the game and, because the location was relatively convenient, I decided to go by car, taking the ferry from Larne at seven in the morning. The fifty-mile drive on the other side wouldn't take much more than an hour and, after the game, I'd be on the evening ferry and back in my own bed that night. The Saturday before, Jim, with his hand in plaster and at a loose end at the weekend, suggested coming along for the ride. I was more than happy to have the company.

As the days passed, a cold snap developed and by the Friday it had become obvious that the frozen pitch at Ayr Rugby Club wasn't going to be playable. With twenty-four hours to kick-off, the game was switched to Murrayfield in Edinburgh, where there was undersoil heating. It was still doable in the car, 130-odd miles one way, but it would make the return journey to the ferry ever so slightly tight. I could have flown, but Jim would have had to pay for his own ticket. We decided we'd take our chances on the boat.

When I was arranging to pick him up, Jim had asked me if I had a tape machine. He fancied having a go himself, just like I had done those few years before. I did have a little cassette recorder, so

I brought that along and we set off in the dark of the first Saturday morning in December 1977. The crossing was uneventful and we rocked up at the Holiday Inn just by Edinburgh Zoo and not far from Murrayfield in plenty of time for lunch, which we took in the lounge, seated at a low table on comfortable couches, a detail that may seem irrelevant at this point but which will prove significant later in the story.

The home of Scottish rugby was undergoing refurbishment at the time and the main grandstand was out of commission. I would do my commentary on the gantry suspended from the stadium roof. But if Jim was going to do one too, he couldn't come with me for fear of being overheard on the air. We negotiated a seat for him at the front of the building site that was the empty stand – something you'd never be able to do in the twenty-first century, but a request that was most affably granted back in 1977. So, while I provided part of the Saturday afternoon soundtrack on Radio Ulster, Jim took his first tentative steps into the world of commentary.

In *The Irish Times*, Edmund van Esbeck reported that 'On a day when winter spread its bleak cloak across the lands, the Irish gave a performance to warm the heart and lift the spirit, as they fashioned victory by a try and a penalty goal to a penalty goal.' Ciarán Fitzgerald, who'd go on to captain Ireland to two Triple Crowns and a Five Nations Championship, led the 'B' XV. Scrum-half Colin Patterson scored the try. Tony Ward converted the penalty.

Commentary done, report completed, we went back to the car and headed for the A702 to the southwest. In the absence of a motorway connection, it was a single-carriageway cross-country trip with no time to spare. Clear of the city and out on the open road as dusk turned to December darkness, we decided it was time for the audition. Jim put the cassette in the player.

I don't think the pair of us have ever laughed as much. It was rough around the edges, but it was hugely entertaining. As we roared, the road veered slightly to the right. The headlights didn't pick this up and, following the line of the verge, we headed straight on. It was only when we found ourselves closing in on some outbuildings that we realised we'd driven into a farmyard!

No harm done, we got back out onto the road and made it to Stranraer in time for the ferry, but we were lacking a vital piece of documentation – my driving licence. At the height of the Troubles, you needed ID to go anywhere. And my driving licence had gone AWOL. The policeman at my window was none too impressed and, for a moment, it looked like they weren't going to allow us on board. Thankfully, our explanation was accepted. The tale of our outing, the fact that we'd papers to show we'd come across on the morning ferry and would have been vetted for that and that we were clearly going home encouraged the application of a fair helping of Scottish common sense. We were cleared to proceed. We could have played him Jim's commentary if we'd needed further proof!

The licence, it turned out, had slipped from my pocket as we'd been having lunch on the low couch at the Holiday Inn. The kind soul who found it handed it in and the hotel posted it on to me. It arrived back in Belfast on the following Tuesday. By then, Jim's tape was with Joy Williams. I'd told her I had this pal who was keen to give broadcasting a go. The one thing that was clear from the comedy cut was that he possessed the perfect voice for it. Before Christmas, he was on the air, reporting on a Senior League Rugby game, ironically enough between my Old Boys team, Collegians and Civil Service. Saturday, 3 December 1977 was a day neither of us will ever forget, for the very best of reasons. And the comedy didn't conclude when we ejected the tape.

On what was a rough enough crossing back, we were, as Jim would put it, 'Hank Marvin'. So, although it might not have been advisable, we sought out something to eat. In those days, there was a restaurant on board, complete with waiter service. Jim and I took our places and were offered menus. Pretty straightforward fare, as you'd imagine, with pâté and soup among the starters. The waiter hovered, swaying gently as the ship rolled. 'What do you fancy?' I asked Jim.

The waiter interjected, 'I wouldn't recommend the soup!' We gave it a wide berth but did partake of something appropriate. We made it back to the Egg in time for the closing ceremony.

That winter was one of the coldest for many years and Ayr wasn't the only frozen pitch to feature, though in the case of the Parc des Princes the following February, they insisted the show must go on. It was the third weekend of the Five Nations Championship. Ireland had begun the tournament with a 12–9 win over Scotland at Lansdowne Road – France had beaten England in Paris on the same weekend – then sat out the second round of matches as France won at Murrayfield and England went down at home to Wales.

Next for Ireland was the trip to the French capital, so on Thursday 16 February, Joy Williams and I headed for Dublin to join the official party on the Aer Lingus charter to Le Bourget.

Visiting Paris for rugby was always a delight, on this particular occasion doubly so, for I'd been advised to pack my dinner jacket. We would be guests at the official dinner after the game.

The BBC studios were on the Rue du Faubourg Saint-Honoré, almost next door to the official residence of Président de la République, the Élysée Palace. It was wonderful having the chance to observe a foreign correspondent in action, and imagine the excitement there must have been for the journalist in question, Stephen Jessel, a busy little man who seemed to be forever en route from one glamorous assignment to the next.

There we would file our previews and be entertained to coffee by Chantal, around whom the place revolved. She'd look after all our arrangements, including the chauffeur-driven car that would collect us on match day from our hotel at the Gare Saint-Lazare and whisk us through the movie set come to life that is Paris, past the Opéra and the Madeleine to the Place de la Concorde, the memory still vivid of moving alongside the Obelisk on the left, with the broad expanse of the Champs-Élysées over on the right, sweeping up to the magnificence of the Arc de Triomphe at the top.

Across the river, the twelve Corinthian columns of the porch of the parliament building, the Assemblée Nationale, straight ahead, then on to the Quai d'Orsay, the Eiffel Tower standing proud beyond the rooftops.

Past the Hôtel des Invalides, final resting place of Napoléon Bonaparte, on through the 15th arrondissement, regaining the Seine downstream by the Pont Mirabeau. Then, to the Porte d'Auteuil, down past the Stade Roland Garros, home of French tennis, to the press gate of the Parc des Princes. There would be a light lunch before we'd take the lift to the commentary boxes at the very back of the futuristic grandstand.

Those commentary boxes were unique, overlooking the pitch from a height through floor to ceiling windows installed in the shape of the bow of a ship. Constructed of thick, shatterproof glass, they rendered the space inside almost completely soundproof. They were all equipped with a little speaker that delivered crowd noise, so that it felt as if you were actually seated among the spectators.

That Saturday in 1978, though, the sight that greeted us was like nothing I'd ever seen two hours before the kick-off of a major international. Down below, the grass was white. The pitch was, quite obviously, frozen. There had been snow in Paris during the week and remnants of it remained despite a clearance operation the day before. Heavy overnight frost had left what remained rock solid. Ground staff were moving across the playing field, doing what they could to alleviate the situation, without any discernible success.

What happened next would have been comical were it not for the seriousness of the situation. The pitch was unplayable, but the French Rugby Federation was determined the game would go ahead. They sent word through their press officer that journalists and broadcasters would be welcome to come down and check the surface. It seemed that someone had had the bright idea that if a couple of hundred pairs of feet marched up and down for half an hour or so, they'd offer any developing thaw some assistance. Some hope.

Given that under normal circumstances the stadium sward was sacred turf and no mere hack would be permitted to set foot on it, this was an invitation that could not possibly be resisted. So down we went and I had the singular experience of standing beneath the posts, gazing up into the stands, imagining a full house and that I was an international goalkeeper (the stadium was home to the French football team as well), then marching out to the centre of the pitch to look back at those same uprights and visualise what trying to convert a penalty from that kind of distance in a packed stadium would feel like. The stands were empty. The small crowd was on the pitch, walking around for fully thirty minutes. It made precious little difference.

When the Irish party arrived about an hour before kick-off, they were appalled by what they saw. They were adamant, van Esbeck reported, that the game should not go ahead. But the French insisted, no doubt fearful of the financial consequences of a postponement. 'I have never previously seen', van Esbeck wrote, 'a game played on a pitch so hard and potentially dangerous to the participants.' The players bore the scars afterwards, in terms of cuts, abrasions and bruises. He described it as one of the most courageous performances ever given by an Irish team. Victory went to France (by a single point, 10–9) but Ireland won the award for valour.

That night we dined in splendour. In our best bib and tucker, we made our way to the Grand Hotel in the Rue Scribe, not far from our own stylish lodgings, superior by a street to what a station hotel would look like back home. The dinner was being held in the Opéra Salon, described as the most renowned ballroom in all of Paris, with its opulent statues and gilding, its fourteen-metre-high ceilings and monumental chandelier, its curved walls a complete circle of mirrors.

Over seven courses including lobster, which I'd never eaten before, I experienced French cuisine at its finest. Among the trinkets at each place was a commemorative cigarette lighter, a little square tower gilded and glossy green, with the match and the date inscribed. It lasted for years, seeing me through many a Villiger cigar.

If there is such a thing as a travel bug, by this stage I had well and truly caught it. I think I can identify when it really took hold. It was in the autumn of 1976 when I found myself at a football match abroad on each of three consecutive Wednesday nights. This was what I really wanted to do. I followed Glentoran to Basel in Switzerland for the second leg of a UEFA Cup tie. The Glens had won the first leg 3–2, so hopes of an upset were well and truly alive. While the team was flying on the day before the match, I was on TV commentary duty back in Belfast, covering Crusaders against Liverpool in the European Cup. This was Bob Paisley's Liverpool, the team of Kevin Keegan and John Toshack, captain Emlyn Hughes and Steve Heighway. The Irish League champions were their first-round opposition and had put up a fight at Anfield in the opening leg, defeated only by a penalty from Phil Neal and a second half goal by Toshack.

The second leg at Seaview – Crusaders' compact stadium on the Shore Road – was more of a cruise for the Reds. David Johnson scored twice; Keegan, Heighway and Terry McDermott also contributed to a 5–0 scoreline. Liverpool were up and running and on their way to their very first European Cup, which they secured with a 3–1 win over Borussia Mönchengladbach in Rome the following May.

So, I was travelling separately to Basel, via Heathrow, on

the day of the game, boarding a British Airways 1-11 for the second leg of the trip. Thirty thousand feet up in a cloudless sky, seated at the back as the tail-mounted engines roared in my ear, I could barely suppress my excitement when I spotted the whole of Paris laid out below me like a carpet and picked out the Arc de Triomphe standing proud at the heart of the Place de l'Étoile, the shape of the architect's star so obvious from up there, the twelve spokes of the avenues leading away from Europe's tallest triumphal arch its visual embodiment. I arrived at the hotel just as the Glentoran party was leaving to head to the stadium. They'd no more joy than Crusaders the previous evening. Conceding two first-half goals, they saw their prospects of progress evaporate. They eventually lost 3–0 on the night and 5–3 on aggregate.

A week later, I was in Luxembourg. Carrick Rangers, a second-tier team, had shocked the local footballing establishment by defeating Linfield to win the Irish Cup for the very first time. Led by Jimmy Brown, a player-manager in his mid-twenties, this 'B' Division side had qualified for Europe. They came out of the hat alongside Aris Bonnevoie and I was assigned to cover the second leg.

For somebody of my vintage, the Grand Duchy meant only one thing – Radio Luxembourg – which we'd tune into on our transistor radios on 208 metres on the medium waveband. Barry Alldis, a trumpeter for Sydney, Australia, was their top jock. Later, a youngster by the name of Noel Edmonds hosted the late show, which began with the salutation 'Multitudinous greetings to you, sons and daughters!' It was effectively the United Kingdom's first pop music station and had been required under-the-bedclothes listening for a whole generation of youngsters starved of the kind of tunes it played.

The team from Carrickfergus in County Antrim had won the first leg 3–1. We were travelling more in expectation than hope. At the time, individual accommodation wasn't always available, so I had a roommate – Bill Ireland of the *Belfast Telegraph*. Not that this hadn't happened before. I'd had the most extraordinary experience as a rookie of sharing in the Shelbourne in Dublin with one of the biggest names in British broadcasting – Peter West, a principal commentator on rugby and cricket for the BBC, and the host of the original *Come Dancing* programme on television. We got on like a house on fire.

Though the Irish Cup holders lost 2–1 on the night, they were through on aggregate – a 'B' Division team through to the second round in Europe! This was sensational and worthy of a report on BBC Radio 2, where John Motson was hosting a football special. Manchester United and Sunderland were locked in a League Cup tie which had gone to a second replay and they had had live commentary. I'd got the request to speak to Motson when I was recording my match report for Radio Ulster.

In the low-tech world of the mid-1970s, this last-minute arrangement would only work if I could find a telephone and, with the press corps busily engaged in filing their own copy, there was nothing else for it but to leave the ground and seek out a phone box on the street. Fortunately, the public realm in Luxembourg was well appointed and I was safely ensconced in one within a matter of minutes.

The connection was made and I awaited my cue. Motty, unsurprisingly, wasn't particularly well versed in the ins and outs of the Irish League 'B' Division and erroneously introduced Carrick Rangers as a junior team from the Republic of Ireland. Not exactly the perfect start.

Carrick's celebrations continued late into the night, to the extent they hadn't left enough time for one of the squad, who should best remain nameless, to get himself back into a state fit enough to fly. There was quite a discussion at the foot of the aircraft steps before the player, still tired and obviously fresh from the emotional celebrations, was cleared to board.

The third Wednesday away was that World Cup match in Rotterdam when Danny Blanchflower took charge of Northern Ireland for the first time, George Best came out of international retirement, the Netherlands of Cruyff, Haan, Krol and Neeskens was held to an unlikely draw, and the BBC1 *Nine O'Clock News* was read twice for the first and, as far as I am aware, only time.

Carrick's Cup Winners' Cup journey continued a fortnight later. They'd drawn Southampton, then managed by Lawrie McMenemy, and as their home ground at Taylor's Avenue wasn't up to European standard, they hosted the tie at Seaview, where Liverpool had been in action against Crusaders not long before.

Rangers did manage to score twice but lost in the end 5–2 on the night, eventually exiting the competition 9–3 on aggregate. Years later, I was involved in a programme with Lawrie McMenemy and I reminisced about the game at Seaview. Instantly, he burst out laughing. The result was one thing, but the most memorable aspect of the evening had been an incident that followed an injury to a Carrick Rangers player.

He'd come off second best in a tackle and needed assistance.

The physio assessed him and indicated he needed to be carried off. The volunteer stretcher party looked like extras from Dad's Army. Once they'd loaded him on board, they hoisted him. The problem was the two at one end were facing one way, the two at the other were facing in the opposite direction, all four with their backs to the injured player. The inevitable happened. One pair dropped the stretcher and the player fell off. He'd gone down because of a problem with his leg. When he was eventually carried away, he was holding his head. Thankfully, no lasting damage was done.

* * *

In the spring of 1977, I was tiring of the early mornings and itching for the chance to do more sports broadcasting. Sometimes you have to create your own opportunities. Happenstance presented me with the chance to combine a bit of business with pleasure. After my year in the Ruhr, I took every opportunity I could to get back to Germany. When it was announced that Northern Ireland had arranged a friendly with West Germany in Cologne that April – funnily enough on the 27th, the date of my parents' thirty-fifth wedding anniversary – I suggested that I should cover the game. Two birds with one stone and all of that. First and foremost, a football game. Second, it featured West Germany, the current World Cup holders. And third, it would take me back close to my old, familiar stomping ground. As it was only a friendly, they wouldn't be 'sending', in the parlance. But if they had a reporter there …

I was taking a leaf from Nevin McGhee's book. Shortly

after he joined the BBC, he proposed that he could cover the Commonwealth Games in New Zealand that year, focusing on the Northern Ireland team. The BBC had no intention of funding such a trip, but when Nevin suggested that he'd pay his own fare if they'd guarantee to pay him pro rata for what he produced, they reckoned they had a deal.

My suggestion wasn't half as dramatic, but I figured if I got myself to Cologne, I could more or less cover my costs if they paid me for my contributions. This would be a labour of love and I could set down a marker for what I would propose down the road – a greater focus on local sport through the contributions of an actual sports reporter.

Media organisations, I've found, can usually be persuaded to pay for material. It's always the expenses that are the killer. The fact that Radio Ulster was going to get coverage of a Northern Ireland international football match abroad, without having to pay for flights and accommodation, was a no-brainer. I was on.

I knew I could make this pay. They would include match updates in the evening schedule, that was a given. With no television coverage, there was, for sure, a market for my reports. I would do previews for the current affairs programmes, post-match interviews for the morning after, and, given that Radio Ulster also includes light entertainment in its schedule, I would offer some German lifestyle for the likes of Gloria Hunniford's mid-morning show, *A Taste of Hunni*. Gloria's approach matched my own. Make it unique, make it different and they'll listen. I was pushing an open door. What better than a German travelogue, particularly when the football team was over there for a match?

So, I contacted David Segel, the Irish Football Association's

London-based travel agent and arranged my flights and accommodation to tie in with the team. I landed in Cologne, hired myself a Volkswagen Polo and headed for the Esso Motor Hotel to plot what would effectively be my pitch for the position as BBC Northern Ireland's freelance sports reporter.

Fully aware that giving up *Good Morning Ulster* could have serious financial implications, there was something else I had to do. The Cologne arm of West German broadcasting – the Westdeutscher Rundfunk – had used me for live reports from troubled Belfast. I was keen to show my face in their newsroom in the hope that a guy they actually knew might spring more often to mind. I placed a call to my contact there. Rainer Assion told me to come on in.

Recollecting my formative years in the broadcasting business, I am struck by how different so much has become. In 1977, I could simply turn up at the front door of the Funkhaus on Appellhofplatz in the centre of the city, say that Herr Assion was expecting me and I'd be directed to the paternoster lift – continuously moving, slowly, with no doors, you simply stepped on and off again when you'd reached your desired floor – named after the rosary prayer. The WDR paternoster inspired a short story by the writer Heinrich Böll, who was born in Cologne and had a home in the west of Ireland, writing fondly of the place in his *Irisches Tagebuch*. 'Doktor *Murkes gesammeltes Schweigen*' ('Dr Murke's Collected Silences') is a satire about a rather odd radio producer who edits together the gaps in taped productions and likes to frighten himself by riding the rolling lift beyond the apex of its ascent into the space beyond the top floor to see what might happen if one day it got stuck.

Stepping out of the paternoster on the appropriate floor, I was directed to Rainer's desk. It was the first time we'd met and he couldn't welcome me because he was on the phone, a typically German device that offered a little cup to hold over your free ear so the noise of the newsroom environment – typewriters and tape machines – would not disrupt your concentration.

He was talking to his wife, who was off on a working assignment and had just checked into her hotel in Prague. This was impossibly exotic for the boy from Belfast. Nobody I knew ever flew off of a morning to somewhere behind the Iron Curtain.

I enjoyed hanging out with Rainer in the newsroom in Cologne, much as I've enjoyed many a visit to studios abroad, meeting the people, watching them at work, looking through the control-room glass as the end product is presented at the top of the hour by somebody doing exactly what I used to do, reading the bulletin.

Matchday minus 1, as they say in UEFA, the day before the game. I had a preview to prepare. There was no problem setting up the Northern Ireland interviews. Wasn't I staying at the same hotel? But what about West Germany? Well, nothing ventured, nothing gained, so I got out the map and plotted a route to the Sportschule at Hennef, half an hour away on the other side of the Rhine, the national team's training base for matches in Cologne.

As a fan of German football ever since my year following the Bundesliga every weekend, I knew the routine. Training in the morning. Lunch. Then at their leisure for the afternoon. I aimed to be there for about half past one and would take my chances. I had no appointment. Access really wasn't a problem in the 1970s.

I arrived in good time, parked the Polo, went into reception and announced myself. Would it be possible please, I enquired in my best German, to speak with the coach? The lady behind the desk didn't think this would be a problem. She made a phone call. Herr Schön will be with you presently. First roll of the dice and I'd hit the jackpot. Herr Schön was, of course, Helmut Schön, the legendary manager who'd taken West Germany to that famous World Cup Final at Wembley in 1966, finished third in Mexico four years later, won the European Championship in 1972, before winning the World Cup two years after that. In other words, he was the current World Champion. And he was leaving his post-prandial R&R to come to the lobby to talk to me, the wee man from the Cregagh Road.

He was the most charming subject. Expecting to be interviewed in German, as I'd introduced myself *auf deutsch*, he could not have been more accommodating when I asked if he'd mind answering my questions in English. I'd got myself a one-on-one exclusive simply by chancing my arm.

Pleased as punch, I headed back to the hotel to send the gold dust back to Belfast. Not a straightforward matter, when you're flying solo on a budget and haven't the wherewithal to book a studio. What I'd learned about broadcast circuits was that they were essentially two telephone lines combined to offer more bandwidth and consequently, better-quality sound. A single telephone line would suffice in extremis and you could improve it, if you bypassed the weakest link, the microphone in the handset.

I'd come to Cologne armed with a cable to connect my tape recorder via a pair of crocodile clips with the innards of the mouthpiece of the phone in my room. That way, the interview with Helmut Schön would sound almost as good as if it had been done in a studio. By the same means, I rigged up a microphone to make my contribution to *A Taste of Hunni* on the morning of the match. It was all going so well, apart from the moment the previous evening when the Polo, overloaded with the Belfast press corps' finest, ended up rather too close to the Rhine for comfort when we took a wrong turn on the way back from dinner.

I was at the stadium in good time for the match, which was just as well. Radio Ulster had stretched to a telephone for me to provide updates throughout the evening. For some inexplicable reason, this had been installed in the TV truck behind the grandstand, not the ideal spot to be covering a game – unless you're involved in the production. Thankfully, Deutsche Telekom's man was able to get it moved to the press box and I was all set for a repeat of Rotterdam the previous year. Northern Ireland against the World Cup holders. But we had George Best.

It was all going really well. Scoreless at half-time – scoreless right up to the 55th minute. West Germany won a free kick in the attacking third, out on the right. Pat Jennings organised the Irish defence. Heinz Flohe, a Cologne favourite, floated the ball into the penalty area and from among the heads rising to challenge for it emerged, like the sword Excalibur, the outstretched arm of the Northern Irish left back, Sammy Nelson, to punch it away like a goalkeeper. Penalty! Rainer Bonhof sent Jennings the wrong way. And that was effectively that. West Germany went on the rampage and it finished 5–0.

From my point of view, it was another ambition achieved. Two months after that, I resigned from *Good Morning Ulster* and moved into sport full time. Well, to say full time is overstating it. The budget wasn't there. They could only employ me for half a day, Monday to Thursday. The Friday slot remained with the primary teacher John Bennett.

Of course, there were other outlets for my reporting and they did give me a radio slot on Friday mornings between nine and ten for a rather more leisurely chat about matters topical that would have been appropriate on *GMU*. I'd Enoch Powell in one morning. No expense spared! But, in truth, I wasn't being stretched, so in the spring of 1978, having noticed a newspaper story that suggested the presenter of RTÉ Television's Saturday afternoon *Sports Stadium* was not flavour of the moment with the station bosses, I wrote to Fred Cogley, the Head of Sport, whom I'd met many times at the rugby, to let him know if he was ever stuck for somebody to front his show, I'd be available.

I don't know what I was expecting to get back, but it certainly wasn't the letter he sent me in which he used a phrase I'd never heard before – I don't want to be raising a hare – which I understood to imply that if he followed through with what he was thinking, it mightn't be the most popular decision. Basically, he was offering me the chance to join the RTÉ team that was going to Argentina to cover the 1978 World Cup.

This was happenstance playing its part again. My letter had arrived at precisely the right moment. The away producer, as the team leader is referred to, was a senior editor called Mike Horgan. He had RTÉ's two regular commentators at his disposal – Jimmy Magee, who did television, and from the radio, Philip Greene. For logistical reasons, because of the vast distances between venues in Argentina, he reckoned he needed four.

Billy George of *The Cork Examiner*, who was a regular contributor to the station's sports programmes, had also been engaged, but they were stuck for a fourth. When the fellow from the BBC up the road was suggested, the ducks were all in a row. In next to no time, arrangements were being made for me to fly with the team to Buenos Aires and then on to the foothills of the Andes, where I'd cover six games in four weeks. This was the stuff of dreams.

My travelling kit arrived: special World Cup luggage labels, various bits and pieces, and, of course, the precious airline tickets. Dublin–London–Madrid–Buenos Aires–Mendoza. (Nobody had ever heard of Mendoza then. We would be among the first Irish to know that it produced some of the finest wine in the southern hemisphere!) There was also the small matter of an inoculation against cholera. No problem. I made an appointment with my GP, who happened to be located just half a mile from the BBC.

One lunchtime, I strolled up the Dublin Road to Shaftesbury Square and presented myself at the surgery. My regular medic was on holiday. The locum was an elderly lady who'd never had to deal with a tropical disease, or football either, I suspect. She was intrigued that somebody would be going to South America. She reached into her fridge and extracted the relevant phial. Squinting at it, she said, 'You're supposed to get this in two separate doses, a couple of weeks apart. When are you going?'

'Next Friday,' I told her.

'Ah well,' she said, 'It wouldn't be wise to give you it all, but I'll give you a dose and a half. That should be okay.'

I trusted her. I knew no better. It was a jab like any other, the sharp prick in my left arm quickly forgotten. I thanked her and made my way back down the Dublin Road to Broadcasting House. Within ten minutes I was there, attempting to push the revolving door. I couldn't. My arm was rigid by my side. The injection had obviously worked. Gear-changing on the way home proved problematic. But that was as bad as it got. A small price to pay for a ticket to sporting paradise.

10

Much Ado About Nothing-Nothing

The World Cup had always held a special fascination for me, since those days of my childhood following Northern Ireland's exploits in Sweden through the gloriously vivid descriptions of Malcolm Brodie in the *Belfast Telegraph* and *Ireland's Saturday Night*, the sister paper that dealt only in sport and shone like technicolour around the grainy images of the tournament. Those black and white shots grew into moving pictures when the World Cup arrived in Chile in 1962. It was so improbably romantic. *Match of the Day* didn't bring its weekly diet of highlights to the small screen until two years after that. Viewers were restricted to the FA Cup Final and the odd international. The players we were familiar with were necessarily those whose names appeared in newspaper coverage or the articles and photographs that would adorn the pages of Charles Buchan's *Football Monthly*.

There was also a relatively new periodical called *World Soccer*, which featured dispatches from contributors all over Europe and beautifully crafted essays from its Buenos Aires-based

South America correspondent, Eric Weil, which brought news of Pelé, who, at seventeen, had become the undoubted star of the Swedish World Cup four years before. We were ready to watch this magical carnival unfold before us on our recently acquired TV screens.

It should have been Pelé's World Cup again, but he was injured early in the competition and the dynamic that drove Brazil on to retain the trophy was provided by another favourite from the Swedish tournament, Manuel Francisco dos Santos, a little right winger who went by the nickname his sister had given him because of his diminutive stature, Brazilian Portuguese for a little brown bird – Garrincha.

I was still going on family holidays in 1966. That year, we went on a road trip 'down south', as Belfast folk would say. My parents would often remind me of my teenage insistence on seeking out B&Bs that had a large TV aerial on the roof, which meant the hosts weren't relying solely on Telefís Éireann for their evening's entertainment. RTÉ was eight years away from its first involvement in the World Cup. A big aerial meant there was access to the BBC and ITV, so I wouldn't be missing out on the early stages of the English World Cup.

On one of the stops on our trip, in Skerries in north Dublin, we got to know a butcher from Finglas and his family. Their view of a good night wouldn't have tallied with the kind of social evening solid Presbyterians would be indulging in, but, hey, we were on our holidays. At least, that would have been the view of my dad and myself, so we accepted an invitation to join them for an evening out. Against her better judgement, mother tagged along.

That summer's evening, a Tuesday, we were directed to a public house in rural County Meath and, over the course of the conviviality there, the singing started. My father, who had a lovely voice that he had put to good use in amateur operatic productions, delivered his party piece, which was 'The Boys from the County Armagh'. Sure, why wouldn't he? He was from up north.

Then one of the crew realised what day it was. 'Hey,' he called across the bar, 'it's the Twelfth of July! Come on Jim, give us The Sash!'

My mother was gobsmacked – halfway between mortification and fear for her safety. My father smiled sheepishly and shook his head. I knew what they were thinking. Northern Prods in a southern setting. This cannot be wise. Our friend from Finglas was reassuring. They meant no harm; they were out for a laugh.

'Come on Jim!' There was no way he was going to escape this encore.

He stood up again. The room fell silent. And as he began, 'It is old …' the roar would have been heard all the way to the Hill of Tara. What amazed me was that they all knew the words and they all joined in. And the applause and the whooping at the end of it even forced a smile from my mother. As Frankie Valli sang in an altogether different context, 'Oh What a Night!'

The rest of the holiday was uneventful enough and we were well home by the time the final rolled around. We watched it, still in black and white, in Rochester Avenue. I was secretly rooting for West Germany. German was my favourite subject at school. I'd be going on a summer exchange the following year. Why not?

It was 2–2 at full time, so into extra time we went. England scored. Or did they? Geoff Hurst's shot smacked down off the crossbar and onto the ground – onto the goal line or behind it? There was no technology, no VAR. The linesman, Tofiq Bahramov from Azerbaijan, signalled a goal. It's been the subject of controversy for over half a century since. Perhaps the most telling insight into the legality of the goal or otherwise is the fact that England's other striker, Roger Hunt, closing in as Hurst shot, immediately turned in celebration after the ball had bounced. Had there been any doubt in Hunt's mind that it had crossed the line, he would surely have smashed it in to make sure, much as Harry Kane needed to follow up his saved penalty in the Euro 2020 semi-final against Denmark.

That, though, mattered not, for England were to score another goal. We were watching on the BBC. My favourite commentator, Kenneth Wolstenholme, was at the microphone. There were just seconds remaining. England attacked again, right to left.

'And here comes Hurst,' said Wolstenholme, 'he's got …'

And then he paused, for he'd just spotted an unusual development.

'Some people are on the pitch. They think it's all over,' he called.

Hurst shoots. And scores.

'It is now! It's four.'

Priceless. A moment that will live forever – captured by a commentator at the height of his powers reacting to the image.

It's truly amazing to think that four years after that, at the World Cup in Mexico where he was the main commentator and still not yet fifty, the BBC was planning to replace him with David

Coleman if England reached the final, only four years after he'd delivered the line that blew everybody else out of the water. You do sometimes wonder how certain decision-makers end up in the positions they occupy.

1974 was the World Cup I would have loved to have been involved in. Freshly graduated with my 2:1 in German and French (class of 1973), I was now a newsreader at the BBC in Belfast. The West German World Cup, like the Munich Olympics, had come around just a little too soon for me.

The final, at the Olympic Stadium in Munich, began in bizarre fashion. The kick-off was delayed when the referee, Jack Taylor, another butcher like our Finglas friend, who worked in his father's shop in Wolverhampton in the English West Midlands, spotted, as the teams lined up, that there were no corner flags in place.

West Germany, made up of players I'd been watching Saturday after Saturday not that long before, were playing the Netherlands. Within two minutes, Jack had awarded the Dutch a penalty. They scored. Midway through the half, he gave the Germans a penalty of their own. They scored too.

There had never been a penalty in a World Cup final. Now, like the 46A, the Dublin bus to Dún Laoghaire, two had arrived at once. Gerd Müller scored for West Germany just before half-time and his goal proved to be decisive. Little did I think that that would be the last World Cup that I'd have to watch at home, as a fan. And little did I know that within four years, I'd be on the plane to Argentina at the start of a journey through some of the greatest moments in sport.

* * *

Before heading off to South America, though, there was to be another World Cup experience with Northern Ireland, a visit to Iceland the preceding summer. In 1977, lacking the satellite technology on which everything now depends, Iceland's remoteness and the absence of a submarine cable connecting the country to a European television feed meant there was no way we could televise this particular match live. We could do it on the radio, though, which is what we decided to do.

But Ulster Television, the competitor station in Belfast, was beginning to flex its muscles. We got wind of their proposal to have the match recorded locally and bring the tapes back to Belfast for transmission the following evening. We would have had the match live on the radio but nobody would have seen it. Having delivered the Rotterdam scoop, which had required the *Nine O'Clock News* to be read twice, the BBC couldn't allow itself to be upstaged like that. A plan was put in place.

The match was on a Saturday afternoon. Given that the result would be known once the final whistle was blown, there would be no appetite for a ninety-minute rerun. A thirty-minute slot would suffice, but that would mean editing once the tapes were back in Belfast. Time would be of the essence.

It was decided that we too would transmit a telerecording and we'd get it on the air before UTV. I would travel to Reykjavik with my radio producer, Brian Dempster, and we'd cover the match live on Radio Ulster. We booked our own recording on two-inch videotape and collected the cargo after the match.

First thing Sunday, we were off to the airport at Keflavík, checking in for Glasgow, which is where flights from Iceland to the UK touched down at the time. UTV were on board too, as concerned as we were that our precious hand luggage would not be contaminated by any overzealous intervention on the part of the security people and their X-ray machines. This had become a bit of a race.

We'd scheduled our transmission for teatime. UTV were aiming for a late evening slot. The connection from Glasgow to Aldergrove airport – now Belfast International – was an afternoon flight. That was UTV's route home. Had we waited, we'd never have got the thing edited down to thirty minutes in time for TX (TV speak for transmission). So, a private aircraft had been arranged, a four-seater Cessna, to take Brian, myself and the precious tapes to a private airfield in Newtownards, just outside Belfast, that's home to the Ulster Flying Club. Jaws dropped when we made our excuses and left the guys from UTV awaiting the scheduled service.

I'd never been on a light aircraft. The prospect was rather daunting. But what we were engaged in was the source of a huge adrenaline rush. We climbed into the Cessna and taxied out to the end of Glasgow's runway 05, meaning we'd be taking off in the direction of the city, then turning round to head across the west of Scotland towards the Irish Sea and our destination in north Down.

There were commercial jets lined up behind us as our pilot wound up the engine and we rattled off on our take-off roll, clambering into the air, shuddering and shaking, looking down on the Glasgow suburbs and the River Clyde. As we banked and went around, I could see below a Trident passenger plane beginning to accelerate down the runway. It was the weirdest sensation observing it from up there.

The transit was as smooth as you'd expect it to be on a

sunny June Sunday, and soon we were descending, down over the Holywood Hills and onto the airstrip alongside the northern tip of Strangford Lough. We were met by a Customs man, who'd had to give up his Sunday lunch to be there to meet this one-off arrival.

Duly cleared, it was straight into the BBC in Ormeau Avenue, where the best bits (and there weren't that many – Northern Ireland had lost 1–0) were distilled. That left just one piece of the jigsaw to be fitted. I'd been commentating on the radio the day before. There was no commentary on the pictures. So, at 5.30 p.m., we went live with the recording and I commentated all over again. The only issue was the perspective. The pictures had been shot from a position directly opposite where I'd been for the radio broadcast. What I was seeing was like a mirror image of what I'd described in Reykjavík.

That can happen when you're live and then it's no joke. On a rainy night in Lisbon in 1995, Jack Charlton's team was battling to earn a place in the European Championship in England the following summer. It was the final qualifier and nothing was certain. Portugal led the group, but if the Republic of Ireland won that night, they would join them on points and move ahead of them by virtue of the fact that they'd beaten them in Dublin, so the head-to-head comparison was in their favour. Even if they drew or lost, which would mean Portugal securing the single qualifying place, they would still have earned a play-off spot.

The commentary position for the game in the Estádio da Luz was behind glass, which wasn't great because the weather outside on that November night meant the windows steamed up. Add to that another factor, something we weren't aware of. Who knows whose fault it was, but the information that the pictures being provided for Ireland were being shot from the opposite side of the stadium never reached the RTÉ personnel on the ground.

When you think of TV coverage of a football game, you'll be aware that there are advertising boards beyond the far touchline. In 1995, some marketing whizz had had the bright idea that you could maximise revenue by selling opposing-team-specific space on the side below the main cameras. But nobody thought about the commentators. With Pat The Baker and the *Sunday World* on boards below our position, viewers in Ireland were getting a completely different perspective from the one that we had in the stadium.

In a way, it was a mercy that the windows were steaming up for that meant we had to rely on our monitors, showing the game from the other side of the ground. To say it was disorientating would be putting it mildly.

I still had some ground to cover, though, before I would get to that night in Lisbon. Back at the 1978 World Cup, I would cover six games in four weeks in a city nobody had heard of then, though it's well known now, courtesy of its status as the wine capital of Argentina. Mendoza was the location for games featuring Peru and Iran, Scotland and my old friends the Dutch, whose first home game in qualifying had been that memorable encounter with Northern Ireland in Rotterdam – my first big live game on TV.

The Netherlands had progressed by winning the group but would go to Argentina without Johan Cruyff. He pulled out of the World Cup and there was all manner of speculation about why. It was suggested that there had been a row with the Dutch

Football Association over sponsorship. At the World Cup in West Germany in 1974, the team kit had been sponsored by Adidas. But Cruyff, their star player, had his own deal with Puma, bitter rivals of Adidas in the sportswear business. The Adidas trademark is three stripes, which featured on the arms of the players' orange shirts. A special shirt had to be made for Cruyff, with only two stripes on its sleeves. Player power.

The back story to this is worth telling. The rivalry between the two companies stemmed from a family feud. Rudolf and Adolf Dassler were brothers from Herzogenaurach in Bavaria who started a company making running shoes in the 1920s. They called it Geda (short for Gebrüder Dassler or the brothers Dassler) and scored a huge success when the Olympics came to Berlin in 1936 and they were able to convince the great Jessie Owens to wear their gear. Owens, the black sprinter from Alabama, won four gold medals in Geda spikes, single-handedly crushing Hitler's theory of an Aryan master race.

After the Second World War, the brothers fell out. Geda was wound up and they set up factories of their own, Adolf founding Adidas (its title made up in the same way that Geda had got its name), Rudolf setting up a factory at the other end of town and calling his brand Ruda (which he subsequently changed to Puma).

It would be thirty years before Cruyff would explain his refusal to travel to Argentina. Playing with Barcelona at the time, he revealed in a radio interview that about six months before the World Cup, he and his family had been the victims of an attempted kidnapping in the Catalan capital. They'd all been tied up and held at gunpoint in their apartment. It wasn't explained how the abduction was foiled, but he did reveal that they had lived under police protection for several months afterwards. He'd withdrawn from the tournament saying, 'There are moments when there are other values in life.'

While I wouldn't have the opportunity to meet Johan Cruyff in Mendoza, I did get the chance to interview him when the Netherlands came to Belfast for the qualifier there, which mustn't have been long before the kidnap attempt. When I asked him on the Windsor Park pitch for his view on how the match the next night might go, he came out with one of the most memorable answers I've ever heard: 'The game is long, the ball is round and before the game is not after the game.' How true! Although he might have claimed he hadn't foreseen it, he was able to look back on a Dutch victory in Belfast, Willy van de Kerkhof scoring the only goal.

Being assigned to the matches in Mendoza gave me the opportunity to reconnect with my old buddy from that night in the Feyenoord Stadium, Kees Jansma, as well as getting to know two of his colleagues from the Dutch broadcaster NOS, Theo Reitsma and the man described by the coach Louis van Gaal (who won the Champions League with Ajax, La Liga with Barcelona, and the Bundesliga with Bayern Munich, before leading the Dutch to third place in the 2014 World Cup, as well as managing Manchester United) as the best football reporter in the Netherlands, Eddy Poelmann.

Eddy was the man who introduced me to calzone – the folded-over pizza that has become my go-to choice – one night in Hilversum, the broadcasting capital, in northern Holland, when I was there doing off-tube commentary for Europa Television, a fledgling satellite station that was based in the city. It was owned by a consortium of public service broadcasters from the Netherlands, Germany, Italy, Portugal and Ireland. RTÉ Sport was heavily involved. It was way ahead of its time but closed down long before anybody had ever heard of Sky.

No calzone in Mendoza. It was baby beef and tomato duque. The Irish contingent – editor Maurice Reidy and myself – felt right at home with the preponderance of fillet steak on the menu. Way ahead of the curve, we also got to know the local vintage at the ultimate wine and cheese party laid on for the journalists, at a ranch outside town, where the entertainment took the form of a polo match, a dazzling display of equestrianism, like hockey on horseback.

It was the most wonderful introduction to the world of international tournament football. The distances between venues were considerable, which is why I was there after all, as the team leader Mike Horgan had decided the best way to cover the tournament was to have four commentators, two of them in Buenos Aires for the games around the capital, one in Córdoba and me in Mendoza. So just the six matches, then, and plenty of time in between to get to know the place and get to know the Dutch, whose three first-round matches were in the city.

We also had the opportunity to explore the region, taking a trip one sunny day up into the Andes on the road to Chile until we reached the snowline. Later that same summer, I'd be in the foothills of the Rockies, in Edmonton, Alberta, as Canada hosted the Commonwealth Games and a seventeen-year-old boxer from Clones in County Monaghan won the bantamweight title, his first major prize. His name? Barry McGuigan.

Argentina was under military dictatorship at the time, its

government headed by General Jorge Videla, who'd come to power two years previously, the result of a *coup d'état*. Following the return of representative democracy, the junta was put on trial for a host of human rights abuses and Videla's final years were spent in prison, where he served life for his crimes.

Of course, there was no evidence of anything for the visiting sports journalists to see as Argentina put its best face forward for world consumption. The only sign that things might have been more militarised here than back at home was that the police wore navy blue fatigues as opposed to the kind of uniform we'd have been used to seeing.

The football was unforgettable. My first match was a 3–0 Dutch victory over Iran, Rob Rensenbrink scoring all the goals, two of them from the penalty spot. Adidas reared its head again. With no Johan Cruyff, the three stripes were everywhere in evidence, even on the backs of the shirts, where they formed the numbers. This rendered 6 and 8 and by extension 16 and 18 identical from a distance. Well in now with KNVB, the Dutch Football Association, I was part of the delegation that made representations to have it made easier for the press pack to identify the players. We were listened to and when they next went into action four days later against Peru, their orange shirts were adorned with plain black numerals. I wasn't the only professional observer who sighed with some relief at the sight.

That game ended scoreless, but it left the Netherlands as good as qualified for the next phase, for they and Peru were on three points (two for a win back then), while Iran and Scotland, the other teams in the group, were both on one, with vastly inferior goal differences. To get past the Dutch and stay in the World Cup,

Scotland, in the remaining group game, would need to beat them by three clear goals.

However unlikely that appeared, the prospects disappeared over the horizon when, after Scotland had had two goals disallowed, Rensenbrink, with his third penalty of the tournament, which happened to be the 1,000th goal in World Cup Finals history, put the Dutch ahead. On the stroke of half-time, Kenny Dalglish equalised. Then just after the resumption, Graeme Souness was fouled in the area, Archie Gemmill converted the penalty and the Scots began to dream again. A whole half ahead of them, they were now a goal up.

With twenty minutes to go, Gemmill scored another, a goal for the ages. Scotland attack, the Netherlands manage to clear. The ball breaks and out on the Scottish right, he sets off. Taking what *The Guardian* described as six of the best touches you'll ever see in a World Cup Finals, Gemmill slalomed through the Dutch cover, caressing an exquisite chip into the middle of the goal over the stranded keeper, Jan Jongbloed.

Two goals clear now, Scotland on top, entering dream-come-true territory.

But within three minutes, the dream had died. Having battled to within one goal of making it through, here came instant deflation in the shape of Johnny Rep scoring the goal that put Scottish progress out of reach. The fact that they went on to defeat the mighty Dutch was of little comfort. The 3–2 scoreline was a Pyrrhic victory indeed.

Scotland headed home and I said my farewells to my Dutch friends, whose second place in the group sent them off to meet Austria, West Germany and Italy on a journey that would take them to the final. My prize was two games involving Brazil, not half bad as a slate for a rookie commentator. I watched them beat Peru and Poland 3–0 and 3–1, and in between, covered Poland's 1–0 win over Peru. Argentina, the team I didn't get to cover in the second group phase, ended their programme by somehow scoring six against Peru – enough to relegate Brazil to the third-place play-off and put themselves in the final against the Dutch. I was back home in Belfast to watch them win the trophy in front of their own passionate fans – in glorious colour, I might add. Though the latest technology was sending the pictures around the world, television transmission in Argentina was still in black and white. It had felt like being in a time warp, following the tournament watching those 405-line grainy pictures again.

* * *

Fresh from my first World Cup, where I'd actually met Pelé and got his autograph in a check-in queue at Mendoza Airport, I was offered a contract by RTÉ. I would soon be on my way to a new career and indeed a new life in Dublin, but there was one more trip on the schedule before I made that move. The combination of compulsive curiosity and overwhelming wanderlust meant that ever since my student year in West Germany, when I'd had the chance to make my first tentative forays beyond the Iron Curtain, I'd been itching for the opportunity to investigate further. Now I had it. Northern Ireland were playing in Bulgaria.

This was in the qualifying round for the European Championship of 1980, which involved a group of five teams battling for the one place available at the Finals in Italy. There was huge significance in the line-up, for Northern Ireland and the Republic had been drawn together, meaning they would meet for the very first time in September 1978.

England were hot favourites. Ron Greenwood's England featured Kevin Keegan, the captain Emlyn Hughes, Phil Neal, Ray Clemence, Terry McDermott – all European Cup winners with Liverpool the previous year – Trevor Brooking, Ray Wilkins and Peter Shilton.

As well as Bulgaria, World Cup participants as recently as 1974, Denmark were in there too, at a time when their team was still managed by a selection committee. It would be 1979 before the Danish FA appointed a full-time professional coach, a German by the name of Sepp Piontek.

The Republic had already posted a 3–3 draw in Copenhagen when the two shades of green squared off at Lansdowne Road. It was a three o'clock kick-off that Wednesday afternoon.

I felt extremely fortunate and honoured to be BBC Northern Ireland's man with the mic on this historic occasion. Sadly, the match didn't live up to it. 'A game conceived in tumult died with a whimper,' wrote Peter Byrne in *The Irish Times*, opening his account of the scoreless draw. Much ado about nothing-nothing. My commentary also made it onto RTÉ, which was fortuitous after my involvement with their World Cup coverage in Argentina. A strike by riggers at the station meant there was no commentary position for Jimmy Magee.

Northern Ireland followed that with a 2–1 home win over Denmark. Next up was the trip to Sofia. The small BBC party joined officials from the Irish Football Association for the shuttle to Heathrow, where we hooked up with Danny Blanchflower's squad for the journey on to the Bulgarian capital, on board a scheduled British Airways flight. Charters, private aircraft? That wasn't part of the deal.

Thanks to my own compulsive curiosity and the sheer uniqueness of it all, it's firmly etched in my memory. The clear skies of a fine November afternoon. The routing that took us over Stuttgart and the thought striking me that down there, 35,000 feet below, was a friend of mine, Winfried Roesner, the South German Radio journalist who'd sought me out as a guide when he'd come to Belfast to report on the Peace People. Landing in Bulgaria at a spartan aerodrome. The long walk from the aircraft to the arrivals hall. Pat Jennings remarking, as we left the chill and entered the building, 'Can't you just smell it?' – the distinctive mustiness of air untroubled by the fragrance of Flash, the persistent reek of the rough tobacco that would never have made it onto Western shelves. We were behind the Iron Curtain.

We didn't go in for co-commentators back then. I had just the one travelling companion – Nevin McGhee, the man who had cajoled BBC Northern Ireland into live coverage of George Best's return in Rotterdam two years previously.

There was plenty of time over our three-day stay, once our pre-match obligations had been fulfilled, to venture forth from our hotel in the centre of Sofia, directly opposite the Bulgarian parliament building, to check out the Orthodox cathedral, to walk the streets where the distinctive exhaust fumes of the limited traffic still lingered on the chilly air, past the windows of the department store with boxes of washing powder on display. Up to the church of St Sophia, where there was the Monument to the Unknown Soldier with its eternal flame. And back down again, to what's known as the Largo – three huge buildings in the Stalinist style where government was based in the communist era – and the Presidency, with sentries outside, just like Buckingham Palace in London. And, as we were to discover, we'd happened upon the location at precisely the right moment – just like at Buckingham Palace, there is a changing of the guard, on the hour, every hour.

It rained on the night of the match. Rained throughout the game. We were in the dry, but conditions were miserable. Cold and wet. For the 11,000 or so spectators scattered across the vast open acres of the Vasil Levski stadium, there wasn't even the consolation of a performance to lift the gloom.

Gerry Armstrong struck early. Billy Caskey scored in the second half to make it 2–0 at the finish. Danny Blanchflower had worked his magic again. Three games in and Northern Ireland were top of the group. It would not be the only happy night I'd experience in that old Soviet-era stadium.

We all made our way back to the hotel. Our work was done. The written press still had its copy to file. In 1978, communications with the West weren't the most efficient or straightforward (though I would soon discover that Irish telecommunications at the time could also leave a lot to be desired!). For the hacks, it now became a waiting game. Book a call with the hotel switchboard, then repair to your room and await their pleasure. One of those was the *Belfast News Letter*'s correspondent, Jimmy Dubois.

The *News Letter*, based in Donegall Street, just the other side of St Anne's Cathedral from *The Irish News* and around the corner from the *Belfast Telegraph* in Royal Avenue, in what would count as the northern capital's equivalent of Fleet Street, remains the longest-surviving continuously published English language newspaper, having first appeared in 1737. It boasts a proud history. Among its scoops, it was the first paper in Europe to report the American Declaration of Independence. Its sports section retains a cutting edge, but that night, not many know how close it came to losing its back page lead.

The Northern Ireland team was back now too, fed and ready to relax, and a couple of those who'd played their part in this significant victory had made their way to the ever-hospitable Jimmy's room. He was the most charming of men, with a cherubic air that always seemed oddly out of place among the hard chaws of the press pack. Somehow Nevin and I ended up there too. The crack was mighty. This was a 'vintage victory' as the *Belfast Telegraph* put it on its back page – a first away win in four years.

It was cold outside. The hotel had boosted the central heating. And with a few celebratory beers being chugged and the obligatory Benson & Hedges being puffed – who wasn't a smoker in those days? – the air in Jimmy's compact apartment became a little on the stuffy side.

The solitary window was pushed wide open. The flimsy tulle of the Bulgarian net curtain began to waft as the warmth being generated by our celebratory beano met the plummeting temperature of the Balkan night. The rain had turned to snow.

Of course, everybody was having a laugh. Those were indeed the days when you could enjoy yourself with the players and they would be happy that you were there, all part of the party.

The principal joker was Allan Hunter, then with Bobby Robson's Ipswich Town, who were big in England's top tier at the time. Allan had won the FA Cup with Ipswich the previous

May, centre back alongside Kevin Beattie as they beat Arsenal, managed by a Northern Irishman, Terry Neill, 1–0. The Arsenal team was captained by Pat Rice and included Pat Jennings and Sammy Nelson. Jennings, who'd observed the olfactory oddities on arrival in the airport, was in goal that night in Sofia, with Nelson at left back.

Hunter, who should have been captaining the side, had been ruled out because of a knee injury but had been brought on the trip nonetheless. Those were the good old days.

The snapshot is as vivid now as it was when the moment froze all those years ago. Allan's eye lit upon Jimmy's notepad, nestled beside the telephone, the ready reference for when the connection was finally made to the copy-taker in Donegall Street. He picked up the spiral-bound pad and scanned the handwritten notes on the top page.

'Is this your match report, Jimmy?'

You could tell what was coming next. 'This is all crap,' he laughed. 'You cannot be serious!' And, no doubt still pumping the adrenaline that should have seen him through the evening on the pitch but had, on this occasion, been fuelled still further by copious refreshment, big Allan fired the notepad at the window. It was caught by the flimsy net curtain, hung tantalisingly inches beyond the sill, then floated away, down into the winter darkness.

Jimmy's face fell, but not being a man to make a fuss, he contained himself admirably. Inside his whole being must have been crumbling. The gasps that had filled the room subsided. Well lubricated by now, nobody else there knew quite where to look or what to say, caught between peals of laughter at the sheer comic madness of what had just transpired and gasps of horror at the thought that the phone would ring any minute now and poor Jimmy would have to make the whole thing up as he went along.

The big brick shithouse of a defender instantly realised that this particular tackle had gone completely over the top. He rose purposefully, saying nothing and strode from the room. We were several storeys up, at the back of a hotel in downtown Soviet Sofia. Goodness only knew what lay below. The mental image was of a sodden notebook lodged between hotel-sized wheelie bins and crates of empty beer bottles.

In no time at all, the hotel room door opened and with a flourish big Allan presented Jimmy with his match report, none the worse for its late-night flight through the Balkan air.

When the phone eventually rang, we left Jimmy to it and repaired to the bar in the hotel basement. I got talking to some locals – in German, which surprised me. It turns out that learning German as well as the obligatory Russian was quite common, because all the principal scientific textbooks in the Eastern bloc came from East Germany. It all made sense.

It was getting late and we'd an early enough start the following morning, flying Balkan Airlines to Zürich in Switzerland on the first of the three legs of our journey home. I was reminded of the story told of a former sportswriter with the *Daily Mirror* in Belfast, Jack Milligan, who'd found himself in a similar situation after a match in a far-flung location and had decided to amuse himself by calling one of his more abstemious colleagues who'd had an early night.

When the phone was answered by a voice belonging to somebody who'd been roused from a deep sleep, Jack announced himself. 'What the hell are you ringing me for?' the unfortunate wanted to know. 'Have you any idea what time it is?'

Jack replied in song. 'It's a quarter to three/ There's no one in the place/ Except you and me … one for my baby/ And one more for the road' was Jack's party piece!

I was with John Roberts when I made my exit. John was the tennis correspondent for *The Independent* for twenty years, but back then he was the north of England football reporter for the *Daily Express*, a beat that included the Northern Ireland football team. Much like myself, John was vertically challenged and he also wore glasses, which gave him the appearance of Don Estelle's character Lofty Sugden in the BBC sitcom *It Ain't Half Hot Mum*, set in India during the British Raj.

When we emerged from the basement, the snow was still falling and it was, believe it or not, a quarter to three. Nothing stirred. The empty, dimly lit streets were blanketed white. I remembered the hourly changing of the guard outside the Presidency. I wondered aloud if they might do it through the night. 'There's only one way of finding out,' said John, so off we marched, our footprints the only imprints on the virgin snow. Up past the department store with its window display of washing powder, on past the few parked cars up Tsar Osvoboditel Boulevard, crunching through the snow that was still falling and lodging itself on the round frames of John's spectacles. Halfway there, it seemed we were on a mad mission but, suitably lubricated, there was no way we were turning back.

As we finally approached the Largo, we stopped in disbelief. In the darkness in the distance, we could see them. The two sentries. Standing to attention. It was five to the hour. We edged closer, wondering now would our presence draw undue attention that might interfere with a return to our beds in the Grand Hotel, a ten-minute walk away.

The silence was broken by a bell tolling. Through the arch behind the two sentries, out marched their relief, in greatcoats, knee-high boots and Russian army-style fur ushanka hats, both bearing a bayonet. The handover was completed with formal military ceremonial, concluding with the two newcomers standing to attention as their counterparts marched back into what must have been welcome respite beyond the Presidency doors. We couldn't quite believe what we'd just witnessed, but our question had been answered. The changing of the guard in Sofia was a 24/7 operation.

11

Flash those Sandy Row Sparklers

It had been snowing the day I moved to Dublin, which happened to be my twenty-ninth birthday, 2 January 1979. I was due to be introduced to my new colleagues at the regular weekly meeting but I arrived to find it had been cancelled because of the weather. I'd managed to get myself a hundred miles down the road, but the few local flurries were enough to encourage the good folk in RTÉ Sport to prolong the Christmas and New Year break. As it turned out, maybe I was being a little harsh. The cold snap persisted and snow was never too far away.

One particular morning, I had been booked to conduct an interview at Donnybrook. The streets were still treacherous and there was precious little traffic about as I joined the dual carriageway just by the church for the final half mile to RTÉ. And there ahead of me was the reason why. The gritters were only out mid-morning and by gritters I don't mean snow ploughs. This was a flatbed truck with two workmen in overcoats standing on the back, shovelling sand out either side. The capital city back then truly belonged to another country.

In contrast to the way things lumbered along generally, RTÉ was like a spaceship that had landed from a different universe. Despite the sure-it'll-do mentality that pervaded almost every aspect of the public realm, this semi-state organisation was actually managing to provide its audience with a very decent service. It was like every other aspect of Irish life that faced out into the world beyond, Aer Lingus, for example; it couldn't survive if its standards didn't match those of its equivalents elsewhere. In that sense, the easy availability of the BBC and ITV did RTÉ a favour. Making this assertion, I can hear hoots of derision, for it's been fashionable, over the years, to knock the station. I would be the last to suggest that the way it's been managed has shone like a beacon of corporate rectitude, but it is fair to say that the professional standards of those who put programmes before the public were rigorously maintained.

I had come to Dublin to expand my working horizons. They'd been happy enough with my work at the World Cup to offer me a two-year contract and that was sufficient encouragement to up sticks, leave the comfort blanket of the BBC in Belfast and test myself in a completely new environment. I'd been persuaded by my experience in Argentina.

I wasn't yet three months through the door when I was dispatched to Limerick for a World Championship event, something that turned into an astonishing Irish sporting occasion.

The previous year, in Bellahouston Park in Glasgow, a young man from County Waterford had run his way into history. 'Ireland's latest sporting hero', *Magill Magazine* reported, 'is a pigeon-toed, wisp-like running machine who looks as though he would have difficulty catching the Dublin–Ballymun bus, let alone winning the world cross-country championships. He's John Treacy, 20, and he weighs barely nine stone.'

John Treacy was defending his title in Limerick in March 1979 and I would be there. RTÉ had given me the World Cup. Now, fresh out of Belfast, I had a World Championship to cover. This was the place to be.

The organisation was a touch on the chaotic side. I recall a bit of a to-do at the Saturday media briefing the day before the event at Limerick racecourse. One of the Fleet Street crew, a very distinguished journalist by the name of Neil Allen of the *Evening Standard*, was so distressed by the apparent insouciance of the local organisation that he tried to raise some kind of mutiny. I recall an impassioned speech about the perceived lack of facilities – in particular telephone lines – to the assembled hacks. In this twenty-first century of mobile communications, it may be difficult to comprehend the difficulties of communication in 1970s Ireland. You could not assume there would be a telephone line. And if you had one, you could not be certain you'd be able to make your call.

When I moved to Dublin in 1979, the landline from my accommodation offered direct dial to Belfast, but anywhere else in Northern Ireland required operator assistance. So Limerick racecourse, an open-air venue, on a spring afternoon that year, was unlikely to offer much in the way of a connection with the outside world.

Neil Allen was like Peter Bowles' character in the popular BBC drama that came later, *The Irish RM*. The incomer just didn't get the locals, but things, somehow, worked out. It would all be, and indeed was, all right on the night.

Mind you, I did have my own problems. As the new boy, I was to commentate on the junior men's race, while RTÉ's main athletics man, Brendan O'Reilly would cover the principal race and I would interview the winner. Proper order.

But the info on the competitors in the junior race was scant and none of these guys were giants. The venue, Limerick racecourse, was like every other racecourse, with rails around the infield – rails that don't impede your vision when the action is on the far side and you're watching thoroughbreds charging along, with jockeys on top, wearing brightly coloured silks. But youngsters trudging through going that could best be described as soft? And just tall enough for those rails to obliterate any chance of spotting a race number pinned to a teenage chest?

Calling the shots was Justin Nelson, a lovely gentle man, who was only on the gig because RTÉ's main outside broadcast director, Michael O'Carroll, had been sidelined by a health issue. A talented visual artist, Justin had begun his career as a press photographer with *The Nationalist* newspaper in Carlow. He moved into television as a cameraman when RTÉ began in the early 1960s, and then climbed the ladder to become one of the station's top TV directors. He was a regular in the outside broadcast truck at All-Ireland finals in Croke Park and he worked too on many of the station's prestigious projects, his highlight, I'm sure, the papal visit to Ireland in 1979.

But RTÉ didn't really do athletics. Maybe the odd filmed report, not a live gig. And the World Championships to boot! I wasn't the only one that day in uncharted waters.

For my race, the first event to be shown in our coverage, Justin played it safe, persisting with what's known as a wide shot, so there'd be no possibility of missing anything. What that meant was that when the runners went out into the country, as horse racing parlance has it, what we saw were diminutive athletes bobbing along, their heads and legs clearly visible, their torsos, bearing the all-important race numbers, neatly obliterated by the barrier rail.

A head-on shot would have broken the visual monotony for the viewer. It would also have given the commentator a fighting chance of identifying the athletes. But we stayed with the side-on wide shot the whole, long length of that back straight.

It was like a moving image of Lowry's matchstick men, progressing right to left across the screen. God knows what I said to see the broadcast through that interminable stretch. But you do remember the good bits, like the relief I felt when they came round the bend and into the finishing straight and there was no other shot available but a head-on. I finally saw a race number and could conclusively identify the Belgian runner who went on to win. Those circumstances have etched his name into my memory: Eddy de Pauw.

It's maybe also worth noting that behind the young Belgian, a future star of middle-distance running was finishing thirty-sixth – none other than an eighteen-year-old Steve Cram, in years to come a World and double European champion and Olympic silver medallist, who, like me, would end up in the commentary box, though with rather more to put in his trophy cabinet than I ever earned.

Later, with Brendan O'Reilly at the mic, our 'wisp-like running machine' defended his world title and that didn't happen for the Irish every day, particularly not on home soil. Or should that be home mud?

I was stationed at the finishing line with a cameraman, ready for the post-race interview, but, of course, when it became obvious that John Treacy was going to win, crowd control went out the window. Yes, we were there, but by now engulfed in a way that only happens in Ireland.

Jostled, in the midst of a heaving, cheering throng, with gardaí in greatcoats doing their best to make sure everybody at least remained standing in underfoot conditions that had been churned into an absolute morass, we got this mud-spattered, spittle-flecked interview shot through with such euphoria that it probably made little sense. But, hey, the world champion had retained his title and we'd got our man. Justin's broadcast ended in triumph. And back in Dublin, the local dry cleaner dealt with my clothes.

* * *

I had two good years in Montrose, fronting the Saturday afternoon *Sports Stadium* programme, which was edited by Maurice Reidy, my travelling companion to Mendoza, and directed by Joe McCormack, whose instruction into my earpiece as the opening titles rolled was to 'flash those Sandy Row sparklers'. It had the desired effect.

I wasn't the only northerner in the place. In fact, there were two of us in the party when we headed for what would be my first Olympic Games, in Moscow, in 1980. The other was Derek Davis, the portly man-about-the-television-station whose career took in everything from reading the news to presenting RTÉ 1's afternoon show *Live at Three* alongside Thelma Mansfield, to hosting the Rose of Tralee. It would also involve some commentary on Olympic sailing.

This was a journey into the unknown for all of us. We assembled at Dublin airport a week before the opening ceremony to travel to London for our onward connection to Moscow. The Aeroflot flight was by no means full, but we'd been scattered across the cabin, most of us sitting alone. When the seatbelt sign went off, a number of us decided it might be more pleasant to pass the time in the company of a colleague or two and made to move. This brought an instant rebuke from the cabin crew, who insisted we return to our assigned seats – allocated on the basis of the stability of the aircraft! Apparently the Ilyushin was exceedingly sensitive to weight distribution and the trim would have been adversely affected had we all changed places.

With Moscow two hours ahead of Dublin, it was well into the evening when we eventually arrived at the Cosmos Hotel. Through the metal detectors we went, checking in before heading for the lift to the assigned floor, where a concierge – they were all fearsome females – handed over the room key. These had to be returned to the relevant lady each time we went out.

So, what do you do when your party arrives late at the hotel? Well, you go to the bar, don't you? And that's exactly what we did, heading for the basement lounge, where it wasn't long before the singing started. Mike Kelly, the money man in the sports department, leant his beautiful tenor voice to 'Heart of my Heart', a 1950s hit by The Four Aces. There was a particularly poignant rendition of a Johnny McEvoy song. One of our number had never been on an away gig before and on this, the first night of three weeks apart from his beloved wife and family, he was finding it all a little too much. 'When I first said I loved only you, Nora,' he sang, 'and you said you loved only me ...' The problem was, his Nora was over 2,000 miles away, in Dublin.

We'd just about got over that, when somebody called from the corner. 'Hey, it's after midnight. It's the Twelfth of July!' I felt like I was back in that pub in rural County Meath. 'You pair,' the voice in the corner continued, as a finger pointed in the direction of Derek Davis and myself, 'Get up and give us The Sash!' And so, in the early hours of that Moscow morning, the Cosmos Hotel played host to the vocal gymnastics of the big man from Holywood in County Down and his somewhat smaller accomplice from the Cregagh Road in east Belfast. And, of course, everybody else joined in.

Moscow, a traffic-choked city now, was very different as the capital of the Soviet Union. Everywhere on the streets there was the putrid stench of rough diesel. Not that there were that many vehicles about. Apart from the sleek black limousines of the apparatchiks, the traffic consisted of occasional small Ladas and large, elderly buses and trucks. Beneath the city, though, there was state-of-the-art transport – the spectacular underground, swift and efficient, its stations famously lit by ornate chandeliers.

We were very well looked after, in a regimented kind of way, though we weren't encouraged to stray too far from the well-trodden path. And, of course, there was the concierge on duty by the lift on each floor, keeping a check on our comings and goings.

That said, we were free to move around the city as we wished. The Olympic laminated pass would grant you a fool's pardon if you found yourself somewhere you shouldn't be. And state censorship didn't seem to apply. *The Irish Times* was on sale in the press centre and there was nobody appearing from the shadows to rebuke you if you decided to read it over coffee at a pavement café.

There was plenty to see but, for a major metropolis, the bright lights were conspicuous by their absence. You'd also notice people with their groceries in old-fashioned string bags. Apparently, you wouldn't go out without one, just in case you came across a commodity that might be in short supply, like oranges or bananas.

Speaking of which, the hotel did pretty well on the food front. There was a large buffet that served breakfast, lunch and dinner, and you'd get your fresh fruit all right, but there wasn't much choice. It became apparent after a while that they'd taken to disguising the absence of any variety in the fare by moving the various containers around on their heated displays, so the peas might be beside the carrots one day but down at the other end on the next. And it didn't really stretch much further than peas and carrots in the vegetable department.

On one of my sightseeing excursions, I took the underground down to Red Square. Unwilling to join the lengthy queue to view Lenin in his tomb, I went across to the other side of that vast open space where the military hardware was paraded every May Day and into the huge building that housed Glavnyy Universal'nyy Magazin, which translates as Main Department Store and is universally known by its initials GUM.

Harrod's or Brown Thomas it most certainly was not, but there were items in there that you couldn't find anywhere else in the city – Soviet Army hats aplenty, for one thing. Its construction certainly facilitated its twenty-first-century manifestation as a shopping mall, for it was built as an arcade, the various storeys rising up on either side of a tall central aisle.

I was taking it all in, curiosity killing the cat, making my way up through the displays of Soviet fashion and footwear, eventually emerging at the top of a staircase into an area devoid of shop counters. I wasn't there long, puzzling over what it was that was on sale up here, when a gentleman approached and spoke to me in Russian. I'd no idea what he was saying, so offered him a look at my laminated pass by way of explanation. At this point, he broke into a broad smile and explained as best he could that I was actually on the office floor where the administrative staff were based and I really shouldn't be there at all, as it was off limits to the public. As in the best of circles, I made my excuses and left, pondering the significance of what I'd just experienced. For one thing, I'd been able to get myself into somewhere that I would have expected to be behind some kind of security. And for another, when I'd been rumbled, there had been no attempt to do anything other than ensure that I could find my way back to where I should have been. As I concluded after two later visits to Russia, for football's Confederations Cup in 2017 and the World Cup the following year, the people there get a bad rap. I can think of places in Western Europe I've been made to feel a lot less welcome than I have in the Soviet Union and the Russia that re-emerged from its disintegration.

On one of the days during the Olympics, I was walking into a track and field session when one of those sleek black Zil limos whooshed past and pulled up at the VIP entrance. I was surprised that it was the front door on the passenger side that opened, for out stepped a very familiar figure, none other than the General Secretary of the Communist Party, the man who ruled the Soviet Union, Leonid Brezhnev. With no visible bodyguard, he'd been a front-seat passenger on the trip from the Kremlin, sitting alongside his chauffeur. Without any formality, the now seventy-three-year-old politician made his own way into the Lenin Stadium.

It wasn't long after my return from Moscow that I got a call from the BBC in London. I don't know what prompted it – maybe they were missing me! Whatever it was, Cliff Morgan, the Head of Radio Sport, who'd been such an important mentor at the start of my commentary journey, and his deputy, Pat Ewing, who, like Joy Williams in Belfast, would go on to become the first woman in the top job, wanted to arrange a meeting. Not that I had itchy feet – I was only just over two years into my involvement with RTÉ – but like anybody who has started in the provincial office of a big-time operation, I was intrigued by the opportunity of a move to Head Office. So, they booked me on a flight to London and we convened in the Post House Hotel right beside the Heathrow exit on the M4 motorway.

Basically, they saw the opportunity of utilising the skills I'd acquired in Dublin – principally the exposure to more major sport that would have developed my commentary, plus the added experience of regular programme presentation. Obviously, my presence indicated a degree of interest. They made me an offer and then took me off on a drive around west London, pointing out the kind of places I'd be likely to consider living if I were to make the move. I'd been made very welcome and this had a good feel to it.

Two years after the drive south in the snow, I was heading for the ferry to Fishguard and the drive across the M4 to begin a new chapter.

* * *

My first assignment was an FA Cup tie, the fourth-round meeting of Shrewsbury Town of the old Second Division and Ipswich Town of the First, then managed by Bobby Robson, who would end the season second to Aston Villa in the League and victorious in the UEFA Cup, the only European trophy Ipswich have ever won.

I'd no idea how long it would take to drive from my new pad in West Hampstead to the Shropshire town. Taking no chances, I set off at nine in the morning and was pulling up outside the ground at 11.30 a.m., a little early for the three o'clock kick-off. In the tight confines of the commentary box at Gay Meadow, Shrewsbury's home then, right beside the River Severn, where they employed a boatman on matchdays to retrieve errant footballs, I was in the company of the former England captain, Jimmy Armfield, a lovely man who had family connections in Dún Laoghaire and played the organ every Sunday at his local church in Blackpool. The object of our broadcasting exercise ended in a scoreless draw.

The Sportsroom in Broadcasting House, just up from Oxford Circus in London's West End, was on the third floor with a view right down Langham Place to Regent Street. Not that there was much window-gazing going on. There was too much to concern us in the world of sport. The day shift would run from 11 a.m. to 7 p.m. and would revolve around the 'desks', as they were known: the bulletins at a quarter to the hour from 1.45 p.m. that formed part of the afternoon schedule on Radio 2. We'd our own studio – 3H, it being on the third floor – where we'd read the two-minute updates and then finish off the day at 6.45 p.m. with a complete round-up of what had been happening. Though we weren't in the same studio, we were all on-air mates with the DJs – David Hamilton, Ed Stewart, John Dunn.

Back in Belfast, my dad, in particular, was an avid listener. On my parents' wedding anniversary, I thought it would be nice to get them a dedication, so I asked Ed Stewart if he'd do the needful and he was only too delighted. Of course, sod's law, that day they were out and missed it. And there was no *BBC Sounds* to reprise it for them.

I was so fortunate to be part of what was, without question, the golden age of BBC Radio Sport. The team that had been assembled was an array of stellar broadcasting talent: Desmond Lynam, Mike Ingham, Peter Jones, Alan Parry, Ian Darke, Peter Bromley, Christopher Martin-Jenkins, Gerald Williams, Tony Adamson and the cast of characters who backed us up – Ian Thomas, Mike Lewis, Emily McMahon, Dave Gordon, Brian Tremble. Graham Jenkins, who accompanied me to the Varsity match at Twickenham in December and produced a hip flask containing a Whisky Mac, a most welcome combination of Scotch and ginger at half-time, had an interesting connection. His brother was none other than the actor Richard Burton (Burton was their mother's maiden name). We often got to enjoy Richard's hospitality *in absentia*. He had a tab at the Dorchester Hotel on Park Lane. Graham used to refer to it as 'my club'. Then there was the one and only Peter Lorenzo, a Fleet Street legend who had ended up in management by accident it seemed, who smiled through every crisis and whose principal concern was to find out who might be nipping out of the office, so that they could fetch him five Hamlet.

Smoking wasn't an issue – remember the Bakelite ashtrays? I'd equip myself with five square Villiger cheroots when I'd go in to present *Sport on Two* – four-and-a-half hours live from the bigger basement studio B9 (B for Basement, of course). I had Tommy Docherty as my studio guest one Saturday afternoon. He'd been manager of Manchester United, famously being relegated in 1974 but bringing them back up again the following season at the first attempt.

I offered Tommy a Villiger, but he turned me down suggesting, in that rasping Glaswegian accent he had, that that was no kind of smoke, you should be having a Havana. Somewhat embarrassed, I lit up anyway and thought no more about it. Some time later, on commentary duty this time, with Tommy as my summariser, I flew up to Manchester for the game. He'd phoned me to arrange a time to meet pre-match and when I told him my travel plans, he said he'd pick me up at the airport. Sure enough, there he was in arrivals. He greeted me warmly and off we went to the car park. Things hadn't ended well at Manchester United. He'd been sacked, hounded out by adverse publicity after it became public knowledge that he was having an affair with the physio's wife. (They subsequently married and remained together until his death on New Year's Eve 2020 at the age of ninety-two.) Though it wasn't the end of his career as a manager, he never had another job with the profile of his position at Old Trafford and the work was pretty intermittent, hence his involvement with BBC Radio.

His dismissal hadn't cost him his good humour. He famously described himself as the only football manager who had ever been sacked for falling in love. That Saturday at Manchester airport, he showed me to his transport, a Volkswagen Polo. In we got and before he fired the ignition, he dug into his jacket and pulled something out. 'I've a wee present for you,' he said in that broad accent of his. It was a cigar case. 'Something for you to keep them Villigers in.' I laughed, remembering his blunt dismissal of my choice of smoke, and thanked him warmly. I knew him to be a man of generous spirit. I didn't realise his generosity extended this far. It was only when I got back to London that night and took the case from my pocket that I realised there was something inside. Three of the finest Havanas. What a gent!

I'd be slower to apply that epithet to Malcolm Allison, one of English football's most flamboyant characters – pretty much the Cockney wide boy, whose career in management took in thirty years, fourteen clubs in four countries and the Kuwaiti national team. When our paths crossed, he was in charge at Middlesbrough, whose goalkeeper was Jim Platt, a Northern Ireland international I knew well. 'Boro' were in the Second Division at the time and had been held at home in an FA Cup tie by Bishop's Stortford, a team from Hertfordshire just north of London, who played in the Premier Division of the Isthmian League, four rungs below Middlesbrough in English football's pyramid. After the 2–2 draw on the Saturday, it seemed that an upset could be on the cards when the big boys came south for the replay at the home of the non-League side, so I was dispatched to cover it.

There was no upset – Middlesbrough won 2–1 – and I went down to the spartan dressing room beneath the small stand to do the post-match interviews. On his way out, Jim Platt spotted me and stopped for a chat. 'We're going back to the hotel for a meal before we go back up the road,' he told me. 'Why don't you come along?' I was delighted but wondered what the management might think. 'No bother,' said Jim, 'I've asked you. That's it.'

So off he went to the coach and I wrapped up what I was doing and made my way to the local hotel to have a quick bite before driving home. The players were seated at a long table with Malcolm Allison at the head, talking loudly, enjoying his glass of red wine. They'd already eaten and the plates were being cleared away. Jim was at the other end of the table. He motioned for me to sit down beside him, introduced me to his teammates close by and made sure that there would be a plate of food for me.

The head waiter was fussing over Malcolm, asking would he like a digestif, would he care for a cigar? Sure, that'd be lovely came the reply. The brandy was produced and out came the humidor. The lid was raised and without so much as checking whether they were Coronas or Churchills, Malcolm plunged in his sizable fist. When he withdrew it, he was clutching at least half a dozen of Cuba's finest.

I had one World Cup and one Olympics with the BBC. The World Cup was in Spain, in 1982, and I was assigned as the reporter and commentator to cover Scotland. After their disappointment in Argentina, the manager, Ally MacLeod, had fallen on his sword and was replaced by Jock Stein, who'd led Celtic to the European Cup in 1967 in the middle of a run of nine consecutive domestic titles.

Scotland failed to qualify for the eight-team European Championship in Italy but made it to the World Cup in Spain. The draw wasn't kind to them, putting them in against Brazil and the Soviet Union, as well as New Zealand. Only two of the four would qualify for the next phase of the competition. Two of Scotland's matches were to be played in Malaga, with the other in Seville, so they based themselves at the San Roque Golf Resort not far from Gibraltar, within decent striking distance of both venues.

The BBC secured accommodation for us in the village of Guadacorte nearby, in a lovely old-fashioned Spanish hacienda, all tiled floors and cool, dark corners.

I'd teamed up again with Nevin McGhee, who was now working for BBC Scotland, and our little group was completed by the Arsenal double-winning captain, Frank McLintock, who'd become my regular co-commentator on First Division games on a Saturday. It was an absolute delight to get to know Frank as a friend. As an Arsenal fan of long-standing, that friendship felt like an astonishing turn of events. And I learned so much from sitting alongside him. The house style was that two commentators would cover a game, each doing a half of each half, so when I wasn't commentating, I was simply a spectator and Frank, when he wasn't making his observations on the air as part of the broadcast with Peter Jones, would turn to me with nuggets about why this or that wasn't working or how it was looking like this was going to happen. It was spellbinding. It was like a coaching session every week.

The hacienda had extensive grounds, with a sizable lawn out the back, and on one of the down days, it was suggested we have a kick around. I don't know who brought the ball, but it might have been the guys from Scottish Television who were stationed nearby. Their presence meant there were enough of us to have a decent bit of a game. We'd jumpers for goalposts and all of that. We were taking it in turns to go in goal and my moment duly arrived. Now, I never did have the physique to be a keeper and this disadvantage became immediately apparent. Frank was playing for the opposition. This wasn't your typical five-a-side. There were fellows showing off all over the place, the ball was in the air more often than it was on the ground. One came floating in towards the area I was defending. I rose to catch it. Next thing I was flat on my back on the ground, with Frank standing over me saying, 'Are you all right?' Once a pro, always a pro. The back lawn at Guadacorte or the penalty box at Wembley – when he was going for the ball, nothing would get in his way.

Thoughts of Wembley bring back one particular golden memory for me. One Wednesday night in 1983, England were down to play Hungary in a European qualifier. Not having much knowledge of the Hungarians, I was given the afternoon off on the Tuesday to go and watch them train. I arrived at Wembley and made my way into the bowels of the stadium, emerging up the players' tunnel and taking a position behind the goal, the better to see the opposition up close. It wouldn't happen these days. Martin Tyler, then of ITV, was already there with a number of other colleagues from the world of television.

It was the stuff of dreams – standing beside the pitch at Wembley, down in front of the terrace where my dad had stood for the FA Cup final in 1953. His brother-in-law, Billy McMurray, worked for British Railways in Belfast. If they could get tickets for the Final, he could get them to London and back by boat and train for a concessionary fare. The match – remembered as the Stanley Matthews Cup Final – ended dramatically. It looked like it was heading for extra time, which the two boys would have had to miss if they were to catch the train back to the Heysham ferry, but, inspired by Matthews, Blackpool – who had been 3–1 down – won with a goal in injury time.

As I reminisced, the Hungarian kitman emerged from the tunnel carrying a net of footballs for the training session that was about to begin and placed it beside the goal. Martin, who never lost the desire to play the game and has carried on a part-time coaching career alongside his television work, decided that this was an opportunity not to be missed. He went and picked out one of the balls and struck it on to the hallowed turf. He trotted out after it and one by one, the half dozen of us followed.

I was simply enjoying the experience, wandering around the pitch, looking up at the stands, imagining what it must feel like with 100,000 fans in making a huge noise. How could you not be inspired by that? I was wearing a fine pair of slip-on brogues, not the boots I'd have loved to have tried out on these sacred acres. The ball came my way and I stroked it back in the direction from which it had come. It was stunning how true it ran on the perfect surface. The gentle passes continued until Martin was in possession again, out towards the corner flag on the right. By now, my meandering had brought me back from the far side of the eighteen-yard area and I was approaching the penalty spot. There had been enough pace on the previous pass to encourage Martin's baser footballing instincts. He saw a teammate perfectly positioned. He swept in a cross, which bounced just as it reached me. I swung my right leg and connected with the perfect half volley. The ball hit the net. My shiny black shoe had made the perfect connection.

My teammates' cheers were cut short by shouts from the tunnel. A large man in groundsman's gear was barrelling out towards us. 'Get off the bloody pitch, you lot!' Sheepishly, we sidled away to await the arrival of the Hungarian squad. It might have ended too soon, but not soon enough to deprive me of my *Boy's Own* moment. My shot had hit the back of the Wembley net.

Back at the World Cup in Spain, Scotland began well with a 5–2 win over New Zealand, whose right back was John Hill, who had once been a regular with my team back in Belfast, the Glens. He would never have played in a World Cup if he hadn't emigrated to the North Island seven years before. He won seventeen caps in all.

Next up for Scotland was Brazil in Seville. They dared to dream again, for after only eighteen minutes an absolutely super drive by David Narey – the words of the ecstatic Radio Scotland commentator David Francey that reached me despite the wearing of headphones and a sizable physical distance between us – put Scotland 1–0 up. Alas and alack, it had an effect similar to prodding a sleeping tiger. Brazil rose majestically and swatted the Scots aside, winning by four goals to one. Scotland returned to Malaga, back in familiar territory, needing goals to progress, for they were level on points with their final group opponents, the USSR, but with an inferior goal difference. A draw wouldn't do, but a draw was all they got – 2–2 – and another World Cup dream died.

During my time with the BBC covering the English First Division, I was contributing a weekly football column to the *Sunday Independent* in Dublin. Because the BBC weren't keen on their people doing jobs on the side, 'nixers' where I come from, this had to be done under an assumed name, so I became Michael Henry.

In the early 1980s, you could either dictate your material over the phone to a copy-taker, like Jimmy Dubois in Bulgaria, or you could have it sent by telex, which is how text was transmitted down phone lines before faxes came along. (I know all of this makes me sound positively antediluvian.)

Michael Henry usually filed his copy from a telex bureau in London, which was quicker than spending the time dictating it over the phone. During the World Cup in Spain, this posed a problem, for there was no telex in Guadacorte. The nearest one was in the post office in the port city of Algeciras, by the Strait of Gibraltar. On deadline day, I took the bus for the five-mile ride and found the post office without difficulty. But then the problems started. The guy behind the telex desk had no English and he wasn't about to try to turn my purple prose into a telex transmission. I'd have to type it all up myself.

Fair enough. My typewriting skills are excellent. Even if I'd never used a telex machine and it had a Spanish keyboard, I was sure I'd manage. Let me at it. What the guy didn't tell me was that a telex message is generally pre-prepared on a kind of tickertape so that when you dial up the number, the text is ready to go and is transmitted in no time at all. You don't type it up as you go.

I was taken into the telex room and asked for the number in Dublin that I wanted to call. Blissfully unaware, I offered it. The connection was made. And I started to type. It probably took the best part of three-quarters of an hour, but I got it done and was pretty pleased with myself.

It was only later that a message reached me from Independent House in Middle Abbey Street. My efforts on the Spanish keyboard had hogged the telex machine there for the duration while I typed and they'd been unable to access all the various news wires until I got to the end of my piece! Alternative arrangements were made for the remainder of the tournament.

My BBC Olympics was the 1984 Games in Los Angeles. I'd covered gymnastics and some athletics in Moscow with RTÉ. Here, with the major events taken by established radio commentators – Alan Parry on the athletics, Peter Jones on the swimming and the ceremonial – I'd be more of a human-interest reporter. This meant I teamed up with Terry Wogan. During big set-piece sporting occasions, Terry's show would move to the venue and he'd present his music and take a sideways look, as only he could, at what was going on around him.

I'd had a bit of a run of this at a previous Commonwealth Games, when Pee Wee Lacrosse had been presented as a demonstration sport. You can just imagine what Wogan made of that. My brief was to attend something away from the mainstream and act as a foil. It was great fun and though very intermittent, we had a wonderful on-air relationship. Of course, Terry was a merciless mickey-taker. Five hours in the heat of a Californian afternoon at the cycling road race, having neglected to apply sunblock, necessitated a visit to the First Aid station when it was all over. 'Your nose is beyond repair,' the nurse had declared. I included her observation in my two-way with Terry. It became something of a leitmotiv for our conversations through the rest of the Games.

There was a touch of showbiz glamour as well. One afternoon, we'd just finished our on-air chat and I was in the control room shooting the breeze with the technical people when a call came through to say a guest for the programme had arrived at the security gate of the broadcast compound and needed to be signed in.

Terry was still live, the studio crew was still busy, so I said I'd go down and get him. It was blazingly hot, living up to southern

California's reputation as a place where it never rains. Didn't somebody write a song about that? Yes, they did, and that person was the man in the white suit who was waiting down at security, none other than Albert Hammond.

12

Platten à la Carte

I had always enjoyed being a radio broadcaster. That's where I had begun and once I got involved with television it became clear very quickly that they are two entirely different media.

A television production has a cast of thousands. On the radio, it can be just you and the listener. When I was a continuity announcer in Belfast, it fell to me, on occasion, to close the station down at a quarter to midnight. It wasn't long before I discovered a constituency out there who would listen right up to the national anthem that ended the day's broadcasting. By and large they'd be alone. And my sign-off – 'A very good night to you' – would feel very much like a personal farewell. I got letters telling me so.

My four years in London with BBC Radio Sport had marked the end of my full-time involvement with radio – what's known in the business as the senior service. I did, though, still have a small amount of skin in that particular game. In London, I'd had an approach from the Head of the BBC German Service, Victor Price, a name I was familiar with from my student days.

Then, I'd done my German dissertation on Georg Büchner,

a nineteenth-century playwright. Victor Price, who'd come to broadcasting from academia, was a world expert on Büchner. He knew me, obviously, as a sports journalist but he was also aware of my occasional involvement as a German language reporter covering the Troubles in Northern Ireland. He put a very interesting proposition to me.

The BBC German Service, an arm of its World Service, was essentially a means of getting Western news and information into communist East Germany. And Western popular culture too. There was a weekly programme called *Platten à la Carte*, hosted by an English lady who was married to a British Army officer. He was being posted to the British Army of the Rhine, a cohort of the NATO forces responsible for the defence of West Germany. She was obviously going too, so there was a vacancy for a German-speaking DJ.

Victor Price arranged for us to meet in the St George's Hotel, next door to Broadcasting House. She talked me through what was involved and having convinced them I could get my tongue around Kajagoogoo and Bananarama, we toasted success. I'd got the gig.

So, each Monday morning, I made my way to Bush House in The Strand where I'd raid the gramophone library matching music to the requests that had come in by post from behind the Iron Curtain. I was never quite sure how the listeners managed it. Clearly postcards – and they were mostly postcards for some reason – from the old DDR addressed to the BBC in London would be unlikely to leave the jurisdiction, or if they did, it would be only after the sender's details had been duly noted. There must have been some kind of dead-letter-box arrangement.

The one thing I had to be careful about when I was reading out the requests and dedications was never to reveal a surname and never to be too specific about a location. So, Klaus-Peter from Potsdam it would be. Even the Stasi would baulk at trying to ferret out a low-level dissenter whose head had been turned by 'Two Tribes' or the Thompson Twins.

There was plenty of mail. I was never stuck for a playlist. And clearly it went down well, because when I announced I was leaving BBC Radio Sport to return to Dublin, Victor asked me if it would be possible to keep the show going from RTÉ.

And that's what I did, bringing the recording forward to Sundays to allow for the tape to get to London. It was a source of some amusement in the booking department in Donnybrook that somebody would be hosting a music show in German in one of their studios, but they took it all in their stride and looked after the shipping of the precious reel of quarter-inch.

This continued for some time until I got a letter from Victor. In it, he told me the budget for the German Service was being pared back by the government and, regrettably, *Platten à la Carte* had to go. I wasn't really surprised, given the economic circumstances of the time. I was by no means the only one to have been given the boot by Margaret Thatcher.

I responded, thanking Victor for the opportunity he'd given me and telling him how much I'd enjoyed the experience. He was so taken aback by my comments, he wrote again to say he'd never expected an expression of thanks from someone he'd just sacked.

It was but a minor setback. I had moved back from London following an intervention by RTÉ that was very similar to the BBC's approach just after the Moscow Olympics. Tim O'Connor wasn't the head of sport in RTÉ, but he ran the place, certainly as far as television was concerned. Fred Cogley had the title but, the most mild-mannered of men, kindness personified, he was not built for the cut and thrust of broadcasting politics as networks began to proliferate and sports organisations saw the main chance. Fred was happy to attend the bunfights, carry on as the principal rugby commentator on the station and let Tim get on with it.

Tim had an idea that would raise the profile of the Saturday afternoon *Sports Stadium* from a glorified purveyor of horse racing and the odd mainstream event – he was a genius when it came to exploiting opportunities. TV rights fees were based on how big an audience you might reach. In that sense, RTÉ, serving a population of around four million, could plead the poor mouth. He would suggest to the sports organisers that even what, by their lights, would be minimal exposure, bringing with it a tiny financial contribution from RTÉ because the Irish market was so small, would still be a bonus. There's a song by 10cc that sums up this view, and it's right on the money – four per cent of something is better than ten per cent of nothing at all.

The Football League bought it and Tim had a product. Now what he wanted was a commentator – an Irish voice that would be identified with that product, not one that had been grafted onto it. I'd been doing First Division commentaries on the radio for four years, and the huge following that English football commanded meant there was a sizable audience in Ireland for *Sport on Two* who would be prepared to listen through the crackles on the medium wave to get their fix. If he could put the BBC guy onto RTÉ's television coverage, he reckoned he'd have a winner.

So there's a meeting over dinner in East Sheen in suburban London and I make the call, telling Pat Ewing at the Olympics in Los Angeles that I'm heading back to Dublin. She thinks I'm mad and I may well be. Ireland in 1984 is a basket case.

I returned to an RTÉ Sports Department that I'd left in the relative splendour of Montrose House, in whose grounds the broadcasting station was built. Named after a Walter Scott novel, it was built by John Jameson, a Scot who came to Dublin in the 1780s and founded a distillery. His granddaughter Annie was the mother of Guglielmo Marconi, the man who invented the radio. Four years after I'd left, it had been repurposed and the Sports Department was now based in what was effectively a warehouse, a newly constructed television studio that the station hadn't the money to equip. What had I done?

Still, Tim was in charge and I kept the faith. Thanks to his vision, we were able to buy the rights to a big game that might pique an Irish audience's interest – a quarter-final of the 1985/86 European Cup. The cup holders were Juventus of Turin and we'd be showing the second leg of their tie against Barcelona. There were no English teams involved for the most dreadful of reasons.

Juventus had become champions of Europe for the very first time in Brussels just the year before in 1985, defeating the holders, Liverpool, 1–0. I'd been due to commentate on the game but family circumstances dictated otherwise. My father was seriously ill and I was given compassionate leave.

Ger Canning was on duty in Brussels. An hour or so before kick-off, I was driving along University Street in Belfast, on my way to visit my dad in the City Hospital. I was listening to my former BBC colleague Peter Jones describing the scenes in the stadium.

There had been an incident of some sort in the crowd – I'd come late to the commentary – and it was obvious from what I heard that there had been casualties. I heard Peter use the word 'bodies', and I said out loud, 'Come on, you can't say that. Casualties aren't bodies.' Or were they?

Thirty-nine people, Italians and Belgians, died. Liverpool fans were blamed for the tragedy, which came about, the BBC reported at the time, when supporters charged at a wall separating them from Juventus fans, causing it to collapse onto the mainly Italian crowd.

In the wake of the Heysel Stadium disaster, the FA in England announced it would not allow its teams to play in Europe. UEFA followed with an indefinite suspension of English clubs. They would not return until 1990, with Liverpool banned for a year beyond that.

On a personal note, I was glad to see the back of 1985 – my father passed away that June, three days after his seventy-seventh birthday – but there had been so many good times together in the glorious game that he, a former Irish League player, had introduced me to, that I was determined to seize the opportunities that would come my way, for I knew how proud he had been as I'd made my way in my chosen career.

Juventus against Barcelona, in the quarter-finals of the competition the following year, came just a week before Jack Charlton's first game as Republic of Ireland manager. Hard to believe now, but Barcelona had yet to win the European Cup. They took the first leg 1–0. The holders had a task on their hands and Barcelona had the popular Scottish forward Steve Archibald. It was perfectly set up. Archibald duly scored. Michel Platini equalised for Juventus. And that was how it ended, 1–1, meaning Barcelona progressed by virtue of their away goal.

RTÉ showed the final of the European Cup each year, but Juve v Barça was the first time that we'd dipped our toes into something earlier in the competition. Maurice Reidy was my minder on the trip – looking back across the years, it's truly amazing how our paths have intertwined.

Maurice and I left the Stadio Communale, exhilarated by what we'd seen, but completely lost in suburban Turin. Out on the street, there were trams passing by, so we boarded one, seeking a ticket from the driver, who couldn't help us.

Schwarzfahren they call it in Germany – 'travelling black', riding without the requisite pass. The tram stopped. There was a lot of movement, passengers rushing off. The doors closed. The tram bell sounded, the journey resumed – and the inspectors moved in. We were stuffed. There was a lot of gesticulating given that we didn't speak Italian, but the transport police were most understanding when we produced our RTÉ IDs. We dodged a bullet, Maurice and I, that evening in Turin.

We had another night to spend there before we moved on to our next assignment, which was the World Cross Country Championships in Switzerland. The two events had tied in nicely for a two-birds-with-one-stone trip.

So we'd Thursday at our leisure in the city and went in search of the Turin Shroud. I'm ashamed to say that we didn't manage to locate it. We did acquaint ourselves, though, with much of what is delightful in that city of arcades and shopping streets with their covered walkways, the better to avoid the vagaries of the winter weather in that particular quarter of Piedmont.

That Thursday evening, we were having a drink when a couple entered the bar – the tramway inspector from the previous evening and his wife! There was more gesticulating and we offered to buy the guy a drink for the courtesy and goodwill he had shown us the day before. He was having none of it. His integrity would have been compromised. We parted amicably, the Irish impressed by this expression of Italian rectitude.

On the Friday, we were booked on a flight from Milan to Geneva, where we were to pick up a hire car and travel on to the cross-country in the town of Neuchâtel. There, we'd hook up with Brendan O'Reilly, who had called John Treacy home when he'd won the event in Limerick seven years before, a man who, as the top Irish high jumper, should have competed at the Melbourne Olympics in 1956 but didn't travel because of a lack of funding. Ronnie Delany had got the gig and came back with a gold medal in the 1500 metres.

There's no obligation on a sporting venue to be handy enough to an international airport and Neuchâtel was not, being situated midway between Zürich and Geneva, 150 kilometres from both. Caselle, Turin's small airport, didn't offer a direct flight to either, so we'd miss the spectacular alpine scenery on departure.

When you fly in on a typical approach from the south, you get the most wonderful views of a rather different kind, Piedmont fog permitting. With landing imminent as you pass over the Juventus Stadium, you've already had sight of the hills that ring Turin, you've seen what became of the former Stadio Communale, now the Olimpico Grande, home to the city's other football club, Torino, and you've had sight of the old Fiat factory in Lingotto, with its rooftop racetrack where they shot the iconic sequence for the comedy movie *The Italian Job*, released in 1969, about a gang of cockney crooks who hijack a consignment of gold bullion and make their getaway in three Mini Cooper cars.

Production at Lingotto ceased in 1982 and the huge factory has since become a venue in central Turin, featuring an exhibition and conference centre, a shopping mall, a multiplex, restaurants and a hotel where we were based on one occasion for a Juventus game in the Champions League.

Now needing to head across to Neuchâtel and with no direct route out of Turin and over the Alps, we took the train the ninety-odd miles to Milan for a flight to Geneva. Taxi, then, from Milano Centrale to Linate airport. And that's when the fun began.

We rocked up at the check-in desk. In view of what happened next, you'd wonder why there was anybody at the check-in desk at all. We presented our tickets. The old paper slips. 'Alitalia is on strike today,' the lady said, like we'd just picked the wrong day. 'There are no flights.'

We were stuffed. Why had we spent an extra day in Turin? Why hadn't we just headed straight off to Geneva? Toss of a coin: an extra night in Turin or an extra night in Switzerland? It could have been one or the other. The Italians were on one of their wildcat strikes, which were pretty prevalent back then.

So we took another taxi back into Milan to get on a train through a tunnel in the Alps to Switzerland. Credit cards sorted that out, but there were two hungry geezers on the station forecourt and credit cards couldn't help us – Italian lire were what we needed for food. We were at the end of our stay in Italy and we'd precious few left. Maurice and I pooled what we had, which stretched to a slice of pizza each.

But the arrangements we'd cobbled together were shot to pieces. The Hertz desk would be well shut by the time we got to Geneva so there'd be no option for a rental car – and in any case, the Hertz desk was at the airport, not at the Gare Cornavin downtown where we were due to arrive.

Five hours after leaving Milan, through the intrepid travellers' first experience of a dark Alpine night (both in and out of the tunnel), our train pulled into Lausanne. It was approaching eleven o'clock, and I was getting concerned. It would be the best part of another hour before we'd reach Geneva, and getting to Neuchâtel after that – a two-hour drive if our original arrangements had worked out – was now entirely out of the question. Yet that was where our beds were.

Never known to be indecisive in a crisis, I jumped up, grabbed my bag from the overhead rack and said to Maurice, 'We're staying here tonight!'

It's funny how roles reverse. In the *Sports Stadium* presenter's chair, I'd hear him in my ear and I'd do precisely as instructed. That's how it works. In the dark Swiss night, though, mine was the voice of experience. So off we got and by dint of an ad in a brochure on a stand in front of the shuttered tourist information desk, we found the address of a *pension* just up the street from the station. Being Switzerland, the accommodation was just so and within thirty minutes, we were tucked up. Neuchâtel had become Saturday's issue. Sure, the event wasn't until the Sunday.

It was a decent enough pit-stop and set us up for what had now become a ridiculous journey. If we'd known we'd be coming by train, we would never have followed this route. Anyway, needs must. We headed south to Geneva to get the car, then north to Neuchâtel. Finally, we were able to check in with RTÉ and inform them that we had actually arrived.

* * *

My hunch that moving back to Dublin would be rewarding was paying off. I was commentating on big matches for television, which was something I had always wanted to do, and my enjoyment in my work was further enhanced by the popularity of the quiz show *Know Your Sport*.

These were halcyon days, a term seldom used any more but a favourite of the sportswriters I read in my youth. They'd be recalling a great team of the past, summers of supreme excellence or the glory of a time there was a gold medal to celebrate.

From the autumn of 1987 to the summer of 1998, the incomparable Jimmy Magee and I brought *Know Your Sport* to the nation.

We'd been commentary box buddies for some time, sharing duties at major events but only ever once sitting side by side – at the World Cup Final in Mexico in 1986 – when the opportunity to collaborate came right out of the blue.

Mary Hogan, a wonderful lady whose sparkling intellect brought many a bright idea to the airwaves, came up with the notion of a sports quiz for the people.

There had been many before, but this would be different, harnessing the pulling power of television. Eighty regular punters, who'd have come through a rigorous process of auditions, would compete for a major prize – the trip of a lifetime, with a brand-new car to come home to, courtesy of the programme's sponsor, Opel.

Michael O'Carroll, the producer in charge, had devised a plan: partner RTÉ's foremost sports broadcaster – Jimmy – with the new lad, not long in from the BBC but becoming a familiar face from hosting *Sports Stadium*, our Saturday afternoon offering of live televised sport.

I was the quizmaster. Jimmy set the questions and he was the referee. But he would also feature in the show's central segment as the Memory Man. He'd be expected to answer whatever sporting query would come his way. I thought this would be part of the smoke and mirrors of everyday TV life, but no.

Jimmy lived up to his billing in spades. Viewers were invited to test the Memory Man on whatever took their fancy. The more obscure the better. Mary and I would sit in the office and decide on what would best put Jimmy to the test. He never got to see the questions beforehand.

At half-time on *Know Your Sport*, the Memory Man would face the music. I'd ask. He'd ponder. He might seek clarification. And then he'd respond. Never once, over more than 300 shows, did he fail to come up trumps. He was some man to set the questions. But he was some man to answer them too.

Despite its obvious success – in a prime-time slot on the principal channel, across its thirty-week run, it was regularly in the top ten most watched programmes – RTÉ grew tired of it. They could never quite accept that it should fall into the light entertainment category which is where its budget had come from in the first place.

Without explanation, it was shunted around the schedule. These days that might not matter, since by-appointment television has become almost a thing of the past. But then, if there was one thing a TV audience liked, it was the certainty of knowing when a favourite show would be on. The station wasn't backing *Know Your Sport* and the figures reflected that.

Low-level industrial disputes were a feature of the 1990s landscape in Donnybrook. One of those that developed impacted the programme. To make a point, the stage hands invoked the rule book, which hadn't been changed to take account of advances in electronics. They reverted to a former work practice, where they had sole responsibility for keeping the score.

Mary Hogan could only watch on in despair as this cumbersome process slowed the slick presentation of her fast-moving quiz show. It wasn't fair to the contestants. It was an embarrassment to us. Quite what the studio audience made of it is anybody's guess. The one thing that was missing from the whole sorry mess was a management effort to address the grievance that was giving *Know Your Sport* such grief.

They allowed their successful sports quiz, which had been pulling in audiences of 750,000 on the main television channel at its peak, to wither on the vine. There was no will to turn it into a staple, like the BBC's *A Question of Sport*.

It would have vanished earlier had Tim O'Connor not stepped in to back it with funds from his budget in TV Sport. But he couldn't sustain it. Broadcast rights for sports events were becoming ever more expensive and not even his renowned acumen as a negotiator could stretch to keeping enough back for *Know Your Sport*. We crowned our final champion in the spring of 1998.

* * *

In retrospect, I see now that these forays into entertainment in the 1980s and 1990s paved the way for what has become one of my most fulfilling and enjoyable roles in more recent years. At the time, though, I was taken by surprise. If my dad had been James Bond instead of Jim Hamilton, I might have been more prepared for what happened in the back of the taxi in an eastern Moscow suburb on a dark September night in 2003. I've learned, though, that good things in small parcels can turn up anytime, anywhere.

That night I'd been to a football game because, by and large, that is what I have done for the best part of my working life, which you might say has been spent avoiding the very thing around which a working life revolves – work. Being a sports commentator is a very privileged way to make a living.

There was still a feel of the Cold War Soviet capital about the place, even then, in the early twenty-first century. Our route to town was through ill-lit streets. We'd gone to Moscow to report on a game that had a bearing on the chances of the Republic of Ireland qualifying for the European football championship for the first time since their initial glorious, though ultimately unsuccessful campaign fifteen years before.

Russia were playing Switzerland that Wednesday night. Switzerland led the qualifying group, a point ahead of the Republic. Russia were three points further behind. Although not as clear-cut as the game in Bulgaria had been, when Scotland had won against all the odds to put Ireland through to Euro 88 – its first ever major tournament – this time, a Swiss win would leave Ireland handily placed to earn a play-off spot. It was a sure-fire ratings winner.

But Russia, as the former Irish Taoiseach Bertie Ahern might have put it, 'upset the apple tart', winning 4–1. The Irish had been shunted back to third. With a visit to the Swiss to come, they were still in the hunt, but your gut said otherwise.

Alongside me, in the back seat of that cab was Stephen Alkin – RTÉ's head of football and an inveterate Chelsea fan – a man of many talents.

Now back then, mobile phones had a terrible tendency to interfere with the broadcast circuits, so there was a strict rule – when you reached the commentary position, you turned your mobile off. Only when I got into the taxi did I think of turning it on again.

We were on our way back into the centre from the venue in a pretty non-descript north-eastern suburb. I was gazing out at nothing in particular, dim city lights casting shadows on dull city streets. I felt the lump in my pocket vibrate. I pulled out the phone. There was a message from somebody I'd never ever met.

'Hi, George, this is Aodán Ó Dubhghaill.' The caller introduced himself as the new head of RTÉ's classical music service, Lyric FM. 'Would you mind giving me a call?' So, somewhere in the dark outer reaches of Moscow's east side, I punched in the unfamiliar number and heard an unfamiliar voice make me an offer that would change and enrich my life. So began my involvement with Lyric FM – an involvement I would never have predicted back in the 1980s as I jetted off round the world covering all manner of sporting events.

13

Charlton Gets the Job

Back in those days, there was one major piece of Irish sports news that I didn't have to get on a plane to cover. Among all the anniversaries commemorated on the island of Ireland there is one date that deserves much more attention than it gets. Friday, 7 February 1986 should be remembered for the impact it had on foot of a major development that very evening in the heart of Georgian Dublin. The next day's *Irish Times* put news of what had taken place on its front page: 'The Football Association of Ireland last night appointed the former English international Jack Charlton as manager of the Republic of Ireland soccer team after a lengthy meeting in Merrion Square.' That didn't even tell the half of it.

* * *

In the run-up to that momentous date, there was another World Cup coming up. I was on the case in the colourfully named Wankdorf Stadium in Bern when Eoin Hand's team secured a scoreless draw with their Swiss hosts, which kept them in the hunt for qualification with two rounds of matches still to be played. But one of those was a must-win game in Moscow.

They lost, and though mathematically qualification was still possible, the *coup de grâce* was delivered when the Soviet Union's defeat of Norway a fortnight later rendered even the abacus redundant. The Republic of Ireland had one more game to play, at home to Denmark. But while their interest in the 1986 World Cup would end with that match, Northern Ireland, under Billy Bingham, were second in their group behind England and still very much in contention for a place in the Finals. On that same Wednesday in November, they would meet England in London secure in the knowledge that a draw would qualify them. The fact that Lansdowne Road had no floodlights, so the Ireland match would be an afternoon one, offered Tim an open goal. RTÉ could show both games. Jimmy Magee would be on duty for the Republic's game and I would go to Wembley, where Northern Ireland secured a scoreless draw and the point that booked their ticket to Mexico.

Frank Stapleton gave the Republic an early lead, but the Danes equalised within a minute. With top spot in the group as the prize, the visitors went for it and, by half-time, they were 2–1 in front. Just before the hour, it became 3–1 when the Danish right back John Sivebæk, soon to be on his way to Manchester United, scored. That was the cue for one of the most wacky tales of sporting endeavour.

In Denmark's line-up that afternoon was Søren Lerby, at the time a crucial cog in the Bayern Munich midfield. Bayern had a game that night – a tough cup tie away to VfL Bochum in the

Ruhr, where there were floodlights to avail of. When Denmark went 3–1 up, Lerby was immediately substituted and whisked away, under garda escort, to a private jet at Dublin Airport.

He made it to Germany well before kick-off, but heavy traffic meant he didn't reach the stadium in time to be included in the starting XI, though he did come on as a sub. Bayern held on for a draw after extra time and won the replay, with Lerby scoring one of the goals.

Denmark's win on that November afternoon in Dublin helped seal the fate of Eoin Hand in his role as Irish manager and cleared the way for a new regime.

* * *

Jack Charlton was certainly not uppermost in the minds of the decision makers at the Football Association of Ireland when the vacancy arose. They had canvassed far and wide across England and had come up with a shortlist. At 80 Merrion Square, the tall Georgian terrace in central Dublin that was home to the FAI in those days, they mulled over the credentials of the candidates.

Bob Paisley, the last of whose six First Division titles with Liverpool had been secured less than three years before, was deemed to be the favourite. There was talk, too, of John Giles resuming where he'd left off in 1980, when he took Irish football by surprise and stepped down as international manager after what had been deemed a successful period in charge.

Jack's name was in the hat as well, but it seemed like stretching credibility to imagine that a stalwart of England's World Cup-winning team of 1966 might take charge of the Irish.

This was a period when the Troubles in Northern Ireland were a running sore. Though Margaret Thatcher had signed the Anglo-Irish agreement with the Taoiseach Garret FitzGerald just two days after the Danish footballing invasion that had created the managerial vacancy at the FAI, diplomatic relations could scarcely be viewed as cordial. Could an Englishman seriously be considered as the prospective manager of the Republic of Ireland's football team?

It was the evening of Friday, 7 February 1986. The media pack was informed that there would be an announcement at 7 p.m., but there would be no formal press conference. If we just turned up, they would let us know. So the representatives of the Fourth Estate assembled outside, huddled by the gardens opposite the faded green front door. We weren't allowed in. The only public area in the building was the cramped front room where fans would queue, awaiting access to the hatch through which they could buy match tickets.

Surprisingly, when it came to a vote, Jack Charlton emerged as a credible candidate. So there was no seven o'clock announcement, just word that there had been a three-way tie and there would have to be a second ballot.

When the process was concluded, the front door opened and the announcement was made to those who were, by now, assembled at the foot of the front steps. It caught everybody on the hop, maybe even the association itself. Jack Charlton was the new manager of the Republic of Ireland.

One of the eighteen delegates around the table had had a change of heart and his volte-face broke the 6–6–6 deadlock to give Jack the extra vote he needed. The news was greeted with disbelief and there was a note of uncertainty too. The choice had been made, but the FAI hadn't been able to get through to their man to tell him he'd got the job.

In those pre-mobile days, it was the house phone or nothing, and Jack wasn't at home. Being the hunting–shooting–fishing type, he'd taken himself off to his place on the Northumberland moors and telecommunications there were non-existent.

I knew Jack. I'd first met him when I was working with BBC Radio in London – Radio 2 on a Saturday afternoon, with second-half commentary from a First Division venue that had to stay secret till everybody had kicked off at three o'clock. That particular week, I was in St James' Park for a Newcastle game. The BBC sportsroom had an enviable reputation and the pick of the crop when it came to co-commentators. Jack was between jobs, as they say – not long out of Sheffield Wednesday.

He was genial and affable when I met him at the ground. Of course, everybody knew him. Though by then a thirty-something, I was still starstruck. This was the guy, after all, who'd come from nowhere to play a starring role at the back for Alf Ramsey's team in 1966, when I was imagining the bright red of those England shirts on the black and white TV back home in Belfast.

St James' Park in 1983 can't have been so different from how it was when Newcastle United were winning the old Inter-Cities Fairs Cup and Doug Weatherall's reports filled the back page of the not-yet-tabloid *Daily Mail*, which used its north-east edition to satisfy readers in Ireland.

Of course, there was an East Stand on what had been the open terrace that provided the backdrop to the action shots of the then number 9, Wyn Davies, banging them in. I can't imagine, though, that the main stand had changed that much.

Radio 2's commentary position was to one side near the front, where an angled partition interfered with the guest's legroom. My abiding memory is of Jack, somehow, shoehorning himself in. Not a word of complaint, though. If there's one thing you could say about Jack Charlton, he just got on with it.

Little did I think then that not only would I be back in Ireland myself, but that Jack, the big, good-natured Geordie, would now be the man in charge of the national team that I was tasked with following.

But before all of that, there was some detective work required. Our press colleagues had been blindsided by the surprise announcement. Puzzled expressions abounded as contacts books were examined for any possible connection that might lead to the new manager of the international team. I was with my close colleague and dear friend, our football editor, Stephen Alkin – his Starsky to my Hutch. He was shaking his head in bewilderment with a what-do-we-do-now expression. 'Come on and we'll have a think,' I said. It was clear we'd been presented with the opportunity for a scoop. Unlike the newspaper correspondents, we'd no deadline for the next morning's back pages.

We left the assembled hacks, turned the corner into Merrion Street and walked swiftly up towards Foley's Bar, right into Merrion Row and on. 'Where are we going?' Stephen wanted to know. To the Shelbourne Hotel, I told him.

After just fifteen months back in Dublin, my little black book was as near as up-to-date with relevant English numbers as it could have been. And in the Shelbourne, we would find a bank of telephone booths right opposite reception. If he took one and I took another, we'd find a way to Jack Charlton in no time; with a bit of luck, we'd be introducing him to the nation on *Sports Stadium* the following afternoon.

The hotel couldn't have been more helpful, plugging us up to let us dial England ourselves. In no time at all, we hit pay dirt. I should have thought of Jimmy Armfield myself, but it was my old buddy, Alan Green, over in Manchester, who reminded me that but for injury, Jimmy would have been the right back to Jack's centre half on England's World Cup-winning team. But Jimmy had been in the squad. There would be no better man.

I dialled his number in Blackpool and he answered with that unmistakable Lancastrian twang. 'Delighted to hear you, George. To what do I owe the pleasure on a Friday night?' I told him. 'Jack's what?'

To say Jimmy was amused when he heard would be putting it mildly. And he was only too happy to join the posse. Observing the appropriate protocol, he offered to ring Jack's wife, Pat – rather than have me, a stranger, call her straight off – and pass on our request for an interview. He'd call us straight back.

At the desk, the receptionist – thrilled to have been part of the intrigue – wanted all the details and, by the time we'd told the story, Jimmy was back on the phone. Jack would be checking in with Pat in the morning and she'd tell him to get into the BBC in Newcastle for lunchtime because Irish TV wanted to present him to his new public. No need to confirm. He'd be there. Stephen and I had got ourselves an exclusive. Those phone calls in the Shelbourne were the best £39 RTÉ ever spent.

From the outset, relations were cordial. Maybe it was the fact that we on TV weren't faced with the challenge of filling page after page, day after day, but there was never the slightest issue when it came to dealing with the Big Man.

In that first interview, he didn't have much to say. He seemed as surprised as everybody else that he'd got the job. What did come across was his affability, his openness, the sense that this was a man who might well take the team in an altogether different direction.

It might not have struck him then, but it would soon become apparent: Jack Charlton was made for international management. No daily grind on the training ground. No chairman in his ear. Just the odd bit of scouting (though that could be left to his sidekick, Maurice Setters) and then, after the monthly get-together with the players, a concentrated spell of coaching and a match or two. It meant that he could get on with what he loved best – the country life – with a little bit of football thrown in.

A section of the support may have been less than happy with the appointment – 'Go Home Union Jack' was the message that fluttered on a banner high in the old East Stand at Lansdowne Road when he sent out his first selection.

It was an inauspicious beginning. Another Wednesday afternoon kick-off. A dreadful surface (groundskeeping technology was rather more primitive in 1986 and Ireland's final game in what was then rugby's Five Nations championship had been played there just ten days before). A 1–0 defeat to Wales.

The opposition left heavy-hearted as well. Their goalkeeper, Neville Southall, who played for Everton, at the time the English League champions, soared to collect a corner swung in from the direction of the new Lansdowne clubhouse. He landed in a divot and broke his ankle.

But even though the local press were disparaging – following on from the Denmark debacle, it couldn't get any worse was the general feeling – the green shoots of recovery would soon become visible. Jack had hit on a way of strengthening his squad. You didn't need to be born in the country to play for it. There were plenty of second- and third-generation Irish in the professional game in England. What became known as the Granny Rule would be exploited to the full. He followed up every lead.

One night, Jack had gone to a game at Oxford United – then in the top division – to run the rule over John Aldridge who, he'd been told, was qualified to play for Ireland. In the Players' Lounge afterwards, he'd offered Aldridge a place in his squad. Aldridge was delighted. It wasn't every night an international manager came along scouting. He was quick to offer his new boss some assistance.

He pointed to his teammate Ray Houghton, who'd played underage for Scotland. 'You know Ray could play for you as well? His dad's from Donegal.'

With that, two international careers were launched, not to mention big moves to Liverpool, and there were many more besides as Jack brought a freshness and a vitality to a team that had lived forever with the tag of nearly men.

In the classic sense, the whole became so much more than the sum of the parts. His philosophy was simple and if the player bought into it, he was part of the framework.

Transition, that vogue word these days for what used to happen when you got the ball back, was what Jack's teams were best at. They'd get it out to the full back and he'd hit it high and long, for Aldridge or Tony Cascarino to chase into the corner.

'Put 'em under pressure' was the slogan, but it was more than just that. It was making swanky players turn and figure out how to play going backwards.

Success bred success and unlikely results followed. England and Italy were put to the sword in big-time tournaments. And in between, there was an appearance in a World Cup quarter-final.

Big Jack was on his way to becoming the most successful manager the Republic of Ireland has ever had. Those ten years he spent at the helm were the happiest of times for Irish football and for the country too. A proud island nation on the edge of Europe, with a culture all of its own, Ireland has always celebrated its distinctiveness. The ancient game of hurling is revered as one of the fastest and most skilful of field sports. The form of football that evolved in Ireland when soccer and rugby were being codified is also fast and furious, but neither Gaelic football nor hurling has found a public abroad beyond the Irish diaspora. They're games enjoyed at home, the fanaticism of the fans contained by the extent of local rivalries.

It took the team moulded by a World Cup-winning Englishman to give the Irish the opportunity to showcase their unique exuberance on a broader stage, and they took that opportunity with relish. They wore their green shirts with pride and represented their country with honour in stadia right across the globe. Big Jack revelled in his role at the heart of it all. And the Irish loved him back.

And I was there, up in the commentary box, as this sporting miracle unfolded. It took somebody special to bring it about, to raise the bar and say, as another outsider did when he came a-calling, 'Yes we can!'

Barack Obama helped win himself the presidency of the

United States with that slogan and endeared himself to the Irish when he said it, in Irish – *Is Féidir Linn* – on a visit in 2011.

Twenty-five years before, Jack Charlton had picked up the sporting baton with a similar sentiment in mind. If his first game in charge had left the home support unimpressed, there was the merest hint of a new dawn in his second, which prompted this opening paragraph in *The Irish Times* the following morning: 'The Republic of Ireland's crusade for respectability in international football was advanced marginally at Lansdowne Road last evening when Jack Charlton's rebuilt team fought bravely and, at times, skilfully to deny the South American champions, Uruguay, the win that pedigree indicated for an attendance of almost 15,000.'

The 1–1 draw was secured by the first goal to be scored by a Charlton team, a penalty by the veteran Gerry Daly. Interestingly, the starting line-up that April afternoon included two League of Ireland players, Barry Murphy of Bohemians and the twenty-one-year-old Liam O'Brien of Shamrock Rovers – 'a revelation at times,' said Charlton: 'I wish someone would bring him to England and provide him with the showcase he deserves.' Six months later, Ron Atkinson did just that, in what turned out to be his last signing for Manchester United.

The game against Uruguay provided another League of Ireland player, Peter Eccles of Shamrock Rovers, with his one and only cap at the age of thirty-three, when he came on as a late substitute for Ray Houghton.

A triangular tournament in Iceland followed – two matches, two wins against the hosts and Czechoslovakia. It was the first time the Republic of Ireland had won an international competition of any description, but it's remembered now mostly as the root of a spat between the manager and the regular centre half David O'Leary of Arsenal, whom he had, to some surprise, left out of his squad in favour of Mick McCarthy. Following several withdrawals, O'Leary was called up but refused to join the party, saying he'd booked a family holiday and wasn't going to cancel it. He wasn't holding his breath for a recall. It would be over two years before he would play for Ireland again, by which time Euro 88 had come and gone. It would be one of the great sporting ironies that in the World Cup shoot-out in Genoa, O'Leary would have the last laugh.

With the satisfaction of its success in Iceland fresh in the mind, the squad began its first competitive campaign under Charlton in September 1986, in the Heysel Stadium in Brussels. Five years previously at the same venue, Eoin Hand's team had lost 1–0 to a late Belgian goal, a result that ultimately denied them a place at the 1982 World Cup. This time, they salvaged a draw with a last-minute penalty from Liam Brady. The point secured in that opening fixture would be decisive in the end.

But there was still some way to go and the portents were not good when Scotland visited Lansdowne Road the following month and finished with a scoreless draw. The year was rounded off with a 1–0 defeat in a friendly in Poland, while Scotland were claiming a routine win over Luxembourg to go top of the group and shunt Ireland to third, with only one team to qualify for the eight-team Euros. Two games without scoring. Away trips to Scotland and Bulgaria up next. A familiar story seemed to be developing.

On a Tuesday afternoon the following January, the Republic of Ireland under-17s had a friendly against their Northern Ireland counterparts in Belfast. We got word that Jack was going to be there, so it seemed like a good idea to go to meet him and sit him down for an assessment of his first seven games in charge.

When we got in touch to ask would he fancy that, the story took a bizarre twist. The FAI didn't want to fly him from his home in the north-east of England, so his plan was to drive to the west coast of Scotland, park up and take the ferry to Larne as a foot passenger. Quite how he was going to get from there to the game at Sydenham he hadn't quite worked out. Stephen Alkin had the answer. 'You pick him up,' he said.

So that Tuesday, I drove the 125 miles to the County Antrim port, collected the manager of the Republic of Ireland and headed for the junior stadium in East Belfast. The ferry's arrival not long before kick-off meant we were never going to make the early afternoon start.

'Jack Charlton made a late but timely arrival at the Junior National Stadium,' the *Irish Independent* noted, 'and the big man's presence seemed to inspire the under-17 side in this friendly affair.' If only they'd known the whole story. 'Before the interval Charlton arrived, and eight minutes into the second half Chelsea's Tony Cousins grabbed the winner.'

The 1–0 victory put Jack in great form for the post-match meal in the Park Avenue Hotel. He made a little speech and was most warmly received. They loved him wherever he went. There was always a smile and time for a word or two.

The drive back to Larne was relaxed. He'd been impressed by Mark Kelly of Portsmouth, who had laid on the goal. Little more than a year later, Jack handed him his first senior cap in a friendly against Yugoslavia at Lansdowne Road. Kelly was still only eighteen and a month short of his full debut for his club.

The Euro campaign resumed at Hampden Park the next month. A quickly taken free kick – so quick, the television director missed it – gave Mark Lawrenson the opportunity to score the game's only goal and the Republic of Ireland's campaign was back on track.

Despite the defeat in Bulgaria that followed, they were still only two points off the early pace set by Belgium (it was still two points for a win back then). A scoreless draw with the Belgians four weeks later at Lansdowne Road was followed by a 2–0 success in the away leg of the double header against Luxembourg. Summer had arrived with Ireland, thanks to results elsewhere, just a point off the new leaders Bulgaria, though with a game more played. Still, the home victory over Luxembourg that followed in September sent Jack Charlton's team to the top of the table.

Bulgaria reclaimed the summit with a 2–0 home win over Belgium, who were now crucially three points behind them. Ireland were second, just one behind the leaders, but with only one game remaining, and that in the penultimate round of fixtures, against Bulgaria at Lansdowne Road. It was all desperately tight.

That last game, 'a surging tempestuous affair' according to *The Irish Times*, 'was in some danger of going wrong [but] was rescued initially by Paul McGrath's 52nd minute goal before another Manchester United player, Kevin Moran, finally pushed it beyond the reach of the pugnacious Bulgarians with a second score, five minutes from the end.'

But as the players celebrated what was now a certain victory, Liam Brady, who'd earlier been booked, was involved in an incident right in front of the referee, which resulted in a second yellow card. Sent off, he faced a two-match suspension, which would mean he'd miss Ireland's first two games at the Euros, should they make it.

The Republic of Ireland led the group again, but only by a point. Their campaign was complete. Bulgaria still had a game to play, at home to Scotland. With their superior goal difference, a draw would be sufficient for Bulgaria to dislodge the Irish from top spot. And they weren't the only danger. Jack Charlton's final qualifier against the Bulgarians had been in the afternoon – still no floodlights in Lansdowne Road – which meant Belgium now knew that a victory that evening in Glasgow, with full points virtually guaranteed from the final qualifier at home to Luxembourg, would hoist them onto eleven points, alongside Bulgaria and the Republic of Ireland, but two wins would ensure that they retained the best goal difference of all three.

That night, Scotland did the Irish a huge favour by removing Belgium from contention. With no chance of qualification themselves, just over 16,000 turned up to watch, but from their reservoir of Scottish pride, they produced a performance that delivered a 2–0 win. Belgium, World Cup semi-finalists in Mexico the previous year, had failed to score since the game before that 0–0 draw in Dublin. Now they were out.

But Ireland still hadn't qualified. They needed another favour from the Scots. Could they repeat the trick in Sofia?

Tim O'Connor felt it was worth the punt, so he sent Maurice Reidy and myself to find out. The simplest way to get to Bulgaria was with the Scottish team. Those were the days when the press and indeed, if they were needed to fill the aircraft, a number of fortunate fans would travel on the same aircraft as the players and officials.

The Scottish FA had its own travel agency – Scotball – and they were only too happy to assign what were effectively the last of the seats to the two Irish broadcasters. Maurice and I joined the party at Glasgow airport for the four-hour Thomson charter flight to the Bulgarian capital, two Paddies all on their own back in Row 32.

Things were rather different from my first trip ten or so years before. Though the Iron Curtain was still in place, Mikhail Gorbachev's Soviet Union was no longer quite the forbidding place it had been and things were thawing in the acolyte states. There was a Sheraton Hotel, for one thing, where we stayed, enjoying the most magnificent tomato soup during an outdoor lunch on the day of the game.

Come the evening, we were back in the Vasil Levski Stadium, where I'd watched Northern Ireland beat Bulgaria in the pouring rain. This time, from a tiny commentary booth behind glass at the back of the grandstand, we watched as the drama unfolded. Bulgaria, World Cup participants in Mexico the previous year, whose last competitive defeat at home had been almost exactly five years before, needed no more than a point to edge past Ireland and into the Euros on goal difference. Surely the Scots, with nothing to play for, couldn't upset the apple cart twice.

But they hadn't yet drained that reservoir of pride. Into the second half, you can hear it in the commentary: 'Suddenly Bulgaria look frail and vulnerable. Could there yet be the surprise that we all want?' Still the clock ticked on and wishful thinking was getting nowhere. 'Astonishing really, if it should stay like this, that it'll be goal difference that knocks the Irish out.'

Less than five minutes to go, it's still 0–0, Scotland kicking right to left. The ball is in the hands of the Aberdeen goalkeeper Jim Leighton. Out of shot, a teammate is calling for it to be played short. Leighton shakes his head. No, this is going to go long. He's not giving up on this one. Right-footed, he thumps it into the night sky and the ball descends deep in Bulgarian territory, where it's deflected out towards the far wing, with Chelsea forward Gordon Durie off in hot pursuit.

'Durie off and battling.' As the ball bounces, he wins a duel in the air. 'He did well to get away there.' But the defender is quickly back on his feet, determined to exact retribution. He comes through Durie with a thundering challenge. A clear foul, but the Austrian referee with a famous name – Helmut Kohl – plays advantage. 'And,' voice rising, 'it's come through now to Mackay.' He adjusts his feet and fires left-footed past Borislav Mikhailov in the Bulgarian goal. 'It's there! It's there! Gary Mackay, the substitute, has put Scotland in the lead and Ireland are surely on their way to Germany. What a remarkable story in Sofia!'

Gary Mackay, on as a substitute for his very first Scottish cap, has scored the goal that will send the Republic of Ireland to their very first championship finals. Jack Charlton has worked the miracle in his very first campaign.

It was straight to the airport after the match and on board the Boeing for the flight back to Glasgow. Reidy and myself, curiosities at the outset, were now cast as ersatz heroes, to be congratulated by all and sundry. We resumed our seats at the back of the plane, high on the excitement of it all, delighted to have been a part of it.

The spare seat beside us was soon occupied by Ian St John, the former Liverpool international, on the trip for ITV. I'd known him from my time with the BBC in London. He felt he just had to spend the time with us. Scotland had won, of course, but we were the passengers with something to really celebrate.

The aircraft had been on the ground since arrival and had not been re-catered. The bar had been emptied on the way out. It was going to be a dry return flight for all but the players. Some beers had been kept back for them. But then we were joined by the Scotball rep. He had a bottle of duty-free Scotch. 'There's no point keeping this for the house after what happened tonight,' he said as he poured. The four of us had a great flight back.

There was another surprise in store. When we landed in the wee small hours in Glasgow and emerged from the customs hall, there to greet the team was none other than Packie Bonner. Ireland's goalkeeper wanted to offer his personal gratitude to the Scottish squad for how they'd helped the Republic qualify for its very first tournament. He couldn't believe it when he saw Maurice and me, for he'd no idea the game had been on live back home. He'd an armful of the next day's papers with the football front page news. He handed them over. 'You guys need to read all about it,' he said. 'This has been one hell of a night!'

That night in Sofia, Gary Mackay became an honorary Irishman. His goal had lit the touchpaper on a remarkable journey under Jack that took the Republic of Ireland's football team to places they'd never been before and, some would have you believe, played a part in encouraging the self-confidence from which the Celtic Tiger grew.

Whatever about that fanciful notion, there is no doubt that the success of Jack Charlton's team created a positive mood in the country. Even the way his team played was an object lesson in how the underdog could survive.

14

A Dream Becomes Reality

Van Morrison's momma told him there'd be days like this. Van the Man hardly had a football match in mind, but for this Belfast boy, the perfect day was Sunday, 12 June 1988. Nothing could compare with the serendipity of Stuttgart on that summer afternoon.

I've acknowledged my soft spot for Germany. The Swabian metropolis, one of the greenest conurbations in the country, nestling in what's known locally as its *Kessel*, or cauldron, along the valley of the River Neckar, with its regimented lines of vineyards marching up the slopes that surround it, is one of my very favourite places. Winfried Roesner, the radio journalist I'd got to know when he came to Belfast to report on the Peace People in the late 1970s, lived with his wife, Margaret, and their two children in the hills behind the city. I became a regular visitor to the tall house in Talstrasse. Indeed, it was my base when the European Athletics Championships were staged in the Neckar Stadium in 1986.

Then in 1988, happenstance had its part to play, for the draw decreed that Ireland's very first match in the Euro 88 Finals would be against England. It could not have been better planned. That last detail placed the event in my adopted German home. Obviously, interest was huge. Aer Rianta reported that a total of twenty-four charter flights – fifteen operated by Aer Lingus, seven by Ryanair and two by Clubair – would carry 3,500 fans. The estimate was that there would be a total of 10,000 travelling supporters, the majority making their way by land and sea.

RTÉ Sport had never covered anything quite like this before. Olympics and World Cups, yes, and the preceding Euros in France that had produced a festival of sparkling football that I had missed. BBC Radio, in its wisdom, chose not to send anyone, because none of their so-called home countries – England, Scotland, Wales, Northern Ireland – was involved. And there had been the inaugural Rugby World Cup the previous year – Ireland had gone out at the quarter-final stage, beaten by Australia – but rugby matches in the middle of the night on the other side of the planet were never going to catch the imagination the way the national football team would.

With the official party due to arrive in Stuttgart on the Wednesday before the game, our departure was arranged for two days earlier. Mike Horgan, the Sports Department's senior editor, was team leader, just as he had been for my first campaign with RTÉ ten years previously in Argentina. With a heavy schedule of travel ahead of us – the best part of a thousand miles – Mike was determined his troops would have a modicum of comfort on the road. He'd made a huge fuss about the kind of vehicle we would need for our trip. And air-conditioning was a must for a hot summer on the autobahn. He won his battle with the bean counters. A two-litre Ford Sierra with temperature control was approved.

Landing at teatime on a wet Monday evening wasn't a great start. Stuttgart airport then, with its single terminal dating from 1938, wouldn't have looked out of place in rural Ireland.

The car hire office was in a portacabin on the far side of the parking area. It's amazing how the positivity of anticipation can evaporate in the rain. The four of us – Mike, Stephen Alkin, production assistant Joan O'Callaghan, and myself – were glad of the shelter when we made it inside.

Things, from Mike's perspective, immediately got worse. 'What do you mean you don't have a two-litre Ford Sierra with air-conditioning available for us?' Even on the other side of the temporary structure, it was impossible to ignore the burgeoning outrage.

Hearing that the contract couldn't be honoured, followed by an increase in the decibels emanating from the larynx of our supremo, becoming overheated at being let down, I stepped forward and touched him on the shoulder. 'Mikey,' I said, 'don't get excited here.' Many's the moment I'd spent in similar situations at hire car locations, but this wasn't part of his skill set at all. 'If they don't have what you want,' I whispered, 'they're obliged to offer you a model that's one step up. See what they say.'

He was grateful for the intervention. Reverting to the clerk at the desk, he turned down the dial. 'Okay,' he said, 'what do you propose as an alternative?' An E-Class Mercedes, came the reply. Sheepishly, Mikey looked over his shoulder with an expression that said, 'Do you think that would do?' I smiled. There was no need for words.

I was on to Winfried right away, and he smoothed our path as we plotted our previews, acting the location producer, the tour guide and, ultimately, Mr Fixit. We were keen to get an interview with the local chief of police for his take on supervising the fans. England against the Republic of Ireland. The old enemies. The Troubles. This was 1988, after all. We had tried, through the press office, and had been turned down. We learned the same thing had happened to the BBC and ITV. We asked Winfried to give it his best shot on our behalf.

He reported back that there was no problem; the Polizeipräsident would be only too delighted to talk to us. 'How on earth did you manage that?' we wanted to know.

Winfried laughed. 'The problem is he doesn't speak English. I said you'd do it in German.' That sealed the deal!

So, in the spacious office at police headquarters, I asked the questions *auf deutsch*, and we had a most congenial conversation about what was a very serious subject – the potential for trouble at this match. He said he saw none, and how right he was.

We played back the tape. I translated the answers. And, in the absence of studio facilities, something was cobbled together in the hotel car park to pass as a dubbing suite. Our engineer, who'd driven his van-load of tricks to West Germany, placed a television monitor on its front passenger seat, attached a little microphone to the windscreen wiper, and Mike – who could deliver a script in the richest of tones when he put his mind to it – stood in front of the vehicle and spoke the lines from my transcription just like a chief of police. To say the boys from the BBC and ITV were miffed was putting it mildly. We'd scored another exclusive.

We were on the tarmac when the team flight landed – EI-ASH, an Aer Lingus 737 – and put together a powerful package setting the scene for what would be a momentous episode in the history of Irish sport.

Before the business began, though, there was an evening out in the Rathaus, Stuttgart's City Hall. The press – Fleet Street's finest and our own Fourth Estate – were welcomed to the reception by the mayor, Manfred Rommel. If the name seems familiar, it should, for his father was indeed the Desert Fox, the Wehrmacht Field Marshal Erwin Rommel, commander of the 7th Panzer Division which led the invasion of France in 1940.

The reply on behalf of the guests was delivered by a jovial Scot, the chief football writer for the *Sunday Mirror*, who happened to share a surname with another notable military figure who fought on the other side in the Second World War. 'This must be the first time,' said Ken Montgomery, 'that a vote of thanks has been proposed by a Montgomery to a Rommel!'

Match day dawned bright and we made our way in good and early from our idyllic base, the Waldhotel in Degerloch, deep in the Swabian forest. The atmosphere had been building all week, as the jolly green army set up camp in town and around. There'd never been this kind of opportunity abroad to be so self-assuredly Irish.

Down in the stadium, the stage was set. The hosts had kicked off the tournament two nights previously and, by now, Germany was in thrall of Euro 88. In the build-up, they sought an Irish perspective from this German-speaking commentator. Deep in the bowels of the Neckarstadion, I faced Walter Johanssen, my equivalent on German TV. His interview covered all the ground: the near misses in the years gone by, the frustrations of watching the big events from afar, and the irony that the man who'd brought us here had won the World Cup for England, yet had been turned down when he went for the job as their manager. Now here he was, plotting their downfall.

'How do you see it going?' Walter enquired, winding up the preview.

'Well, a scoreless draw would be good. We're quietly confident, and are expecting nothing less. But one–nil would be even better. That would be our dream.'

Up into the stand we went to take our places among the serried ranks of the world's commentators, ITV and ourselves in pole position as the stations covering the match for the participating countries. Walter was just a couple of places away – the host nation comes next in the pecking order!

At precisely 3.30 p.m. local time, under a bright central-European blue sky, Siegfried Kirschen, the East German referee, set the game in motion. The 51,373 who painted a most colourful backdrop – predominantly green, white, and orange – weren't to know it, but history was in the making. The tentative early sparring eventually led to an Irish free kick. The match was just five minutes old. From midfield, Kevin Moran struck the ball long, diagonally. A catalogue of English errors began as Gary Stevens, the right-back, was impeded by his own centre half, Mark Wright, as he attempted to clear. The ball broke free to Tony Galvin, who ballooned in a cross.

And this is where my mental image comes into really sharp focus. Kenny Sansom miskicked. John Aldridge bustled in, the blast of war blowing in his ears. The ball looped towards Ray Houghton, fifteen yards out towards the right side of the goal. He arched his back and, like an Irish King Henry, stiffened the sinews, summoned up the blood and let fly from his forehead. Up it curved, over the stranded Peter Shilton and into the far corner of the net.

Houghton wheeled away, arms raised in celebration, Aldridge in hot pursuit. Jack Charlton, unseasonably attired in a grey tweed jacket, soared from his seat on the bench, smacking his head on the perspex roof of the dugout. By the time the camera caught him, he cut the figure of a man bewildered by what had happened, shaking his head and rubbing it, as if trying to figure it all out. Maurice Setters, his assistant, was grinning from ear to ear. The goal was only the half of it!

There could have been no more dramatic overture and it set the scene for a drama of unprecedented emotional intensity. Ireland dominated until half-time. Not only were they there, in the thick of a major tournament, they looked like they belonged.

Walter left his commentary position to come along and share in the excitement. He wondered if they could possibly sustain this tempo. All eyes were cast in our direction. With the team in the dressing-room, the focus was on their TV station!

Down below us, in England's own private space, Bobby Robson was having harsh words with his troops. They tore at Ireland from the restart, transformed. In the words of the official UEFA report, 'the second half was one long England attack'. The spotlight shifted to Packie Bonner.

Defending the goal in which Houghton had planted that historic header, he made no fewer than seven crucial saves – four of them from Gary Lineker, who also struck the woodwork.

In the midst of this, a piece of paper was pushed in front of me. On it, Walter had written, '*Wie sagt man "ein Traum wird*

Wirklichkeit" auf englisch?' ('How do you say *"ein Traum wird Wirklichkeit"* in English?')

On a clear-headed day, I'd have said 'a dream is coming true'. But in the swirl of excitement and no little emotion, I sent word back through Mike Horgan. 'Tell him "a dream becomes reality"' (the absolutely literal translation!).

I think I made a small contribution to the English language that day, for Walter slipped it into his German commentary and though I'd never heard the expression used before, I have certainly heard it since.

A dream becomes reality indeed. Herr Kirschen's final whistle created paroxysms of pleasure the length and breadth of Ireland. Oh, sweet release. For us, though, the job was only half complete. Of course, we could share in the immediate euphoria, and the congratulations came rolling in from all around, led by Walter and his team. Any chance of a post-match comment? Off we went in German again. The rest, a blur of interviews with the ecstatic participants, then finally the wrap, a piece-to-camera as we know it, a report on an extraordinary day. An extraordinary report it was too, filmed at precisely the spot on the pitch from which Ray Houghton had launched his missile and launched himself into Irish sporting folklore.

'Who put the ball in the English net? Rayser, Rayser!'

A good two hours passed before we eased ourselves into our waiting Mercedes for the drive back up the hill to Degerloch. It was somehow fitting. A Merc, in the city where they're built, which had just become Ireland's hometown. But thoughts were already turning to the next assignment. One that would be approached with burgeoning confidence. The following day, we'd be off up the autobahn, a drive of around 300 miles into the heart of Lower Saxony. On Wednesday, it would be Hanover, against the USSR.

Up the winding road through the Stuttgart suburbs, on into the forest, we pulled up outside the Waldhotel, by now awash with Irish supporters savouring every moment of this most famous occasion. It was all we could do to battle our way through the throng in the lobby to our rooms, all ideas of dinner dissipated by the desire to dump our work gear and get back to the celebrations.

The enduring image of the evening back in the team hotel in the woods above the city is of Jack at the heart of the party. For him, on this night of nights, open house for the fans was part of the deal, and he was the life and soul.

From Ray Houghton came the tale of how he'd been reprimanded as he left the pitch, swathed in a winner's smile.

'Don't ever do that again,' Jack had scolded.

'What? Score against England?'

'No,' Jack boomed, 'don't ever score that early again. That was the longest afternoon of my life!'

That delightful feeling of triumphant fatigue. We may not have played the match, but like every Irish person there, we had shared in the success of the day. With a deliciously deep intake of breath, as I eased my back against the closing bedroom door, I drank in the enormity of it all. The Republic of Ireland had beaten England, had stood the form book on its head. This was heady stuff. Jack Charlton's team had delivered the result that promised a unique evening, a celebration the like of which Irish soccer had never, ever known.

And then I saw it. On the table. A cake, iced in the form of a football pitch, with a little footballer upon it. And a bottle of *Sekt*

– the Germans' champagne – with a tiny knitted scarf around its neck, in green and white. And a card. Heartiest congratulations from Margaret and Winfried.

I took it down to the lobby and it became the talk of the night. It was almost too good to eat but eat it we did, with delight, as we toasted Jack and his squad.

There was a message as well from Bertram Burgert. Twenty-one years after I'd spent a summer with him, and almost as long since we'd spoken, he'd seen me on television that afternoon and remembered. Days like this? Seldom repeated. In fact, the perfect day. It was rounded off in the room we'd converted into a makeshift studio. Last thing at night, we joined Vere Wynne-Jones as he filed his piece for the breakfast-time news bulletin. 'This morning,' he began with relish, 'thousands of Irish hangovers are on their way to Hanover.' There was nothing more to say!

* * *

They'd won the match they should have lost. Now it was time to face the Soviet Union – the match they should have won. Ronnie Whelan's acrobatic volley off his shinpad following the long throw by Mick McCarthy – a goal to grace any footballing occasion – put the Irish in the box seat just before half-time and they appeared to be heading for another famous victory, when the commentator stepped in with one of those crucial interventions that have, apparently, been statistically proven to be responsible for 87 per cent of the goals the Republic of Ireland have conceded. The innocent remark, 'Bonner has gone 165 minutes of this tournament without conceding a goal – he's heading for his ninth consecutive shut-out,' was made when play was deep in opposition territory, and morphed within a moment into a transfixed shriek. 'Danger here!' For in those few seconds, the ball had travelled over half the length of the pitch and was now at the feet of Oleg Protasov. He promptly dispatched it beyond Bonner's reach into the Irish net. Ouch!

They'd drawn the game they should have won, but it was by no means the end of the world. With two to qualify for the semi-finals, Ireland shared top spot with the Soviet Union with an identical record, three points from the two games, two goals scored, one conceded. The Netherlands were a point behind, with England nowhere after two defeats. A draw against the Dutch would ensure the Republic finished ahead of them, guaranteed a place in the semis.

It was a sublime state of affairs, without doubt, but from there, things went, as they say, pretty much to the ridiculous. The base for the USSR game had been the Sportschule Barsinghausen, a residential training facility and conference venue run by the Lower Saxony Football Association. So far, so wholesome. For the final group game against the Netherlands, in the heart of the Ruhr, at the home of the Bundesliga club Schalke 04 in Gelsenkirchen, the FAI had chosen accommodation in the neighbouring town of Marl. The Hotel Restaurant Loemühle, as the name suggests, lays as much emphasis on the gastronomic aspects of its offering as it does on its accommodation. It's gorgeously atmospheric, a Fach-werk building in that typically German half-timbered style, with a terrace, gym, sauna and swimming pools, both indoor and out.

What the FAI appeared to have overlooked was that a venue like this, in high summer, would attract locals in huge numbers, who'd make use of the outdoor facilities in a fashion that is also typically German. This we discovered when we were summoned immediately after check-in to Mike Horgan's room. It overlooked the large lawn which surrounded the outdoor pool. The view took in wall-to-wall sunbathers and swimmers, not one of them wearing a stitch of clothing. This wasn't what Jack Charlton would have had in mind for his players, but they were stuck with it!

The Dutch were based in Düsseldorf, about forty minutes away, and I was tasked with getting some player interviews for our preview programme. Their stars were the captain Ruud Gullit and Marco van Basten, Serie A champions with AC Milan. Arnold Mühren had spent seven seasons in England with Ipswich Town and Manchester United. The goalkeeper, Hans van Breukelen, was well known from his time in the First Division with Nottingham Forest. And they all spoke impeccable English.

There was, though, a seemingly intractable problem. The situation in which they found themselves was pretty dire, with elimination staring them in the face. The pressure was on their coach, Rinus Michels. In response, he had banned his players from speaking to the press. There was no way he would agree to a request from us for access. But I had a friend at court. Kees Jansma, the TV commentator I had introduced to George Best all those years before in Rotterdam, was embedded in the Dutch camp, staying in the team hotel. I gave him a call. Kees said he would sort things. The only thing I had to do was arrive ostentatiously carrying a couple of video cassettes. I'd have had them anyway to record the material. Kees insisted I should have them on show.

I arrived at the team hotel at the appointed hour and waited in the car park. Kees appeared. 'We've a studio set up in one of the bedrooms on the ground floor,' he told me. 'I've explained to Rinus that you've some material you need to play out and you've no studio of your own.'

I made sure I had the cassettes in my hand as I entered the lobby with my co-conspirator. Rinus Michels was seated in an armchair, his eyes fixed on the front door. He was personally enforcing his embargo. I wasn't introduced. That might have been pushing things. Instead, we walked with purpose towards the bedroom corridor and made our way down. We stopped at 106 and Kees knocked. The goalkeeper Van Breukelen opened the door. The NOS cameraman was at the ready. We were miked up and interview number one was underway.

Kees left to fetch subject number two, Arnold Mühren. And so it went on, till I had half a dozen in the bag. This would be some preview. I thanked the crew and shook Kees by the hand. He had done me a huge favour. He'd a small one to ask of me. It was approaching lunchtime and the squad would be out and about. 'I don't want to remind Rinus that you've been in here,' Kees said. 'It could well look like you've been talking to the players. Would it be OK if you didn't go back out through the lobby?'

'Sure, no bother.'

I expected he'd point me in the direction of a fire escape. But no, that was too risky. I'd be on public view in the corridor. Who knew who else might be knocking about? 'Do you mind climbing out the window?' I made my somewhat undignified exit, but I had what I'd come for. I'd had a very lucky break.

Sadly, the Netherlands got theirs eight minutes from the end of the match in Gelsenkirchen. It was still 0–0, a scoreline that would have put the Republic of Ireland into the semi-finals of the European Championship. The Dutch, facing elimination, pushed forward once more. A cross came in from their right. It was firmly headed clear. Ronald Koeman was twenty-five yards from goal as the ball dropped. He swung his right leg, miscuing his volley, which smashed onto the ground and rose, whirling into the Irish penalty area. Wim Kieft beat Paul McGrath to it in the air, but his attempt at a header was more of a deflection. That took the ball beyond the reach of Packie Bonner. It bounced, then bounced again, the vicious spin directing it just inside the goalkeeper's left-hand post.

In the words of my other Dutch friend, Eddy Poelmann, commentating on the game for his audience back home, '*een lucky, maar wat geeft het*' – a lucky one, but who cares. In similar circumstances, I'd have been saying the same.

Ireland had lost the game they should have drawn. That defeat relegated them to third, behind the Netherlands. The Soviet Union, 3–1 winners against England (who lost all three of their games in the tournament), finished on top. So near and yet so far. The first Finals had clearly demonstrated Ireland could compete at this level. Jack Charlton had delivered. The fact that it was the two who'd qualified from Ireland's group who went on to contest the final underlined just how far they had come.

In a delicious irony, Kees Jansma, my friend who had masterminded our undermining of the manager's best-laid plans, went on to serve for ten years as the press spokesman of the Royal Dutch Football Association, the KNVB. Poacher turned gamekeeper indeed.

That final in Munich featured one of the greatest goals it's been my privilege to call. 1–0 up at half-time, thanks to Ruud Gullit, the Dutch were in control. The match was put beyond the reach of the USSR in the fifty-fourth minute. Adri van Tiggelen drove purposefully forward from midfield, then picked out Arnold Mühren, wide on the left. Without breaking stride, Mühren – just turned thirty-seven – looped a diagonal cross to the far side of the Soviet penalty area. There, at an absurdly acute angle to the goal, Marco van Basten, with an economy of effort, met the dropping ball with a right-footed volley that rifled past the goalkeeper high into the net. A goal for the ages to secure what remains, as World Cup 2022 approaches, the Netherlands' only major international trophy.

Jack's squad didn't have long to wait to get back on the horse. The first qualifying game for the Italian World Cup was only twelve weeks away and involved a trip to Windsor Park in Belfast to face Northern Ireland. It didn't prove the most auspicious of starts. The match failed to ignite and it finished scoreless. Four weeks later, in Seville, it got worse. Spain's 2–0 win left Charlton's team and Malta as the only sides in the group without a win.

There wasn't much optimism around that Christmas and things weren't looking a lot better in the spring. A trip to Budapest produced another scoreless draw. With three games played, Ireland had yet to score. The silver lining was that the only remaining game away from Lansdowne Road was in Malta, scarcely a journey to fill a visiting football team with dread.

The first goal of the campaign finally arrived in the first of four-in-a-row at home. Ironically enough, it was an own goal by the Spanish midfielder Michel, who turned a cross from Ronnie

Whelan into his own net. That set up Ireland's first win – 1–0 – and when Malta and then Hungary were both beaten 2–0, the Republic were right back in the mix. The 3–0 win over Northern Ireland that followed was celebrated as if the team had qualified for Italia 90, but as it was an afternoon game at Lansdowne (still no floodlights), confirmation had to wait until Spain would gain their expected victory in Budapest later that evening. It didn't happen. Hungary fought back for a draw. But Ireland could still do it with a point in Malta in the final group game. They did better than that and won 2–0 with plenty to spare. As it turned out, Spain's decisive win over Hungary in their final game in Seville meant Ireland would still have made it to Italia 90, even if they had lost.

Three weeks later, 9 December 1989, we were at the draw for what would be the Republic of Ireland's very first World Cup, in the Palazzetto dello Sport in Rome. Tim O'Connor, Maurice Quinn – head of Radio Sport – and myself in among a vast bank of commentators as Sophia Loren and Luciano Pavarotti drew the names under the watchful eye of FIFA's General Secretary, Sepp Blatter. When it was all done and dusted, Ireland had England and the Netherlands again, with Egypt added into the mix. The opener would be Stuttgart revisited, in Sardinia in six months' time.

15

Things Would Never Be the Same Again

Bags packed, the adventure began on the morning of 4 June 1990.

'You have two good engines.' We're heading down runway 28 at Dublin Airport early on a Monday morning, Captain Pat Galvin in command of the Aer Lingus 737. Those are his words as the pace picks up and the pilot flying – a two-stripe first officer – accelerates towards V1; make-your-mind-up time as far as take-off is concerned.

He's twenty-one, with braces on his teeth, and he's flying us to Italia 90. Several weeks would pass before the nation held its breath. Right now, back in 3A, Tom Flanagan is holding his.

Tom isn't much of a flyer. It's fair to say that the thought of taking to the skies fills him with a profound sense of foreboding. As we settle into our seats, he confesses he can't wait to be on the ground in Milan. This is going to be three hours of torture. The fact that Aer Lingus has recently taken advantage of European deregulation, expanding its catchment area by adding a stopover in Manchester on six of its continental routes, one of them the one we're taking, only deepens Tom's sense of dread by adding an additional take-off and landing to the trip.

I'm the opposite. I love the whole idea of flying. It's great to reach your destination but I'm fascinated by the journey. No two flights are ever the same.

Tom Flanagan is a floor manager, the member of the television production team who looks after the guests and the presenters in the studio. We worked a lot together in the days before I developed a face for radio. Back then, I was a regular on small screens in Ireland, hosting the long-lamented quiz programme *Know Your Sport* with Jimmy Magee, fronting the Saturday afternoon marathon *Sports Stadium*, when I wasn't off at a match, and popping up to introduce the snooker, the cycling or the Circuit of Ireland Rally. I was even on the shortlist to present the Eurovision Song Contest!

For the 1990 World Cup – the Republic of Ireland's first – Tom was assigned as my wingman. In those days, co-commentators were conspicuous by their absence. RTÉ deployed two-person teams to cover the games. Tom's task, apart from keeping me on the straight and narrow, was as our point of contact, both for base in Dublin and the host broadcaster at the various venues. He was also a warm and entertaining companion at dinner on the rare evening off.

With five weeks of an Italian summer on the road, taking in seventeen World Cup games, there was plenty to look forward to, so there was at least a significant distraction for the reluctant aeronaut beside me. But he was going to have to get used to this. As well as our passports, we'd a concertina of those old red carbon paper tickets, all stapled together, that was going to grant us access to the airways of Italy for the duration.

It all began with the pre-flight announcement. *Tá fáilte romhaibh ar bord a dhaoine uaisle.* Welcome on board. It was Pat Galvin's rich Kerry baritone. Pat happened to be a man I knew.

In the sunlit past, pre-9/11, my endless fascination with aviation inveigled me into many a cockpit, and it was just such sweet talking that led me to meet him. For many years, when players, press and a few well-connected supporters would all travel together, Pat regularly took command of the Irish football team's charter. Today, it was pure chance that he happened to be in the cockpit on our flight.

The mission, for Tom and me, was to cover the main matches, diverting to join the RTÉ team for the Irish games, then resuming our grand Italian tour. So we started with the opening game – Cameroon's astonishing victory over the holders, Argentina, in the San Siro in Milan – then took in Brazil against Sweden in Turin before flying to Sardinia for Ireland's game against England. We had accommodation right in the heart of Cagliari, which offered us the perfect vantage point to observe the comings and goings of the fans. Just two short years after Stuttgart, the game itself was a tense affair. The tables were turned. This time England scored early through Gary Lineker, but where they had come up short, the Irish found a way through, Kevin Sheedy seizing on an under-hit pass by Steve McMahon, just on as a substitute for Peter Beardsley, to fire home an equaliser.

Ireland's next engagement was six days later in Sicily, by which time Tom and I had taken in the Netherlands against Egypt in Palermo, Italy versus the USA in Rome, and England against the Netherlands back in Cagliari. In the midst of this, we had some flight adjustments to make and visited a local Alitalia office. As our wad of paper tickets unravelled, the counter clerk's eyes widened in disbelief. 'Oh my,' he said, 'you're going up and down Italy like a yee-yo.'

'A yo-yo,' his colleague corrected. 'It's not a yee-yo, it's a yo-yo!'

The best thing that can be said about Ireland's two games in Palermo is that the results qualified the team for the last sixteen. The scoreless draw against Egypt was dreary. The meeting with the Netherlands petered out when Niall Quinn equalised Ruud Gullit's early goal and it became clear to all on the pitch that if they simply played out time, a draw would put them both through. The fact that they ended up with identical records meant a drawing of lots, as it's described, was required to determine which country would go where. The 1986 World Cup finalists West Germany awaited one of them in Milan. We know where the other road led.

* * *

The city of Genoa had gone green for the day.

Myself and Tom drove down from Milan. We were on our way to a football match. Not just any old football match. This was the Republic of Ireland bidding for a place among the last eight at the World Cup.

We'd set off after breakfast in good spirits. The previous night, we'd covered a thundering tie, West Germany's 2–1 win over the Netherlands in front of 74,000 spectators in the San Siro. And now it was Ireland's turn. What nobody was to know was that this Monday was going to turn into possibly the greatest day in the history of Irish sport.

Down the road we drove in our Ford Sierra, in blazing sunshine, amusing ourselves with rather reckless imitations of our commentating colleagues – it's funny what you do to calm your nerves. One way or another, this was going to be quite the experience.

As an insurance premium so to speak, we each had an overnight bag in the boot. We were meant to drive back to Milan straight after the match, but if there was going to be reason to celebrate, we wanted to be there, and those celebrations, if they happened, would be in the lovely seaside town of Rapallo, which was where the team was quartered.

We needed a B&B, and we found one, a smart little *pensione* not far from the waterfront, with room to park the car and a welcoming fan over the bed in the simply furnished room with its polished tiled floor and shutters offering a shield from the heat of the day.

Genoa was just half an hour away.

We made it to the official car park and then walked to the stadium; it's right beside the local prison and named after Luigi Ferraris, a former player killed in action during World War I.

We took our places in the commentary area and did our thing as the game unfolded. Romania, with Gheorghe Hagi – the Maradona of the Carpathians they called him – pulling the strings, looked the better team. There was that feeling, familiar to anybody who's ever followed the Irish, that, at any moment, this could all go horribly wrong.

But it didn't, and as the game went on, it became increasingly clear that this was a match the Boys in Green might not be about to lose.

The ninety minutes went by without a goal and extra time began. And the longer this went on, the less likely it seemed the outcome would be anything worse than a scoreless draw. And we knew what would follow that.

So penalties it was. As the teams huddled and the formalities were being completed, I had a message from the control room back at base. There, it was not long after six o'clock. The News was on TV. The big story was the press conference at the end of the first day of a European summit as Ireland's six-month Presidency of the EU approached its conclusion. But in Dublin Castle, Taoiseach Charles J. Haughey had called for a pause. There was breaking news in Genoa. RTÉ was putting the shoot-out on the News.

There were only two Irish channels at the time. The one we were on – Network Two as it was known then – and RTÉ 1. Anybody who was watching Irish TV was watching our pictures. 2.9 million people. The biggest audience RTÉ Television has ever had.

Hagi scored. Sheedy equalised. Houghton, Townsend and Cascarino matched the Romanian successes. It was now 4–4. Daniel Timofte stepped forward to take the fifth spot kick for Romania. Packie Bonner stood tensed and ready on his goal line. Timofte shot. Bonner dived to his right and saved. Yip! The breakthrough! If Ireland converted the next penalty, they would be in the quarter-finals of the World Cup.

There isn't the space to feel any more tension. You're live on the air, in a heightened state of awareness. The principal concern is that you've got this right, that this next kick will in fact be decisive. But Tom Flanagan has been keeping score too. And of course, there's a graphic on screen as well.

'David O'Leary is entrusted with the responsibility of taking the penalty', a surprising choice as the potential match winner, 'that could send Ireland to the quarter-finals of the World Cup.' In that maelstrom of information that is swirling around your brain you trust your instinct to pluck the most relevant fact to release at that moment. 'This kick can decide it all.' And the most relevant fact was that the whole of the country was watching. 'The nation holds its breath … Yes, we're there!'

* * *

That evening in Genoa has its very own place in Irish sporting history. The team reached the quarter-finals having scored only twice, without winning a single match (the last-sixteen meeting with Romania is officially recorded as a draw). The celebrations at the team hotel in Rapallo went on long into the night. It was as if they didn't quite believe what they had achieved.

While Tom and I resumed our Cook's tour, the Irish expedition moved on to Rome and a new base at Castel Gandolfo, near the papal summer residence to the south of the city. Every day there would be crowds at the entrance to the grounds of the hotel, many of them claiming family ties to the one member of the Irish squad who they might well have been connected to – Tony Cascarino.

RTÉ had couriered out a video compiled by Niall Cogley, broadcast after the Romania shoot-out, reflecting how Dublin reacted. There were pictures of a great street party, all set to the strains of the theme of the movie *Dirty Dancing* – '[I've had] The Time of My Life'. The RTÉ crew was taking in the amazing scenes in a private viewing room in the hotel. Ronnie Whelan poked his head around the open door, wondering why the music was playing. He couldn't believe his eyes either. 'Can I bring the boys round?' he asked.

They trooped in, in ones and twos, as the tape was played again and again. Cocooned for the best part of a month, they were stunned by the impact they'd had.

The quarter-final evolved a bit like the final game at Euro 88, with a fortunate goal for the opposition – for Wim Kieft, read Toto Schillaci – though, this time, after the final whistle, there was a lap of honour for the man who'd made it all possible, Jack Charlton. At his shoulder, basking in the reflected glory was none other than Charlie Haughey.

* * *

Italia 90 was followed by the abortive qualifying campaign for Euro 92 in Sweden, which concluded in heartbreaking fashion. Ireland were well placed to qualify when they went 3–1 up in their penultimate game, away to Poland in Poznań. It was shaping up as the perfect counter to the 0–0 draw Poland had achieved in Dublin. But two goals conceded in the final fifteen minutes – that was me again, counting chickens – meant Ireland dropped another point. It would prove crucial.

In the final round of matches, England were in Poland, while Ireland travelled to Istanbul to face a Turkish team that had lost every match. The atmosphere was unspeakably hostile. There was a huge crowd milling around outside the Beşiktaş stadium when the media coach arrived. We were dropped, quite possibly on purpose, at the wrong entrance. What followed was frightening as we struggled to make our way through the throng, seeking the gate where we would be allowed in. And the problems didn't stop there. The commentary positions were inside a glass enclosure in the main grandstand. Beside and below in the seating area, it was chaos, totally overcrowded with Turkish supporters filling the gangways. We became aware of a group of Irish marooned among them. One of them was a lawyer from Drogheda, Vincent Hoey, well known as a stalwart of Drogheda United. We managed to get him in to sit beside us. Vincent would often recall the night RTÉ came to his rescue in Istanbul. It was that bad.

After the game, back at the magnificent Swisshotel, which stood in stark contrast to what was happening outside, where locals had bears on chains, the gravity of the situation became clear. The coaches carrying Irish fans had been attacked. The lobby was like a field station as the cuts and bruises were attended to.

In the circumstances, the result – a comfortable 3–1 victory – seemed irrelevant. The win would have been enough had Gary Lineker not scored late on in Poland. England's 1–1 draw put them through a point ahead of Jack Charlton's team. Had Ireland not conceded those late goals to the Poles, they'd have been level on points with England and would have made it to Sweden on goal difference. Had they done better than 0–0 against the same opposition in Dublin earlier in the campaign, there would have been none of the late drama.

Euro 92 was one that got away. I firmly believe it's a

tournament they could have won. The Irish squad was still young, yet experienced enough. In the end, the Euro 92 champions were Denmark, who only got to take part because Yugoslavia were thrown out, on account of what was going on there at the time. It could and should have been the Republic of Ireland's finest hour.

The disappointment of missing out on Euro 92 was tempered somewhat by an invitation to take part in a mini-tournament arranged by the United States Soccer Federation. This was arranged, as much as anything, it appeared, as a familiarisation exercise for the locals, who'd be involved in the running of the World Cup two years hence. Italy, Portugal and the Republic of Ireland, all runners-up who hadn't made it to the eight-team Euros in Sweden, joined the hosts in a four-nation round robin. RTÉ, already committed to coverage of the Euros, managed to secure rights for this US Cup as it was known, but too late to put in place broadcasting arrangements at the venues in Washington and Foxborough, Massachusetts, where Ireland would be in action. Instead, we'd cover the games off-tube.

Off-tube is the term used when the commentator isn't actually in the stadium but is covering the game remotely, following it in a studio or a voice-over booth back in a broadcasting centre, watching on a television screen – 'off-tube' exactly as you would be at home or in the pub. For it to work, it depends on the expertise of the commentator and his or her ability to con the viewer. 'Con' may seem like too strong a word, but when you consider that an off-tube commentator is seeing no more than the pictures you as a viewer have at your disposal, and oftentimes the monitor he or she is relying upon is way inferior to your high-definition huge-screen model, it's something to bear in mind. It has become an easy way for broadcasting stations to save money. It would be helpful, to put it no more strongly than that, if they would be honest enough to acknowledge that they are not prepared to invest in allowing their commentators to attend the events and that the commentaries they are offering are being provided by broadcasters who are not actually there.

Off-tube commentary is fraught with danger. What happens if the vision circuit goes down? This actually happened when I was covering a game from the floor of Studio 8 in the RTÉ Television Centre, home in those days to *Dempsey's Den*, a children's programme based in a set that reflected the demands of its audience, with a reliance on a vast array of zany props that were scattered all around. I had all of this extraneous stuff around whilst pretending to be in a stadium somewhere. To describe it as ludicrous is putting it mildly. Next time you shaft a commentator, reflect on that.

The screen went blank. There was nothing. I could no longer see what was going on. I'd obviously been pretty successful in providing decent enough coverage, for in the control room, the director Max Mulvihill reacted to the loss of vision by suggesting I carry on with radio commentary until we got the picture back. He'd completely forgotten I wasn't at the venue at all but was in the studio next door!

If you ever needed a reason why off-tube commentary should be avoided – quite apart from the fact that to my mind it's an unacceptable delusion – I'll give you one: Ireland's second game in that US Cup. Ireland were playing Italy in Massachusetts and I was on duty back in Dublin. Midway through the second half, with Ireland 1–0 down, Italy attacked, left to right. We'll let

Noel Dunne in the *Irish Independent* take up the story. 'Roberto Mancini split the Irish cover with a great ball to Giuseppe Signori and as he closed in on the goal, [Packie Bonner] was adjudged to have tripped him.'

Noel reckoned it was a dubious decision, but for me, 3,000 miles away, it was a foul by the Irish goalkeeper and, as he denied Signori a clear goal-scoring opportunity, it was a red card offence. The replays started. On and on they went. I had no co-commentator. There was no picture to back me up for we were still watching replays. I was living by my wits. I called it. 'Packie Bonner has been sent off!' There was no visual confirmation. Nor was there any sign of the substitution that would inevitably follow, with an outfield player being sacrificed to allow the introduction of another goalkeeper.

You can imagine the relief when the camera settled on the Irish penalty area as Alessandro Costacurta readied himself to take the kick, for there on the goal-line was Bonner's replacement, Gerry Peyton. I'd made the right call. But I had been on my own, hung out to dry. No safety net. My expertise alone.

Costacurta duly converted, and Ireland were now down to ten men. Bonner had indeed been sent off. But who had made way for the new keeper? Painstakingly, as I saw them on screen, I ticked off each remaining Irish player in turn, until there was only one left. At that moment, I declared a reshuffle in the Irish defence, which was now without its first-choice left back, Denis Irwin, who'd been the one to make way for the goalkeeper sub.

* * *

The next journey had already begun. The qualifying rounds for USA 94 had kicked off in the spring of 1992. We had a taste for this now and the World Cup in America would be quite the adventure. Spain again. Northern Ireland again. Denmark, who had delivered the *coup de grâce* to the previous regime. Albania, Latvia, Lithuania too. A long, hard road. Twelve matches in all. Before the US Cup, Albania had been beaten in Dublin. The campaign resumed with a visit from Latvia in September. A hat-trick from John Aldridge helped the team to a 4–0 win. Draws in Copenhagen and Seville, then a win over Northern Ireland and a draw with Denmark at Lansdowne Road – this was all shaping up nicely.

Albania, Latvia, Lithuania twice ... Ireland were top of the table with two games to go. Then, disaster – they lost 3–1 at home to Spain. Denmark had emerged as a third force in the group and had taken over at the top of the table, and Spain's win had shunted Ireland back to third. But Jack Charlton's team was still in control. If they won their final game against Northern Ireland in Belfast, they would be through. Even a draw would be enough, if Spain beat Denmark on the same night in Seville.

Tension was high in Windsor Park. The security situation in Belfast was precarious. Billy Bingham, the Northern Ireland manager, stoked the flames of antagonism with a series of incendiary remarks, among them a reference to Charlton's squad as 'a bunch of mercenaries'. It was no surprise the game was edgy. Northern Ireland were out of the hunt, but their boss was determined to spoil Big Jack's party. It looked like he might be able to do just that when his centre forward, Jimmy Quinn, put the home team ahead with just sixteen minutes to go. Defeat would have meant the end for the Republic. But in no time at all, Alan McLoughlin fired in an equaliser and they got to the final whistle all square at 1–1. It still depended on what happened in Seville, where Spain and Denmark were still playing. Ger Canning was on the touchline in Windsor Park, all set for the post-match interviews. But they couldn't happen until the final table was clear. Ireland had finished on eighteen points. Denmark were on eighteen, 1–0 down, with five minutes to go. As it stood, Ireland were ahead of them on goals scored, but if the Danes were to draw, they'd move ahead of Ireland on nineteen points and Spain would end on eighteen, like Jack Charlton's team but with a vastly superior goal difference.

As the Republic's players celebrated, unaware that the result in Seville had yet to be decided, the decision was made to broadcast the final moments from Spain. The pictures were punched up on my monitor on the roof of the stadium in south Belfast. I'd no team sheets, no information other than that Fernando Hierro had scored for Spain and if it stayed 1–0 Ireland would be through. It was eerie but, in circumstances like this, experience carries you through, and having covered Spain and Denmark twice in the qualifying tournament, I was pretty okay with the players involved. It was what television does best and it ended with the right result. Spain 1, Denmark 0. Alan McLoughlin's equaliser – his first international goal – provided the passport to USA 94.

If it couldn't be England–Ireland again, then Italy–Ireland was the next best thing. The opening game in New Jersey brought together two teams representing the two biggest immigrant communities in the area. Ireland won the supporters' contest hands down. Giants Stadium was a sea of green. I had Niall

Quinn alongside me in the commentary box. Injury had kept him out of contention. We were housed behind glass, an unfortunate circumstance given the heat and humidity. The sheer surprise of what Ray Houghton did to score – floating a shot past four defenders and over the head of Italy's keeper, Gianluca Pagliuca – and the majesty of the performance of Paul McGrath as Ireland held on to win that day will live forever for me. And I won't quickly forget what happened afterwards either.

The Irish squad, and with them all of the RTÉ team with one exception – myself – flew off directly after the game to their next destination, Orlando. We had travelled around New York and New Jersey in a minibus, which we'd arranged through a hire car company called Dollar. My final duty after the win over Italy was to drive my colleagues to Newark Airport in this minibus. I would then drive back to our base in Parsippany, New Jersey and move on the following morning, catching a flight from LaGuardia to Washington, where I was down to cover the game involving the other two teams in Ireland's group, Norway and Mexico.

On our way to the drop-off at Newark, I spotted the Dollar compound. I was shattered after a long day and an exhilarating occasion that had drained me of all energy. I suggested to our team leader, Michael O'Carroll, that I just call it quits with the minibus, leave it off there and then, and take a taxi the thirty miles back to Parsippany. 'No,' he said, 'taxi to Parsippany, taxi tomorrow to LaGuardia (a further forty miles), that'll cost a fortune. Take the minibus to LaGuardia and leave it there.' I really didn't fancy the drive, but it was Michael's call, so we said our farewells at the terminal and I headed off for one last night in New Jersey.

I rose early, checked out and set off for the airport. Heading east along Interstate 80, with a good eight hours in the land of nod behind me, my reluctance of the previous evening had long since evaporated and I was enjoying the drive, cruising on a Sunday morning. Past Paterson, cradle of the industrial revolution in the United States, then the leafy, upwardly mobile suburb that inspired the singer's disdain in Billy Joel's 'Movin' Out' – who needs a house out in Hackensack? – across the George Washington Bridge over the Hudson River, down through Upper Manhattan and Harlem, and on to Queen's and the airport named after the mayor of New York at the time it was built, the attorney Fiorello LaGuardia.

I saw the signs for hire car returns. I saw Avis and Hertz and Thrifty and plenty more besides, but none for Dollar. I was now in the kind of intricate road network you find around airports, which will take you miles from where you want to go if you're not careful about following the signs. But I had no sign for Dollar. I ended up in a side street, beside a diner-cum-motel. I pulled up and went inside. There were families enjoying their eggs over easy, easy like Sunday morning. And there was this guy with a minibus parked outside, doing his best to address two incompatible imperatives – how to get rid of the vehicle and get himself onto the 10.30 shuttle to DC.

I approached reception. Did they perhaps know where the Dollar compound was? The folk behind the desk didn't appear to be aware they were even close to an airport. Back to the minibus I went and did what I probably should have done before I set off. I called the Dollar number. The answer to my question put my predicament in stark perspective. 'No sir,' said the voice at

285

the other end of the line, 'we do not have a facility at LaGuardia. The nearest Dollar locations are JFK and Newark' – where I'd dropped my colleagues the previous evening and had wanted to end my relationship with the oversized Ford.

What now? Norway and Mexico would kick off at 4 p.m. and I had to be there. I headed for Avis. There was a barrier and a guy in a security hut who wanted papers. I was getting very close to the wire. But my tale of woe and the fact that I was wearing a World Cup laminate encouraged him to bend the rules. 'I'll let you in,' he said, 'just go to the desk and see what they have to say.'

Well, it was Avis or abandon it by the side of the road. In fairness, they looked after me really well. Apparently, this happened all the time. Well, why not? Dollar charged a 500-bucks retrieval fee if you didn't bring your vehicle back. Avis even had a special hook for Dollar keys. The paperwork could stay in the minibus. Their courtesy driver took me to the terminal and I walked straight through and onto the flight. All was well, but the taxis would have been a lot cheaper.

Tadhg de Brún was my minder on the American trip. He was the floor manager on so many significant RTÉ outside broadcasts that he seemed almost a part of the Sports Department. We flew coast to coast following the football, at one point leaving our luggage in the Essex Hotel in Chicago while we headed off on a detour to California. We stayed on Eastern Time while we were there, having dinner in the afternoon. It was the only way to keep the body clock in check.

We shared a wonderful interlude with Jack at the end of the group stage. His team had lost to Mexico in Orlando, but back in New Jersey, they had drawn with Norway and that put them into the last sixteen. Second to Mexico in the table, they would meet the winners of the section that comprised Belgium, Morocco, the Netherlands and Saudi Arabia. The final matches in that group were on the day after Ireland secured qualification.

Belgium were the most likely opponents. With two wins out of two, they were top and had a game against Saudi Arabia to close out the first phase. The Saudis had beaten Morocco but lost to the Dutch, who, themselves, having been beaten by Belgium, were unlikely to go through in first place. So it had been arranged for Jack to go and watch the Belgians. Belgium against Saudi Arabia also happened to be the next match on our schedule.

Tadhg and I flew down on the morning of the game. Jack was on the same flight. RTÉ, under Tim O'Connor, looked after its personnel in the field. The same could not be said of the FAI. Tadhg and I were up at the front of the plane. Jack was down the back. Tadhg, ever the man to look after the stars of the show, made representations to the American Airlines cabin staff. 'You may not be aware,' he said, gently getting around the fact that while association football may be the most popular sport on the planet, its World Cup was coming in a distant second to what was uppermost in the host country's consciousness, 'the tall gent who's just gone down the aisle is a main man in the big soccer gig.'

'Oh really?' Well, they could not have been more attentive. He was summoned to the first-class cabin and treated with the absolute respect he deserved. It was clearly not what the crew were expecting, but they made the most of it. He was introduced to the captain and his presence on board was announced. He loved every minute.

When we landed, there was a driver holding a 'Coach Charlton' sign. Jack did the decent thing. 'OK, you lot, get in. You don't think I'm going to let you get a taxi.'

Belgium against Saudi Arabia got off to a sensational start. You often find teams at the World Cup whose players are not used to the conventions of the upper echelons of the elite game. They just do their own thing. Like Cameroon, who had beaten Argentina in the opening game of Italia 90, Saudi Arabia played like young puppies let off the leash. There were just five minutes on the clock when a Belgian attack broke down and Saeed Al-Owairan took possession in what, in old money, would have been the left half position. And off he went, slaloming past each opponent who challenged until he'd covered two-thirds of the pitch and reached Belgium's penalty area. He fired and Saudi Arabia took the lead.

Tadhg was charged with bringing Jack to our commentary position for a half-time comment. He was being looked after in the VIP seats and it took some persuading to prise him away from the interval refreshments. When he came into our box, he sat with his back to me throughout the interview, his way of making the point that he didn't want to be there.

Saudi Arabia held on to win the game 1–0 and throw everything into confusion. The result meant the Netherlands, who had beaten Morocco while the Saudis made a mockery of the odds against them, were top of the group. They would be Ireland's opponents in the last sixteen. Jack's scouting mission had been a complete waste of time.

What happened after the game, I'll tell you in Tadhg's words: 'He came back up to us and told us he was meeting an old friend of his for a meal and would we care to join them.' We did, as their guests. There was a lot more to Jack Charlton than met the eye.

Of course, another dodgy Dutch goal sealed Ireland's fate. Already 1–0 down after Dennis Bergkamp scored under the searing midday sun in Orlando, a tame shot from Wim Jonk somehow went through Packie Bonner's hands. There would be no way back from that second goal. Ireland went out, but the RTÉ roadshow rolled on.

Placing the tournament in the United States demanded early kick-offs to satisfy the European audience. It meant the games were played in insufferable heat. It was no surprise that Ireland had eventually wilted. The tournament itself suffered. The show-piece games – the semi-finals and final – were thundering disap-pointments, with tired teams playing at a snail's pace in the blister-ing conditions. It was so hot in Pasadena, my stopwatch melted.

The final was the first to end without a goal and the first to be decided on a penalty shoot-out. (You take the Finals to America to sell it to the locals, all of whose games demand score after score, and you deliver what should be the *pièce de résistance*, which ends up lasting two hours without producing a goal, never mind a winner. Surely there was a lesson in that.) Brazil won the trophy – or rather Italy lost it. Roberto Baggio missed from the spot and that gave Brazil the Cup.

But there is one precious memory from that World Cup Final weekend in California. The night before the main event, in the LA Dodgers baseball stadium, one of the greatest acts ever assembled took to the stage for only the third time.

The Three Tenors – Carreras, Domingo and Pavarotti – had first performed under that banner prior to the final of the 1990

World Cup. There was a selection of arias and Neapolitan songs for each to sing on his own, plus a medley for the three of them which brought the house down. That open-air concert, amid the ruins of the ancient Caracalla Baths, had been conceived as a fundraiser for Carreras' charity, which he'd set up when he recovered from leukaemia some years before.

There had been no indication of the phenomenon The Three Tenors would become. When it came to discussing performing rights for the CD and video that would follow, the singers settled for a flat fee rather than taking a percentage of sales. They may well have rued that decision, for the concert, which reached a worldwide television audience of 800 million, spawned what became the biggest-selling classical recording in history.

Pavarotti's promoter, a US-based Hungarian impresario called Tibor Rudas, saw a huge opportunity. He'd already taken the tenor out of the opera house, putting on shows in unlikely locations from a marquee in New Jersey's casino capital, Atlantic City, to Central Park in New York, racking up lucrative pay-days for his client along the way.

For a reprise of The Three Tenors, the first World Cup in the United States would provide the perfect setting. Bringing opera to people who are not part of the opera world, as Rudas put it, would not only fill the Dodgers baseball stadium in Los Angeles on the night before the final, it would deliver stellar viewing figures right across the globe.

The tenors, football fans themselves, were at first reluctant to recreate what they'd regarded as a one-off, but they were won over by the fact that this concert, unlike the one in Rome, would be part of the official World Cup programme.

And that was where we came in. Quite literally, from behind the stage and onto the outfield. The organisers had set aside seats for the TV broadcasters. RTÉ got three, meant for the great and the good of the rights-holding organisations. But while directors-general and chief executives from all of the major stations were there in abundance, the Irish broadcaster was represented by Tadhg de Brún, Maurice Reidy and myself. Tadhg, a musician of considerable accomplishment, was thrilled to have the opportunity, though, like Jack Charlton at the Belgium game, Maurice took some convincing. Classical music wouldn't be all that big in Castleisland, County Kerry, where he comes from.

We entered the diamond facing the audience. In the front row was a vast array of famous faces. I spotted Bob Hope and made a beeline for him. How often would you get the chance to meet, or more precisely gatecrash, a global superstar? He was eighty-seven at the time, but he sparkled, clearly very happy to engage. His wife, Dolores, was seated beside him. Tadhg, who'd been left a bit behind in my starstruck rush to shake Bob Hope's hand, arrived at my shoulder and I introduced him as my colleague from the west of Ireland. 'Well,' said Mrs Hope, 'we have something in common.' She and Bob weren't long back from a family reunion in Galway.

I would never have believed a spontaneous interaction with a personality like Bob Hope could have gone so well. We parted all smiles, the four of us grateful for the chat. Maurice had maintained a respectful distance.

Making our way along the front row towards the aisle that would lead us to our seats, I spotted another famous face. I tried the Bob Hope approach once more but didn't get close. Two large men in black suits converged blocking sight of my target. One of them spoke. 'Mr Sinatra doesn't want to speak to you.' Ol' Blue Eyes, I reckon it was your loss.

The show was spectacular. On a stage that featured classical columns, waterfalls, fake rocks and abundant green foliage – a southern Californian rainforest, according to its creator – The Three Tenors went through their routine with Zubin Mehta conducting the Los Angeles Philharmonic and the chorus of the Los Angeles Opera.

The American World Cup had one last surprise in store. Taking my seat on British Airways 747 back to Heathrow, I glanced across the aisle. Who was by the window on the other side? None other than Luciano Pavarotti.

***

It's hard to put a finger on when the end of the journey appeared on the horizon. It certainly wasn't apparent when the next qualification phase began. Euro 96 in England would have been the perfect stage for Jack Charlton's Ireland. Three Lions on the shirt and thirty years of hurt? And one of those Lions of '66 back to haunt them? Latvia, Liechtenstein, Northern Ireland – three wins, eleven goals, none against. Surely, they were on their way again. Dropped points in a draw at home to Northern Ireland seemed no more than a flesh wound, for that result was followed by a home win over Portugal, the principal rivals. The Republic of Ireland were still top of the table.

At that point, metaphorically speaking, I had to don my scrum cap. I had a dual role then. I missed Jack Charlton's next assignment for I was off at the Rugby World Cup in South Africa. They didn't do so well in my absence. It was 0–0 in Liechtenstein. A blot on the copybook. But though that cost them group leadership, they were still second, with four games to go. You could get away with one aberration and still qualify. And they could redress the balance the following weekend when Austria would be in Lansdowne Road.

That Saturday I was in Ellis Park, the great rugby cathedral in Johannesburg, calling the game as South Africa defeated Western Samoa 42–14 on their march towards their historic World Cup triumph a fortnight later when, in that very same stadium, Nelson Mandela would present the Webb Ellis Cup to the victorious skipper, Francois Pienaar. It was one of those pinch-me-did-I-really-do-that memories. I walked from the stadium to the hire car with my suitcase already in the boot, drove the ten miles to the airport and boarded the overnight flight to Heathrow for a connection to Dublin that would deliver me to Lansdowne Road in time for the Sunday afternoon kick-off against Austria. I might be unique in having covered two major internationals continents apart on consecutive days!

Well, if the one I'd missed had been a blip, then the one I came back for confirmed that some sort of rot had set in. Who knows why these things happen? The best part of ten years is a very long time in international management. Ray Houghton did put Ireland in front, but they conceded three times in the last twenty minutes. And when a similar 3–1 defeat followed in September in Vienna, you feared the end was nigh. Portugal were disappearing into the distance. Austria and Northern Ireland were closing in on that potentially qualifying second place.

The Republic did defeat Latvia at home, but going down 3–0 to Portugal on a dreadful wet November night in Lisbon, when the commentary position was on the opposite side to the cameras, eloquently juxtaposed the difficulties the squad now faced with our broadcasting predicament. They held on to second, but only just, equal on points with Northern Ireland but ranked ahead on the basis that, with a win and a draw against them, their record was superior.

But the points they had dropped in the closing matches of the campaign meant they were the worst of the second-placed teams in qualification and that put them in a play-off with the next worst. It would be the Netherlands again.

Wednesday, 13 December 1995. The Republic of Ireland football team would head to Anfield, ninety minutes from its destiny. Beat the Dutch or exit the European Championship. Jack Charlton, their manager since early 1986, had spun the thread as far as it could go. This was it. Make or break.

The conclusion that the era was ending had been taking hold for some time. Four points from the last five games in qualifying had landed Ireland in this play-off.

Jack knew the writing was on the wall. Pre-match, in Chester, the mood in the team hotel was subdued.

I'm ready to go. It's four in the afternoon. Mark Kennedy is strutting in the corridor wearing only a towel. Jack Charlton is in the lobby of St David's Park, chatting to old acquaintances, relaxed, with the appearance of a man off whose sizable shoulders a boulder has rolled.

I'm on my way to the game. It's three hours to kick-off. I shake his hand, wish him well, and he thanks me warmly. This may well be some sort of a conclusion. I think he knows I know. It's dark as I set off alone. Most of my colleagues have been at the ground since lunchtime.

Alone, behind the wheel of an unfamiliar car, I'm up for the match, perhaps a little edgier than usual, uncertain which radio station would be the better companion. Key 103, rock music from Manchester, Five Live from the BBC – maybe I don't want to hear what they might have to say about this match. It's rather too personal for that. What about RTÉ, crystal clear in this part of the UK? I settle for M-People on a cassette.

Ninety minutes before kick-off, I am in the van – North 4, the BBC outside broadcast truck. Anne Cassin is filing material for the news, but I am waiting for the live piece from Tony O'Donoghue, setting the scene on the teatime bulletin.

The team coaches have disgorged the gladiators; the pre-match ritual has begun. In the truck, with Stephen Alkin our director, are Brian Moran, the RTÉ engineering manager, and BBC technicians, among them Frank Parker, now Manchester-based, who worked on sound on my earliest broadcasts back in Belfast in the 1970s. Broadcasting is like that, almost a club.

There would, of course, be one last heave, but the superiority of the Dutch became all-too-evident. And there was something almost inevitable about that too. The Dutch, who finished the fairy tale in West Germany and the USA, were doing it again. And doing it courtesy of two goals from Patrick Kluivert – just nineteen and on his way to greatness. Jack Charlton's days were done.

It's the dignity of the departure that is most striking. If ever there could be pride in disappointment, it was evident that night at Anfield. Jack Charlton's ninety-fourth match had ended in defeat to the Netherlands – again. There would be no reunion with England at Euro 96. It's Jack's gesture to go onto the pitch with Maurice Setters, his assistant, to salute the fans who were part of the family he and his team had created that lives with me from that night. Yes, dignified is the best way to describe it. They had been ten glorious years. It had been an extraordinary adventure. It had helped sow the seeds of self-confidence in a nation. Things would never be the same again.

Acknowledgements

We'd never have got to the point of holding our breath if it hadn't been for the support of great friends, many long gone. Joy Williams, Bill McLaren, Cliff Morgan, Pat Ewing, Fred Cogley and Tim O'Connor showed such faith in me I was able to fly. Once airborne, there were colleagues aplenty to supply the wind beneath my wings.

Special mention to Tom Flanagan and the late Tadhg de Brún, who went above and beyond at two of my World Cups. Mary Hogan and Michael O'Carroll made *Know Your Sport* what it was. John D. O'Brien minded me on many an occasion. The team at RTÉ Lyric FM are unstinting in their support. A salute, too, to my broadcasting buddies, Peter, Tony, young Tony the imposter, and Jim, and to those stalwarts who soldiered alongside me over the years – Jim Beglin, Ray Houghton and Ronnie Whelan. Friends for life.

Thanks to Conor, Pa and all at Merrion Press for their infinite patience, something Brenda and Eddie have shown in abundance as well. I promise we'll be pounding the paths again soon.